ALASKA BY C[...]

O9-BTZ-362

DOCUMENTATION
Passenger Name _____
Ship Name _____
Captain's Signature _____
Date of Voyage _____
Cabin Number _____

ALASKA
By Cruise Ship

ANNE VIPOND

FIFTH EDITION

YOUR PORTHOLE
COMPANION

™

OCEAN
CRUISE
GUIDES
Vancouver, Canada   Pt. Roberts, USA

Published by: Ocean Cruise Guides Ltd.
Canada   USA
325 English Bluff Road   PO Box 2041
Delta, BC V4M 2M9   Pt. Roberts, WA 98281-2041
Phone: (604) 948-0594 Email: info@oceancruiseguides.com
Printed and bound in Canada.
Fifth Edition. **Visit our web site: oceancruiseguides.com**
Editors: Mel-Lynda Andersen, Diane Luckow, Duart Snow
Contributing Editors: William Kelly, Michael DeFreitas, Katharine Dawe
Artwork by Alan H. Nakano.
Cartography: Reid Jopson, Doug Quiring, Cartesia, OCG.
Design: Ocean Cruise Guides Ltd
Publisher: William Kelly

Library and Archives Canada Cataloguing in Publication

Vipond, Anne, 1957-
        Alaska by cruise ship / Anne Vipond. -- 5th ed.

Includes index.
"Your porthole companion"
ISBN 0-9688389-7-9

        1. Cruise ships--Alaska--Guidebooks. 2. Cruise ships--British Columbia--Pacific Coast--Guidebooks. 3. Alaska--Guidebooks. 4. Pacific Coast (B.C.)--Guidebooks. I. Title.
F902.3.V56 2005   917.9804'52   C2005-900433-9

Kenai River

CONTENTS

PART TWO

THE VOYAGE & THE PORTS

A laska – the Great Land – is best seen by ship. With nearly 34,000 miles of shoreline, Alaska is very much a coastal state. For centuries its waterways were the natural routes for canoes, sailing vessels and steamships. Modern cruise ships use the same waterways as travellers of bygone days and passengers are treated to the same ongoing panorama of mountains, forests, glaciers and fjords. Much can be seen from the ship's rail: tree-clad islands, hanging water-falls, glaciers dropping their ice straight into the sea.

Just as native villages once thrived along this coast, many of Alaska's towns are located on the water's edge – wedged between mountains and sea. Their pioneer history is kept alive by today's Alaskans – people who embody frontier hardiness and community spir-it in a wilderness that cannot be tamed. Whales still travel these waters, bears roam the land, eagles soar overhead, and schools of salmon swim homeward to the rivers that gave them life. The natural wonders are there for all to see, but there's more to Alaska than meets the eye. This book is designed to help you, the traveller, better appreciate the splen-did scenery gliding past your porthole.

Scientists and naturalists have long been fascinated by Alaska, where tectonic forces are nudging mountains skyward and where active tidewater glaciers are a direct link to the last ice age that created the deep channels and broad valleys of this vast region. The massive scale of the landscape puts our human exploits in perspective when a 90,000-ton cruise ship is dwarfed by granite peaks and steep-sided fjords, their sheer rock faces carved by retreating rivers of ice.

Perhaps no traveller loved Alaska more than John Muir. A natural-ist, mountaineer and writer, Muir was a man of strong opinions who quickly lost patience with others who didn't show sufficient interest in

the natural forces – glacial action in particular – that have shaped and are still shaping the land-scapes of Alaska. "Most people who travel look only at what they are directed to look at," he wrote in *Travels in Alaska*. "Great is the power of the guidebook maker, however ignorant."

As the maker of this particular guidebook, I can only hope that Mr. Muir – were he alive today – would not call me ignorant and that he might agree with some of the sentiments expressed here about his beloved Alaska. As for you the traveller, I hope this book will help you see things that might otherwise go unnoticed as you cruise one of the most spectacular coast-lines in the world. – *Anne Vipond*

Sitka National Historical Park

(Top) Glacier Bay
(Above) Ketchikan
(Left) Misty Fjords
(Bottom) Kodiak Island

PART I

GENERAL INFORMATION

WHEN TO GO

The Alaska cruise season stretches from mid-May through September, with late June to mid-August being the peak season. June and July are the brightest months, with early dawns and daylight lasting well into the evening during the northern summer. Flowers are in full bloom, and Pacific humpback whales can be sighted in local waters, for coastal Alaska is their summer feeding grounds. In late July, salmon start swimming upstream along riverbeds and creeks, and passengers have numerous opportunities to witness the fascinating and heroic efforts of these sleek fish returning to their natal streams to spawn. Salmon lure other wildlife out of hiding, as brown bears and bald eagles appear along shorelines and streams to feed on the weary fish.

The shoulder seasons of spring and fall offer more than just reduced fares and fewer people. Springtime brings heavy run-off from mountain snowfields, producing a multitude of cascading waterfalls along the steep channels and inlets of the cruise route. The southern ports of Seattle, Vancouver and Victoria are pleasantly warm in spring, and their surrounding mountain peaks look their most stunning, still crowned with snow at higher elevations. Fall is the time of year to see Pacific white-sided dolphins rejoice in their annual rite – mating – and their acrobatics are a delight to watch when dozens of these swift swimmers make a beeline for a large cruise ship to leap in its bow wave.

Alaska is said to be a place where you can experience all four seasons in one day. The weather is unpredictable and localized, with rain always a possibility along the coast, even in the middle of summer. Fog can also occur in late summer and early fall, but is not prevalent in spring or early summer.

Parks and gardens of coastal Alaska, nurtured by moisture and moderate temperatures, retain their splendor throughout the summer.

WHICH ITINERARY?

The selection has never been better for travellers pondering an Alaska cruise. The ships servicing this region range from some of the newest and largest, carrying 2,000-plus passengers and offering a myriad of on-board amenities, to small cruisers carrying less than 100 passengers and able to get close enough to a berg to plunk ice into your drink.

The majority of cruises depart from Vancouver or Seattle in the south, and from Seward or Whittier (both located near Anchorage) in the north. Weekend departures are the most popular and seven-day itineraries are widely offered. Longer itineraries of 10 or more days are also available, notably on ships departing from San Francisco, and a few three- to five-day cruises are also offered out of Vancouver and Seattle, usually at the beginning or end of the season. Organized shore excursions can be taken at each port of call, and for passengers who want to see more of interior Alaska and Canada, extended land tours are offered by most cruise lines. (These are described in the next section.)

The large ships trace two main routes: the Inside Passage – a loop cruise from Vancouver or Seattle to the Panhandle and back; and the Gulf of Alaska – a one-way cruise between Vancouver and Seward or Whittier. The small ships that service these routes call both at major ports and minor ones not normally visited by large ships, and they offer imaginative itineraries into less-travelled fjords of the coast. The Inside Passage can also be travelled by government-operated ferries, which follow the same channels as the cruise ships but they don't make sightseeing detours into glacier-fed inlets and their schedules don't always provide ample time in port to fully enjoy the local attractions.

The Alaska fleet is one of the newest in the world, with most ships built within the last decade.

The Inside Passage to Alaska is so named because it lies 'inside' a long chain of coastal islands that act as a protective buffer from the open seas of the North Pacific Ocean. Rugged capes, cliffs and fjords define this coast, and each hour of cruising brings another spectacular scene into view. This route remains extremely popular for very good reasons: dramatic scenery, friendly Alaskan ports, numerous port-of-call attractions, and a mild, maritime climate.

The Inside Passage cruise is an excellent introduction to Alaska. Usually seven days in duration, this round trip will whisk you past hundreds of miles of intricate coastline as the ship threads its way along narrow, winding channels, past forested islands and mountain-bounded inlets. Starting and ending in Vancouver or Seattle, the turn-around point is Skagway (at the top of the Inside Passage) or Hubbard Glacier, near the top of the Panhandle. This cruise will stop at three or four ports-of-call and will include a close-up look at a tidewater glacier.

A full day is spent travelling to Alaska and the exact route a ship takes is often at the captain's discretion, depending on the weather and and other factors. Time constraints are the main reason most ships departing from Seattle bypass British Columbia's Inside Passage, instead heading up the west side of Vancouver Island and the Queen Charlotte Islands on their way to and from Alaska. Ships departing from Vancouver travel inside waters, transiting Seymour Narrows (a major pass of the Inside Passage) and Johnstone Strait, where killer whales are often sighted when the ship is southbound. The route taken along British Columbia's north coast is at the captain's discretion and depends on various factors, including visibility (i.e. fog) and whether commercial fishboats are clogging any of the narrow channels.

Prince Rupert is British Columbia's northernmost port of the Inside Passage, but the main ports-of-call are in Southeast Alaska: Ketchikan, Juneau, Skagway and Sitka. Passengers disembark at several of these for a day of shore activities. The highlight of an Inside Passage cruise is

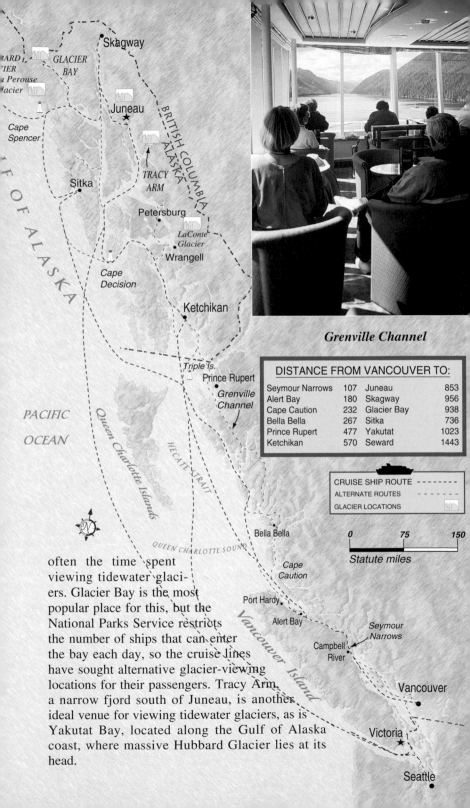

Skagway

GLACIER
BAY

a Perouse
acier

Cape
Spencer

Juneau

BRITISH COLUMBIA
ALASKA

TRACY
ARM

Sitka

Petersburg

LaConte
Glacier

Wrangell

GULF OF ALASKA

Cape
Decision

Ketchikan

PACIFIC

OCEAN

Queen Charlotte Islands

HECATE STRAIT

Triple Is.

Prince Rupert

Grenville
Channel

Grenville Channel

DISTANCE FROM VANCOUVER TO:			
Seymour Narrows	107	Juneau	853
Alert Bay	180	Skagway	956
Cape Caution	232	Glacier Bay	938
Bella Bella	267	Sitka	736
Prince Rupert	477	Yakutat	1023
Ketchikan	570	Seward	1443

CRUISE SHIP ROUTE - - - - - - -
ALTERNATE ROUTES - - - - - -
GLACIER LOCATIONS

QUEEN CHARLOTTE SOUND

Bella Bella

Cape
Caution

0   75   150

Statute miles

Port Hardy

Alert Bay

Seymour
Narrows

Campbell
River

Vancouver Island

Vancouver

Victoria

Seattle

often the time spent
viewing tidewater glaci-
ers. Glacier Bay is the most
popular place for this, but the
National Parks Service restricts
the number of ships that can enter
the bay each day, so the cruise lines
have sought alternative glacier-viewing
locations for their passengers. Tracy Arm,
a narrow fjord south of Juneau, is another
ideal venue for viewing tidewater glaciers, as is
Yakutat Bay, located along the Gulf of Alaska
coast, where massive Hubbard Glacier lies at its
head.

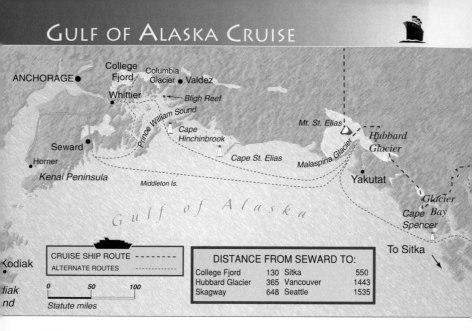

ANCHORAGE

College Fjord Columbia Glacier • Valdez

Whittier ★← Bligh Reef

Prince William Sound

Cape Hinchinbrook

Mt. St. Elias

Hubbard Glacier

Seward

Cape St. Elias

Malaspina Glacier

Homer

Kenai Peninsula

Middleton Is.

Yakutat

Gulf of Alaska

Glacier Bay

Cape Spencer

To Sitka

Kodiak

diak nd

| CRUISE SHIP ROUTE - - - - - - - |
| ALTERNATE ROUTES - - - - - - - |

0   50   100

Statute miles

DISTANCE FROM SEWARD TO:			
College Fjord	130	Sitka	550
Hubbard Glacier	365	Vancouver	1443
Skagway	648	Seattle	1535

These increasingly popular Gulf of Alaska cruises not only weave past the evergreen islands and turquoise fjords of the Inside Passage, but proceed further north into the Gulf of Alaska along one of the most rugged and remote coastlines in the world. A seven-day glacier cruise runs between Vancouver and Anchorage, spending four days travelling the Inside Passage and visiting several popular ports, such as Ketchikan, Juneau and Skagway. The Inside Passage portion of this itinerary often includes a day of glacier viewing in Tracy Arm or Glacier Bay.

Cruise ships bound for Hubbard Glacier at the top of the Alaska Panhandle will usually bypass Glacier Bay and proceed along Icy Strait into the Gulf of Alaska, taking passengers past one of the most spectacular stretches of coastline anywhere. Here the snow-covered mountains of the Fairweather Range rise abruptly from the ocean's edge, their steep summits glistening with ice. Fishing boats look like toys as they pass beneath these magnificent peaks, where the sprawling La Perouse Glacier discharges its icebergs directly into the open Pacific. More glaciers are found in Prince William Sound, where College Fjord is often the highlight of a Gulf of Alaska cruise because of the numerous glaciers lining this stunning inlet. Situated at the top of the Gulf of Alaska, the Sound's mainland shores are surrounded by snowcapped mountains and indented by dozens of glacier-carved fjords containing Alaska's greatest concentration of tidewater glaciers, 20 of them active. Columbia Glacier, near the port of Valdez, is the Sound's largest glacier and one of Alaska's most active.

Ships visiting Prince William Sound will pass within a few miles of Bligh Reef where the *Exxon Valdez* ran aground in March 1989. Cruise companies were just starting to venture into this area when the oil spill

A ship visiting College Fjord nudges close to a glacier's snout where chunks of ice will drop with a thunderous crash into the sea.

occurred and several cruise lines donated substantial funds to assist with clean-up efforts. There is little visible evidence today of the spill, although ongoing studies continue in coves and bays where foreshores and salmon streams were adversely affected.

Cruise ships pick their way carefully through the ice-clogged waters in front of Columbia before proceeding to College Fjord, its slopes lined with glaciers named in 1899 after the various Ivy League Schools associated with a team of research scientists exploring the region by steamship. Nearby is the port of Whittier, beautifully situated in a fjord of Prince William Sound. Whittier is an emerging cruise port with rail and road access to Anchorage but few amenities for visitors.

Seward is the other base port for cruises between Vancouver and Anchorage, and is located west of Prince William Sound, at the head of Resurrection Bay. Lying at the foot of the Kenai Mountains, this fishing and cargo port offers restaurants, lodges and the opportunity to visit the Alaska SeaLife Center. The town is also the headquarters for Kenai Fjords National Park, with boat excursions departing daily for tours of the nearby glacier-carved fjords.

CHOOSING A SHIP

Once you've decided which areas of coastal Alaska you want to see, the next step is deciding which cruise line to book with. This is not a simple decision but the cruise companies make it a pleasant exercise with handsome brochures containing information on their ships and itineraries. The on-board experience is fairly consistent throughout each of

Small ships can cruise closer to the scenery (above); large ships have more facilities (below).

the major cruise lines' fleet, and a good cruise agent will be able to explain the individual style of each cruise line. Let your cruise agent know what you're looking for in terms of atmosphere and activities, i.e. a casual, family-oriented vacation versus a more subdued and elegant ambience.

The cost of an Alaska cruise can vary dramatically, depending on your choice of cruise line and month of travel. Stateroom selection (ranging from an inside cabin to an outside deluxe suite with balcony) is another factor in the cost of a cruise. While it is possible to incur few additional expenses once you board a cruise ship, most passengers buy optional shore excursions and these also vary widely in price, depending on the excursion's length and mode of transportation.

Cruise ships have been compared to floating resorts, with the large ships offering an astounding array of onboard facilities and entertainment. The small ships offer more intimacy and closer proximity to the scenery. They also tend to be more casual than the large ships, the latter retaining traditions from the golden age of ocean liners, such as a Captain's Gala and dress codes for dinner, although optional casual dining is becoming a standard feature on the large ships.

Although cruises can be booked online, this isn't necessarily where the best deals are or where good advice can be found. Cruise lines are very loyal to cruise agents and if a hot price or

Cruise ships are floating resorts, offering a daily change of locale.

new itinerary is coming, agents almost always know about it first. However, it is best to use a qualified cruise agent when booking a cruise. A growing number of travel agents now specialize in cruises and are affiliated with **Cruise Lines International Association** (CLIA) – an independent marketing and training organization for the North American cruise industry. CLIA offers a course for travel agents which earns them Cruise Counselor Certification and provides them with a high level of expertise in cruise travel. Veteran cruise agents have gained their expertise through years of experience and will be able to guide you through the maze of ship choices, cabin considerations and itineraries.

Cruise lines reward people who book early with generous discounts, shipboard credits and, if the opportunity arises, free upgrades. If you know when you want to take your cruise vacation, book early and purchase cancellation insurance. Another advantage of booking early is the opportunity to make specific requests regarding your stateroom. If you are booking an outside stateroom on a northbound Gulf of Alaska cruise, ask to be placed on the starboard side of the ship so you will have views of the coastline from your cabin. If yours is a southbound cruise, ask to be on the port side. The same applies to flights to or from Anchorage – the starboard seats provide the best views when flying north; the port seats are best for southbound flights.

LAND TOURS

There is more than one Alaska. The vast and varied landscape of Alaska encompasses several ecosystems, from temperate rainforests to arctic tundra. A relatively short distance inland from the glacier-carved fjords and coastal ports visited by cruise ships lies the land of legend, where gold prospectors once toiled by the light of summer's midnight sun and where sled dogs are still used to travel the snow-covered mountain valleys and frozen rivers of winter.

To experience Alaska's interior entails booking a land tour in combination with a cruise, or independently arranging a pre- or post-cruise land trip. The major cruise lines offer an assortment of land tours that must be confirmed when you book your cruise, the complete package referred to as a cruisetour. Ranging from three to 11 days in duration (in addition to the cruise), these land tours cover hundreds of scenic miles by road, rail, river and air. They are not be to confused with 'shore excursions', which will be explained in the next section.

Although the rugged scenery of coastal Alaska is best enjoyed from the deck of a cruise ship, the inland regions can be well viewed from a rented car, a motorcoach, rail car or riverboat. Although wildlife sightings are less common on land than on water alert travelers often catch glimpses of moose and occasionally caribou along some of the remote interior routes.

Organized land tours often include driver-guides who explain the sights and whose local knowledge includes entertaining anecdotes about the various places you are visiting. If you prefer a bit more flexi-

bility, independent cruisetours are offered in which your accommodations and transportation are pre-arranged, and a tour company representative is on hand to answer questions, but you are free to do whatever you like at each stop. For total independence, you can rent a vehicle or ride the Alaska Railroad, following the same routes as an organized land tour and staying at the same hotels and wilderness lodges used by the cruise lines.

Mt. McKinley dominates the horizon north of Anchorage, where the scenic Parks Highway leads to Denali National Park.

The **Alaska Railroad** has provided a vital transportation link to Alaskans since 1923 and now caters to summertime visitors, providing regular rail service as well as an assortment of tour packages which include overnight accommodations and side trips. The Denali Star provides service between Anchorage and Fairbanks, with stops at Talkeetna and Denali National Park. The Coastal Classic runs south from Anchorage to Girdwood and Seward, and the Glacier Discovery runs between Anchorage and Whittier with stops at Girdwood and Portage. The cruise lines' private railcars also ride the Alaska Railroad and these provide luxury rail travel with their large domed windows providing panoramic views of the passing scenery. The cruise lines book their guests into their own lodges or those of comparable quality to ensure their passengers a consistent level of accommodation and service on the land portion of their cruisetour. Optional guided side trips are available at each destination, including river rafting, sportfishing and flightseeing. Or a person can just sit back and relax, enjoying the lodge's pristine setting and nearby nature trails.

The train ride to **Denali National Park** is slightly more scenic than the parallel highway, for the train traces the shorelines of lakes and generally provides a more intimate look at the countryside. The advantage to travelling by car, however, is that you can set your own schedule and be spontaneous, stopping anywhere you like along the way to take advantage of the many viewpoints and hiking trails. Major rental car firms are located in Anchorage, Fairbanks and throughout Alaska at communities serviced by an airport.

Cruisetours to Denali include luxury rail travel on private railcars.

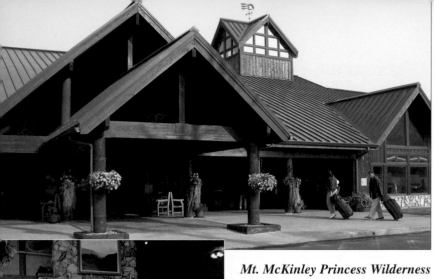

Mt. McKinley Princess Wilderness Lodge is a classic example of the lodges visited on cruisetours.

If you're travelling independently, you should reserve your overnight accommodations well in advance during the peak summer season, when many of the lodges often become fully booked. The advantage of taking a cruisetour is that all arrangements are taken care of by the cruise line, leaving you free to focus entirely on enjoying the scenery.

One of the most popular land tours is the trip to **Denali National Park and Preserve**, home to the tallest mountain in North America – Mt. McKinley. Rising above the surrounding countryside and visible from Anchorage on a clear day, this massive mountain's twin peaks stand in isolation, often shrouded in clouds that collect at the summit. Mt. McKinley is part of the 600-mile long Alaska Range, and the rail journey between Anchorage and Fairbanks provides breathtaking views of this range. Overnight accommodation is provided at lodges located just outside the entrance to Denali Park, which is 240 miles north of Anchorage and 120 miles south of Fairbanks. There are regular shuttles from these lodges to Denali Park, where park buses transport visitors to scenic landmarks, wildlife viewing spots and hiking trails. More lodges are located south of the park, near Talkeetna, where the views of Mt. McKinley are stunning.

There are many variations of Alaska cruisetours, some including a visit to the Copper River Valley. Others focus on Canada's Yukon where the Klondike Gold Rush can be relived in Whitehorse and Dawson City. Some tours (specifically those offered by Holland America Westours) begin or end at the Alaskan port of Skagway, where disembarking passengers are whisked by rail over the Chilkoot

Visitors hike the tundra-covered slopes of Kluane National Park in Canada's Yukon Territory.

Mountains to retrace the Trail of '98 to Dawson City. The Yukon's rugged and remote landscape encompasses **Kluane National Park**, which contains the most extensive non-polar icefields in the world, and the sub-arctic terrain of **Tombstone Territorial Park**. Another way to see this beautiful Canadian wilderness is by rented vehicle from Anchorage or Fairbanks.

Gates of the Arctic National Park lies north of Fairbanks, nearly 100 miles north of the Arctic Circle, and it too can be visited on a cruisetour, as can Prudhoe Bay, on the shores of the Beaufort Sea and the source of the Trans-Alaska Oil Pipeline which runs the length of Alaska to Valdez. To cover these vast distances in a reasonable amount of time, air travel to or from Fairbanks is used in addition to highway driving. This can also be arranged independently in Anchorage through tour companies which are often stationed in the larger hotels.

Another, more accessible region to explore by land tour is the **Kenai Peninsula**. Passengers embarking or disembarking in Seward will have an opportunity to see some of Kenai's magnificent mountain scenery while transferring to or from Anchorage by railcar or motor coach. However, those who opt to spend a few days in the area can visit **Kenai Fjords National Park** by tour boat from Seward, as well as Exit Glacier, where a trail leads from the parking lot right to the face of the glacier. Other attractions include the scenic fishing port and artists' enclave of Homer, situated on the shores of Kachemak Bay. Luxury lodges in the area include the Kenai Princess Wilderness Lodge, nestled on the banks of the Kenai River, and the Seward Windsong Lodge, located in a forest setting along the road to Exit Glacier.

At the head of Turnagain Arm, where a neck of land connects the Kenai Peninsula with mainland Alaska, is the Portage area. This area can be visited with an organized cruise tour; the luxury Alyeska Prince

Hotel & Resort near Girdwood is the area's premier accommodation. The nearby **Portage Valley** is ideal for independent travel, with numerous hiking trails, including one that winds along the edge of a meltwater stream to Byron Glacier where you can climb onto its snow-covered snout and gaze down the green valley that was once filled with ice.

Whether you book a cruisetour, or travel independently, the lodges owned or utilized by the cruise companies are an integral part of the Alaska land experience. Princess is the leader in this category, owning an impressive network of luxury lodges in Alaska, including the Denali Princess Wilderness Lodge near the park entrance and the Mt. McKinley Princess Wilderness Lodge near Talkeetna. Also in the vicinity is the Talkeetna Alaskan Lodge, operated by Alaska Heritage Tours, which is an Alaskan-owned and operated company whose resort properties include the Seward Windsong Lodge and whose services include day cruises of the Kenai Fjords and Prince William Sound.

The Westmark chain of hotels (owned by Holland America Westours) has properties throughout much of Alaska and Canada's Yukon. In Anchorage, the choice of hotels ranges from the Hilton and Sheraton to family-owned motels. The Coast Anchorage is a mid-priced hotel conveniently located near the airport on the shores of Lake Spenard, where floatplanes regularly land and take off, and where flightseeing tours depart. Longer flights available from Anchorage include one to the Eskimo village of Kotzebue, north of the Arctic Circle on the Bering Sea Coast. You can also fly to Nome – a town rich in gold rush history and the location of the finish line for the famous Iditarod Trail Dog Sled Race which is held each March, starting at Anchorage. The return fare to Nome and other points north is about $500 per person.

Kenai Princess Lodge

One of the most enduring land tours available to Alaska cruise passengers isn't even in Alaska. It's the ever-popular trip to Canada's Rocky Mountains where **Banff National Park** has drawn visitors for more than a century to its famous mountain lakes and river gorges. The Canadian Rockies can be reached by road or by rail from Vancouver and Seattle. Passengers on a pre-cruise land tour usually fly to Calgary, situated an hour's drive east of Banff in the foothills of the Rockies, and proceed from there by train or motorcoach to Banff National Park where famous sights include the turquoise blue waters of Lake Louise and the Banff Springs Hotel, which resembles a Scottish castle on the banks of the Bow River. From Banff, a tour might proceed north along the scenic Icefields Parkway to **Jasper National Park** and an overnight stay at the Jasper Park Lodge before turning westward, past Mount Robson (highest peak in the Rockies) toward Vancouver, stopping overnight in Kamloops. Rocky Mountaineer Railtours, which has hosted Bill Gates and other celebrities, is often used by the cruise companies for these classic land tours. **Whistler**, a ski resort to the north of Vancouver, is another popular pre- or post-cruise destination, as is the British-flavored city of Victoria and nearby Butchart Gardens. Victoria, the provincial capital of British Columbia, is also a popular port of call for cruises out of Seattle.

For more detailed information on specific places mentioned in the above Land Tours section, refer to the Table of Contents or Index.

(Above) Hiking at the base of Byron Glacier in the Portage Valley. (Below) Enjoying a relaxing soak before dinner at the Kenai Princess Lodge.

SHORE EXCURSIONS

A cruise to Alaska offers many highlights, and shore excursions often top the list. These port-of-call activities are purely optional but usually worth the additional expense as most cruise lines offer a wide selection of high-quality excursions. The following is an overview of the shore excursions being offered in Alaska. (For detail on each port's attractions, many of which are within easy walking distance of the cruise dock, please turn to the applicable chapter in Part II of this book.)

Captivating as the ports themselves are, their outlying wilderness areas are what many people envision when they think of Alaska. And there's no better way to see a large wilderness area in a short time than from a floatplane or helicopter. The floatplanes usually take off right beside the ship or a short distance from where it's docked, and heli-copter lift off at nearby airports.

Weather checks are made every hour and if your flight is cancelled, you will receive a full refund. However, aircraft still fly in cloudy weather – when the crystal blue ice of a glacier looks even bluer and the fjords are said to be their most beautiful, with mist rising from the water. A few of the day-long excursions depend on evening light for return flights and may not be offered late in the season, but most run throughout the entire cruise season in all types of weather. Headsets are provided with commentary to keep you informed while in flight, but such narration is secondary to the incredible landscapes passing beneath your aircraft.

Glaciers come in many forms and from the air you'll gain a different perspective of them. You'll see entire valleys filled with ice and thick

Although expensive ($200 plus), a helicopter flight to a glacier is one of the most exciting shore excursions offered on an Alaska cruise.

sheets of snow blanketing mountain-sides. You'll also see blue ice hanging from valley walls, and row upon row of icy pinnacles frozen in a downhill march. If you choose a helicopter tour, your pilot will land the plane right on a glacier and in the moon boots provided you will walk on the surface of a glacier and peer down its deep crevasses. Some heli-seeing flights include a visit to a dog-sled camp where you have the opportunity to meet dog teams that compete in the Iditarod Trail Sled Dog Race and mush with them across a glacier before reboarding your helicopter. In late summer, however, this ice can become too soft to continue the sled-dog excursions and these will be cancelled in such conditions. Also, the air temperature on these icefields is considerably colder than at sea level, so pack a warm jacket, wool hat and gloves if you plan to go dog-sledding.

Shore excursions are the best way to see Alaska's wildlife and glaciers up close.

Flightseeing trips are not the only adventures offered while in port. Water-borne excursions abound: river rafting, lake canoeing, sea kayaking, sportfishing and whale-watching are all offered. Even seemingly sedate tours by coach are informative, entertaining and a good way to get an overview of a port before setting off by yourself on foot. These tours also give you an opportunity to meet the people who live and work in Alaska, and to ask them a few questions.

Each port has excursions unique to its area and these are detailed at the end of each chapter. For instance, Ketchikan is the flightseeing base for the Misty Fjords, which is a post-ice age landscape of forests, fjords and pristine mountain lakes, upon which your floatplane will land for a few idyllic minutes. Also popular in

(Above) A kayaking excursion heads up Ketchikan Creek. (Below) Good value can sometimes be had with independent tour operators.

Ketchikan are the native culture tours to Saxman Village and Totem Bight Park.

Juneau is one of the main ports for taking flights over the massive Juneau Icefield with its many glaciers. Landing on a glacier in a helicopter is a thrilling experience, as is flying over the icefield to Taku Inlet for a salmon bake at a wilderness lodge. Coach tours and shuttle buses take passengers to Mendenhall Glacier and the Mount Roberts tramcar is right beside the cruise dock where it whisks visitors to an alpine setting above the Gastineau Canal. Golfing and gold panning are also offered in Juneau, as are excellent whale-watching boat tours.

Skagway, at the head of Lynn Canal, is another port of call offering unique shore excursions. This is where thousands of gold rush prospectors began their trek to the Klondike, and Skagway's tours reflect this colorful past. Most impressive is a ride on the narrow-gauge railway across gorges and through tunnels to the White Pass Summit – one of the gruelling routes taken by stampeders and their pack animals when following the Trail of '98. The Chilkat Bald Eagle Preserve at nearby Haines is also worth seeing.

More wildlife watching is offered at Sitka where sea otters are often sighted. Sitka's Russian and native history is highlighted in city tours which include the totem-lined paths of Sitka Historical Park.

For passengers choosing a Gulf of Alaska cruise to Anchorage, excursions include a boat trip across Portage Lake to view the Portage Glacier, and city tours of Anchorage.

Reserving: Shore excursions can be viewed at each cruise line's website and once you've booked a cruise, you can reserve shore excursions online. Those worth booking in advance are the ones that have limited capacity, such as flightseeing, and these are sold on a first come/first served basis. Your cruise line will enclose, with your ticket, a booklet of information on their shore excursions. These are grouped by port of call, with their activities described and their prices indicated. In addition to advance booking now offered by many of the cruise lines, once you're on board the ship you can book (or cancel) your excursions right up to the evening before you pull into that port – assuming a particular shore excursion isn't sold out.

The ship's Shore Excursion Desk is there to help with bookings, answer questions and provide information. The shore excursion staff can help you co-ordinate your excursions if you decide to take two while in a port and are concerned about a conflict in timing. If you book your shore excursions through the cruise line, there's no need to worry about getting back to the ship on time – the shore excursion staff will make sure everyone's back on board before the ship departs.

It's also possible to book shore excursions with **independent tour operators** (which have kiosks at the docks of most ports), either on the spot at the port or in advance. Prices are about 10 per cent cheaper and should you decide to do this, bear in mind that you're responsible for getting yourself back to the ship before departure and if you are late, the ship will leave without you.

Travellers to Alaska should adopt a bit of pioneer spirit if they are going to get the most out of their port visits. This means preparing for the changeable weather by dressing in layers to stay warm and dry (shirt, sweater, jacket, rain poncho). Also, when selecting your shore excursions, try to allow time for a leisurely stroll at each port of call so you can soak up your own impressions.

Rock climbing near Skagway has become very popular with cruisers.

(Top) Ships departing Vancouver's scenic harbor pass beneath the Lions Gate Bridge.
(Below) The Seattle skyline fades astern as a ship departs for Alaska.

(Above) The Empress Hotel, Victoria.
(Left) Alaska's Russian heritage is showcased in Sitka.
(Below) Colorful Creek Street in Ketchikan.

(Above) The fishing town of Seward is a northern base port for Gulf of Alaska cruises.
(Left) The northern base port of Whittier is situated in scenic Prince William Sound.
(Below) Anchorage's Town Square.

(Above) *Juneau, Alaska's state capital, is scenically situated on the shores of Gastineau Channel.*
(Right) *Haines is located near Skagway in Lynn Canal.*
(Below) *Streetcar tours of Skagway help visitors relive the town's gold rush days.*

Documentation & Currency

A valid passport is the best proof of citizenship a traveller can carry and one that may be mandatory by 2007 for all U.S. and Canadian citizens taking a cruise to Alaska. Meanwhile, American citizens entering Canada must carry proof of U.S. citizenship, such as a birth certificate, accompanied by an official photo identification, such as a current driver's license. Canadians must carry similar proof of citizenship upon entering Alaska. If you're a non-U.S. citizen residing in America, verify with your travel agent the existing identification requirements. Most cruise lines post the current passport and visa requirements on their websites.

Before your departure, leave a detailed travel itinerary with a family member, friend or neighbor. Include the name of your ship, its phone number and the applicable ocean code, as well as your stateroom number – all of which will be provided with your cruise documentation. With this information, a person back home can place a satellite call to your ship in an emergency. Another precaution is to photocopy, on a single sheet of paper, the identification page of your passport, your driver's license and all credit cards. Keep one copy of this sheet with you, separate from your passport and wallet, and leave another one at home.

Travel insurance is recommended. A comprehensive policy will cover travel cancellation, delayed departure, medical expenses, personal accident and liability, lost baggage and money, and legal expenses. You may already have supplementary health insurance through a credit card, automobile club policy or employment health plan, but you should check these carefully. Carry details of your policy with you and documentation showing that you are covered by a plan.

American currency is used in Alaska of course, and is also accepted by most Canadian businesses, but you'll receive the best rate of exchange at a bank or currency exchange service when in Canada. Automatic tellers in Canada and Alaska are connected to major ATM networks. Visa, MasterCard and American Express credit cards are widely accepted.

From the ship's rail, a pair of binoculars will give you a closer look at the snow-covered mountains and tidewater glaciers of Alaska.

WHAT TO PACK

Bring casual attire for daytime wear – both on board the
ship and in port. The weather in Alaska can change rapidly,
so dress in layers. Start with slacks and a light shirt, then a
sweater or sweatshirt, and end with a rainproof jacket. Also
take an umbrella or wide-brimmed hat, in case you get caught
in a downpour. If the sun shines, you can peel off a couple
of layers, and if the sky suddenly clouds over, you won't be
cold. Also bring resort wear – on sunny summer days it will be warm
enough to sunbathe by the swimming pool. The southern ports of
Vancouver and Seattle can reach temperatures of 80 F in summer, as
can the interiors of Alaska and Canada's Yukon. Nights can be cool.

Footwear is also important. Your shoes should be comfortable, with
thick soles and good ankle support, and leather is preferable to canvas
in wet conditions. Give your shoes a good spray of all-weather protec-
tor before packing them and bring along a second pair in case your first
pair gets soaked and needs time to dry. A woolen hat is also recommended for brisk days at sea or when your ship is approaching a tidewater glacier, where the air is cool. Sunglasses are another must. There
is always some glare off the water, even on overcast days. If you plan
on taking a helicopter excursion to a glacier, be sure to pack a warm
jacket, wool hat and gloves. Boots will be provided by the tour operator. If you're heading inland on a cruisetour, bring insect repellent.

Your evening wear should include something suitable for the one or
two formal nights held on board the large ships. Women wear gowns or
cocktail dresses on these occasions and
men favor dark suits or tuxedos. For infor-
mal evenings, women wear dresses, skirts
or slacks, and men wear a shirt and tie, or a
sports jacket with an open-necked shirt.

Check with your travel agent regarding
your ship's on-board facilities, such as
whether there will be a hair dryer in your
cabin, and whether the ship has coin-oper-
ated laundrettes with irons and ironing
boards. Those that don't will provide a
laundering service (the cost is approxi-
mately $15 for a bag of clothes, washed
and pressed), and hand washing can be
done in your cabin. Dry cleaning is another
service offered on the large ships. Basic
toiletries can be purchased aboard the ship.

*Pack mostly casual attire, except for the
one or two formal nights on your ship.*

Keep any valuables (jewelry, travellers cheques, camera, etc.) in your carry-on luggage as well as all documentation (tickets, passport, etc.), prescription medicines and eyeglasses. Keep prescribed medication in original, labeled containers and carry a doctor's prescription for any controlled drug. If you wear prescription eyeglasses or contact lenses, consider packing a spare pair. It's also prudent to pack in your carry-on bag any other essentials you would need in the event that your luggage is late arriving.

HEALTH PRECAUTIONS

All large ships have fully equipped medical center with a doctor and nurses. Passengers needing medical attention are billed at private rates, which are added to their shipboard account. This invoice can be submitted to your insurance company upon your return home.

Sea sickness is not a widespread or prolonged problem on Alaska cruises, especially in the protected waters of the Inside Passage. Modern ships also use stabilizers to reduce any rolling motion when in open seas. However, if you're susceptible to motion sickness, there are a number of remedies. One is to wear special wrist bands, the balls of which rest on an acupressure point. Over-the-counter medications include Dramamine or Gravol pills, which should be taken ahead of time, before you start to feel nauseous. Another option is to chew Meclizine tablets (usually available at the ship's infirmary). Check first with your doctor before taking any medication. Natural remedies include taking ginger in capsule form or sipping on ginger ale and nibbling on dry crackers. Fresh air is another antidote.

SHOPPING

Luxury goods are sold (tax and duty-free) at the on-board shops, but if Alaskan handcrafted items are what you're looking for, the ports of call

are where you'll be doing much of your shopping. The shopping districts at most Alaskan ports are located within walking distance of the ship or tender docks. The shops themselves are often housed in or among the town's historic buildings and are part of a walking tour – so you can mix sightseeing with shopping.

If you're looking for 'authentic' Alaskan souvenirs, be sure the item carries one of two symbols: the Silver Hand on authentic native handicrafts from Alaska,

Ivory carvings, often using walrus tusks from the Bering Sea, are popular items for purchase in Alaska stores.

or the Made in Alaska polar bear on items made by Alaskans. In the southern port cities of Seattle, Vancouver and Victoria, native handicrafts and works of art sold at local galleries and gift shops include items made by native peoples of Washington State and British Columbia, as well as Inuit carvings from Northern Canada. (See the Native Art section on page 100 for more detail.)

Northwest Coast native crafts include engraved silver jewelry, wood and soapstone carvings, silkscreen prints, ceremonial masks and beaded moccasins. Different native groups specialize in different art forms and use a variety of materials, including argillite (a compact, grayish-brown rock used primarily by the Haida) and soapstone, a soft rock with a soapy feel that ranges in color from gray to green. If a sculpture you are considering for purchase is warm to the touch, it is likely made not of soapstone but of resin. Stone is cool to the touch and is heavier than plastic.

Look for these logos of authenticity on Alaska souvenirs.

The quality of native art can vary, and the price usually reflects the level of artistry or craftsmanship that created the piece. Shop at reputable venues, i.e. museum gift shops or galleries recommended by the cruise line, and ask for written proof of an expensive piece's authenticity. If you buy an ivory carving, the U.S. Fish & Wildlife Service requires that you buy an export/transit permit unless you choose to mail it home. In Canada, whalebone and walrus ivory are both banned imports, but not mammoth tusk ivory which has beautiful honeycomb patterns. Walrus ivory is a popular medium in Alaska, and only Native Alaskans are allowed to carve a piece of new walrus ivory, its thin black lines occurring naturally when a walrus experiences abrupt changes in temperature as it leaves its rock haul-out and dives into icy cold Arctic water.

Gold nugget jewelry is another popular Alaskan souvenir. These nuggets are sold in their natural shape – unaltered and mounted with prongs onto pendants. Each nugget is unique and has a gold content of 70 to 95 percent (compared to 41 percent in 10 karat gold and 58.5 percent in 14 karat gold). The nuggets are weighed by troy ounce, which is slightly heavier than a standard ounce. Every gold nugget is unique, and a gold expert can identify its source creek by examining the nugget's color and texture. Local gems include jade (in a variety of colors) and blue topaz – also called 'glacier ice.'

Smoked salmon comes vacuum-packed and is handsomely packaged for take-home gifts. Russian stacking dolls, lacquer boxes and hand-painted icons are other popular items.

VACATION PHOTOS

There is much to photograph during a trip to Alaska and photography buffs will enjoy the challenge of capturing on film the region's unique landscapes, seascapes and wildlife. A zoom lens is mandatory for shooting wildlife but a large supply of patience is even more critical. Professional photographers spend days, even weeks, waiting to get a good shot of a whale breaching or an eagle plucking a salmon from the water. Count yourself lucky if you get a good action shot of an animal in the wild. Natural lighting is also unpredictable because of Alaska's changeable weather, but northern skies – especially around sunrise and sunset – often provide dramatic lighting conditions.

For automatic cameras, 200-ASA print film is your best choice for all-around lighting conditions, and this speed of film is less likely to be damaged by the powerful X-ray machines now used at airports. Exposed but undeveloped film should not be put in checked luggage but placed in a carry-on bag where it can withstand about five X-rays at walk-through security checkpoints before becoming damaged. Another option is to place your rolls of film in a see-through plastic bag and ask for a hand inspection, or have your film developed on board the ship before returning home.

If using a digital camera, be sure to have a total of at least 128 mb of flash card memory storage and shoot at a fine setting for print quality reproduction. A laptop computer will of course provide lots of storage, and most on-board photo departments can develop digital images into prints. Print film can be bought on most ships or in the ports of call, but slide

Taking big pictures with small cameras is one of the joys of visiting Alaska.

film is sometimes harder to find. Put fresh batteries in your camera before leaving home, or pack an extra battery pack if you're using a digital camera. Flash cards can be purchased in most ports in Alaska.

Phoning and E-Mailing home

In addition to sharing the longest undefended border in the world, Canada and the United States also share time zones. Most of British Columbia and Yukon Territory are part of the Pacific Time Zone. Alaska has its own time zone, which is one hour behind Pacific Time. Long-distance calls can be made between Canada and the U.S. without dialing a country code. Cell phone service is available, with most of Southeast Alaska serviced by the same cell zone, and your phone should get reception in roaming mode. Perhaps the easiest and cheapest way to contact family and friends back home is the Internet. Most ships have computers on board and offer flat-rate use (about $10 for 15 to 20 minutes). Recently, some lines have lowered this cost and some even allow passengers to use their own computers to plug into the ship's connection, which is about a 56k speed or better, so emailing images of your trip to friends and family is an easy procedure.

Passengers log into the internet through their shipboard card, issued on boarding, and within seconds are online. At the end of the session most ships systems show the passenger time on the internet and total cost. No matter where you are, at sea or in port, you can send an e-mail instantly from almost all of the ships of the current Alaska fleet.

There are excellent internet cafes on most of the newer ships, such as this one on the Diamond Princess.

The romance of a cruise ship derives from many sources: a change of routine, meeting new people, and returning to a time when travel was slower and more intimate. Literature, movies and television have all contributed to the allure of ships. Even the language of the sea is exotic.

The complexities of safely operating ocean-going vessels prompted mariners to develop their own nomenclature, its conciseness transcending the descriptive power of landlocked words and phrases. Its colorful vocabulary has been adapted with lyrical precision to describe each task. As quoted in Smythe's Sailor's Word-Book, "How could the whereabouts of an aching tooth be better pointed out to an operative dentist than Jack's, 'Tis the aftermost grinder aloft, on the starboard quarter.'"

Cruise ships have plied the waters of the Inside Passage to Alaska for well over 100 years. The noted writer and naturalist John Muir first arrived in Alaska by steamship in 1879 and his writings about Glacier Bay sparked tremendous interest in the area. Soon more ships, including those of Canadian Pacific, were bringing travellers to view this unique area. However, it wasn't until 1957 that Alaskan cruises came into their own. In that year, Westours became the first dedicated Alaska cruise-ship operator when it purchased two 110-passenger steamships, *Coquitlam* and *Camosun*, from Union Steamships Ltd. of Vancouver. Westours was founded by a Fairbanks tour operator named Chuck West who pioneered nearly every element of Alaska's travel industry and eventually sold his company to Holland America Line. In 1969, Westours was joined by P&O's Princess Cruises and the cruise business grew into an industry which today employs thousands of people.

*P&O's **Arcadia** was one of the first large liners to cruise Alaska's Inside Passage in the late 1960s. Built in 1954, she was 30,000 tons and carried 647 first-class and 735 tourist-class passengers.*

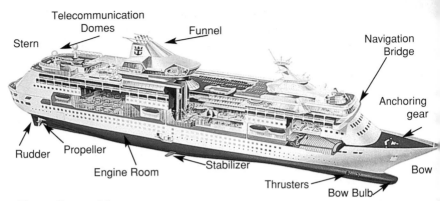

HOW SHIPS MOVE

Ships are pushed through the water by the turning of propellers, two of which are usually used on cruise ships. A propeller is like a screw threading its way through the sea, pushing water away from its pitched blades. Props can be 15 to 20 feet in diameter on large cruise ships and normally turn at 100 to 150 revolutions per minute. It takes a lot of horsepower – about 50,000 on a large ship – to make these propellers push a ship along. The bridge crew can tap into any amount of engine power by moving small levers which adjust the angle (or pitch) of the propeller blades to determine the speed of the ship. In addition to propelling the ship, the engines generate hot water and electrical power. Cruise ships normally travel at about 16 to 20 knots between ports.

The amount of soot smoke from today's ships is a fraction of that produced by earlier ships of the last century. Today, all ships use diesel engines to transmit the power by supplying electricity either to motors that smoothly turn the prop shafts or to motors mounted on pods hung from the stern of the ship, like huge outboard motors, which can swivel 360 degrees. The fuel used by ships on the Alaska run is a higher grade than normal, producing minimal smoke and pollution.

The majority of cruise ships currently sailing Alaskan waters were built in the last decade – a testament to the booming cruise industry. These new ships have been dubbed 'floating resorts' for their extensive on-board facilities, from swimming pools and health spas to show lounges and casinos. Cabins, formerly equipped with portholes, now are fitted with picture windows or sliding glass doors that open onto private verandas. Modern cruise ships are quite different from those of the Golden Age of ocean liners, which ended on a high note with the launch of the SS *France* (which became the *Norway*) in 1960 and the *Queen Elizabeth II* in 1969. These ships were designed for the rigors of regular year-round ocean crossings and some of the worst weather imaginable. Constructed with heavy riveted plating, their design features included a deep draft (more stability in rough seas) and a low profile (less windage, more maneuverability in storms).

The streamlined look of a modern cruise ship includes glass-enclosed outside elevators. Shown here is Royal Caribbean's Serenade of the Seas, launched in 2003.

Ships built today are generally taller, shallower, lighter and powered by smaller, more compact engines. Although their steel hulls are thinner and welded together in numerous sections, modern ships are as strong as the older ocean liners because of advances in construction technology and metallurgy.

An Alaskan cruise is mainly along protected coastal waters and rough conditions are uncommon. The two areas where some ocean swell will be felt are in Queen Charlotte Sound and north of Glacier Bay in the Gulf of Alaska. Challenges for the crew when navigating Alaska include times when ships execute a tight turn around one of the many islands of the Inside Passage. Officers begin the turn well ahead of time and the stern – because of the ship's flat bottom – seems to slide across the water for some distance before it gains way or speed in the new direction. Large ships generally travel at speeds of 10 to 20 knots on Alaskan cruises, depending on distances to be covered from port to port. Distances at sea are measured in nautical miles (1 nautical mile = 1.15 statute miles = 1.85 kilometres).

THE ENGINE ROOM

Located many decks below passenger cabins is the engine room, a labyrinth of tunnels, catwalks and bulkheads connecting and supporting the machinery that generates the vast amount of power needed to operate a ship. A large, proficient crew keeps everything running smoothly, but its size is a far cry from the hundreds once needed to operate coal-burning steam engines used before the advent of diesel fuel.

Three recent technical advancements below the ship's waterline include the bow bulb, stabilizers and thrusters. The *bow bulb* is just below the waterline and displaces the same amount of water that would be pushed out of the way by the ship's bow. This virtually eliminates a bow wave, resulting in some fuel saving because less energy is needed to push the ship forward. *Stabilizers* are small, wing-like appendages that protrude amidships below the waterline and act to dampen the ship's roll in beam seas. These are normally not needed during an Alaskan cruise. *Thrusters* are port-like openings with small propellers at the bow and sometimes also at the stern, located just below the waterline. They push the front or rear of the ship as it is approaching or leaving a dock and greatly reduce the need for tugboat assistance.

THE BRIDGE

The bridge (located at the bow or front of the ship) is an elevated, enclosed platform bridging (or crossing) the width of the ship with an unobstructed view ahead and to either side. It is from the ship's bridge that the highest-ranking officer, the captain, oversees the operation of the ship. The bridge is manned 24 hours a day by two officers working four hours on, eight hours off, in a three-watch system. They all report to the captain, and their various duties include recording all course changes, keeping lookout and making sure the junior officer keeps a fresh pot of coffee going. The captain does not usually have a set watch but will be on the bridge when the ship is entering or leaving port, transiting a pass or approaching a tidewater glacier. Other conditions that would bring the captain to the bridge would be poor weather or when there are numerous vessels in the area, such as commercial fishboats.

An array of instrumentation provides the ship's officers with pertinent information. The electronic Global Positioning System (GPS) uses a system of satellite signals to provide a fix of where the ship is, accurate to within a few feet. This position is displayed in a series of numbers indicating the latitude and longitude, which is compared with a chart (usually an electronic chart) to determine the ship's location.

The bridge on a modern cruise ship has space age features, such as small joy sticks with which officers manoeuvre the ship while seated.

Radar masts are positioned at the top of every ship.

Radar is used most intensely in foggy conditions or at night. Radar's electronic signals can survey the ocean for many miles, and anything solid – such as land or other boats – appears on its screen. Radar is also used for plotting the course of other ships and for alerting the crew of a potential collision situation. Depth sounders track the bottom of the seabed to ensure the ship's course agrees with the depth of water shown on the official chart.

The helm on modern ships is a surprisingly small wheel. An automatic telemotor transmission connects the wheel to the steering mechanism at the stern of the ship. Ships also use an 'autopilot' which works through an electronic compass to steer a set course. The autopilot is used when the ship is in open water.

Other instruments monitor engine speed, power, angle of list, speed through water, speed over ground (which is affected by the numerous currents encountered in the Inside Passage) and time arrival estimations. Along intricate sections of coastline, large ships must have a **pilot** on board to provide navigational advice to the ship's officers. These pilots have local knowledge of every back eddy, stray current and dangerous reef in their territory, and help thread the big ships through the narrow passes and channels that make Alaska cruises so thrilling. Canadian pilots are on board when a ship is travelling the inner channels of British Columbia's Inside Passage, and American pilots are on board when the ship is inside Alaskan coastal waters. These pilots embark and disembark the ship at various pilot stations along the cruise route. When a ship is in open waters, a pilot is not required.

There are many navigational challenges encountered on an Alaska cruise. Those commonly cited by pilots and officers include: Seymour Narrows (fast currents), Cape Caution (lumpy seas, reefs and occasional poor visibility), Snow Passage (fast currents, shallow and twisting passage), Cape Decision (choppy seas and often poor visibility combined with a blind corner), Cape Spencer (steep seas and contrary currents) and Cape St. Elias (lumpy seas, poor visibility). The Gulf of Alaska, between Glacier Bay and Seward can also be quite rough during storms. On the positive side, icebergs are generally not a safety factor because they usually melt before they drift into the shipping lanes, with the exception of the icebergs calving off Columbia Glacier near the Port of Valdez.

SHIP SAFETY

The cruise lines treat passenger safety as a top priority. The International Maritime Organization maintains high standards for safety at sea, including regular fire and lifeboat drills, as well as frequent ship inspections for cleanliness and seaworthiness.

Cruise ships must adhere to a law requiring that a lifeboat drill take place within 24 hours of embarkation, and many ships schedule this drill just before leaving port. You will be asked to don one of the life jackets kept in your cabin and proceed to your lifeboat station (directions will be displayed somewhere in your cabin). Ship's staff will be on hand to guide you through the safety drill but it's wise to pay attention so you know what to do in the unlikely event of an emergency. These safety instructions are similar to those issued on aircraft, and passengers shouldn't become apprehensive – cruise ships are one of the safest modes of travel.

On the ship's bridge, a large area of instrumentation is devoted to the monitoring of numerous fire alarms placed throughout the ship. If an alarm sounds, it rings on the bridge and is illuminated on a ship's diagram so that its location is immediately known and the officers can promptly secure the area to prevent the blaze from spreading. Next to ship navigation, the threat of a fire is the most serious concern for the ship's officers, and deck crews regularly practise fire safety drills.

HOTEL STAFF

The Purser's Office/Front Desk is the pleasure center of the ship. And since a cruise is meant to be an extremely enjoyable experience, it is fitting the Hotel Manager's rank is second only to that of the Captain. In terms of staff, the Hotel Manager (or Passenger Services Director) has by far the largest. It is his responsibility to make sure beds are made, meals are served, wines are poured, entertainment is provided and tour

The Front Desk is centrally located in the atrium area of the ship.

(Above) The hotel manager oversees a large and highly trained staff.
(Below) An outside suite with verandah.

buses arrive on time – all while keeping a smile on his face. Hotel managers generally have many years' experience on ships working in various departments before rising to this position, and usually have graduated from a university or college program in management. Often they train in the hotel or food industries, where they learn the logistics of feeding hundreds of people at a sitting.

A Hotel Manager's management staff includes a Purser, Food Service Manager, Beverage Manager, Chief Housekeeper, Cruise Director and Shore Excursion Manager. All ship's staff wear a uniform and even if a hotel officer doesn't recognize a staff member, he will know at a glance that person's duties by their uniform's color and the distinguishing bars on its sleeves. The hotel staff on cruise ships come from countries around the world.

LIFE ABOARD

Cruise ship cabins – also called staterooms – vary in size, from standard inside cabins to outside suites complete with a verandah. Whatever the size of your accommodation, it will be clean and comfortable. Telephone and television are standard features in cabins on almost all ships, and storage space includes closets and drawers ample enough to hold your clothes and miscellaneous items. Valuables can be left in your stateroom safe or in a safety deposit box at the front office, also called the purser's office.

If your budget permits, an outside cabin – especially one with a verandah – is preferable for enjoying the coastal scenery and orienting yourself at a new port. When selecting a cabin, keep in mind its location in relation to decks above and below. Being above the disco is fine if that is where you'll be to the wee hours, but if you are below the kitchen or dining room, you'll hear the scraping of chairs as a wake-up call. For those prone to seasickness, cabins located on lower decks near the middle of the ship will have less motion that a top outside cabin near the stern. If you have preferences for cabin location, be sure to discuss these with your cruise agent at the time of booking.

Both casual and formal dining are offered on the large ships, with breakfast and lunch served in the buffet-style lido restaurant or at an open seating in the main dining room. Dinner is served at two sittings in the dining room and, when booking your cruise, you will be asked to indicate your preference for first or second sitting at dinner. Some people prefer the first sitting as it leaves an entire evening afterwards to enjoy the stage shows and other venues. On the other hand, the second sitting allows plenty of time, after a full day in port, to freshen up before dinner. Many ships also offer alternative dining – small specialty restaurants that require a reservation and for which there is usually a charge (about $20 per person). Room service is also available, free of charge, for all meals and in-between snacks.

Alternative dining in specialty restaurants, in addition to meals served in the main dining room, is now offered on most large ships.

EXTRA EXPENSES

There are very few additional expenses once you board a cruise ship. Your cabin and meals (including 24-hour room service) are paid for, as are any stage shows, lectures, movies, lounge acts, exercise classes and other activities held in the ship's public areas. If you make use of the personal services offered on board – such as dry cleaning or a spa treatment – these are not covered in the basic price of a cruise. Neither are any drinks you might order in a lounge (although you can certainly sit there and enjoy the ambience without ordering a drink). You will also be charged for any wine or alcoholic beverages you order with your meals. Optional shore excursions are another additional cost.

Tipping is extra, with each cruise line providing its own guidelines on how much each crewmember should be tipped. On some cruise lines tipping is a personal choice while on others it is expected. A general amount for gratuities (in US dollars) is $3.50 per day per passenger for both your cabin steward and dining room steward, half that amount for your assistant waiter, and 10 to 15 percent of your total wine bill for the wine steward (unless this is automatically added to your receipt). Tips for these staff are usually given the last night at sea and preferably in American cash. Some cruise lines offer a service that automatically bills a daily amount for gratuities to your shipboard account; however, if you prefer to personally hand out your tips, you simply notify the

front desk and these automatic tipping charges will be removed from your account. Most ships are cashless societies in which passengers sign for incidental expenses which are itemized on a final statement that is slipped under your cabin door during the last night of your cruise and settled at the front office by credit card or cash.

Birthdays and anniversaries are celebrated with a complimentary cake.

ALASKA'S BUMPY BEGINNINGS

Alaska, were it rated by Hollywood censors, would receive an "R" for violence. A battle scene on a planetary scale is occurring along the west coast of North America where sections of the earth's crust – called tectonic plates – are colliding.

As the Pacific plate rams into the North American plate, dramatic action is taking place along the Gulf of Alaska coastline. Here, some of the world's tallest coastal mountains, caught between these two plates, are being shoved upwards. Others are slipping into the sea as they are dragged under along the collision zone. Something's got to give with this constant pushing and pulling going on, and that something is the occasional earthquake or volcanic eruption. Mountains twist, shake and heave tons of snow and rock from their slopes, or spew from their cores a fiery ash that turns day into night.

The tectonic tug of war that eventually formed Alaska, started when the earth's crust began dividing into plates – a process which seems to have started shortly after the crust was formed. As these large plates rubbed against each other, pieces chipped off and became terranes. These fragments could move more freely than the large plates and the earth's crust became a sort of jigsaw puzzle as pieces slowly moved from one location to another. An island, perhaps where the Philippines are today, gradually made its way across the Pacific Ocean to lie off Canada's West Coast and become part of Vancouver Island.

Over the last few hundred million years, terranes off the Pacific Plate have been pushed, as if on a conveyor belt, up the west side of the North American Plate where they docked against ancestral Alaska, and against one another, at the top of the Gulf of Alaska. These terranes are

Alaska's dramatic Gulf of Alaska coastline was formed by terranes – pieces of the earth's crust – being jammed between two major plates.

The Aleuts wore ceremonial cloaks made from the skins of hundreds of tufted puffins.

still moving today, with the Yakutat terrane riding on the Pacific plate but also docking against the earlier arrivals. If the terrane upon which Los Angeles sits continues moving north at its rate of two inches per year, it will reach the northern Gulf of Alaska in 76 million years.

The current era – the Cenozoic – began 65 million years ago. It began with volcanism and huge slices of crustal rocks stacking one upon the other to form the Rockies and other mountain ranges. Early whales appeared, as did the hardwoods and redwoods of North America. Then the warm, humid climate cooled and fur-bearing animals such as the bear, seal and raccoon came into being. As the climate continued to cool about five million years ago, the widespread giant ape evolved into a manlike ape, and the earliest human artifacts date from this era, which ended about two million years ago.

The Pleistocene era – the age of glaciers – came next and it contained four or five separate periods of major glacial advance and retreat. These rumbling fields of ice eroded rock and transported huge deposits of clay, sand and gravel across large sections of North America.

When the glaciers staged their most recent retreat 10,000 years ago, the landscape they left behind included lakes, valleys and fjords. Channels of the Inside Passage mark the location of inactive faults, their weakened rock eroded by glaciers to form U-shaped valleys that were eventually flooded by the rising sea. Some mammals (such as the sabertooth tiger) didn't survive the Great Ice Age, but homo sapiens did.

THE FIRST ARRIVALS

Ice covered much of Alaska during the age of glaciers, extending across the northern Gulf of Alaska. Sea levels were also lower, and an ice-free corridor of land connected Alaska with Siberia via the Bering Land bridge – now referred to as Beringia. About 30,000 years ago, humans began to migrate from Asia to North America, where they established hunting camps in Alaska's interior and Canada's Yukon. Others may have come not by land, but by water, working their way around the Pacific rim and using as stepping stones the ice-free coastal refuges that were exposed by retreating glaciers when the last great ice age drew to a close some 15,000 years ago. When the glaciers began staging their retreat, these giant bulldozers of ice left behind valleys that would

Sitka Sound was already a popular port of call for British and American ships when Russian fur traders built a fort here in 1799.

eventually become channels and fjords of the Inside Passage. Initially, however, the land uplifted when relieved of the massive weight of ice fields, and it was during this era of retreating ice and dropping sea levels, before the growing torrents of glacial meltwater further inland swelled the oceans and turned valleys into waterways, that a migration of ancient seafarers likely took place along the edge of today's Inside Passage. Sea levels finally stabilized about 5,000 years ago, and the Inside Passage as we now know it became permanently inhabited by people. The maritime climate was mild, the rivers were filled with salmon, and the lush forests of cedar, spruce and hemlock provided an endless supply of building material.

Prime waterfront locations were snapped up as groups established summer and winter villages within their fishing and hunting territories. These highly organized societies thrived along the entire Inside Passage, from Puget Sound in northern Washington State to the top of the Alaskan Panhandle. The rest of Alaska's coastline was inhabited by Eskimos and Aleuts, while Athapaskans – possibly the region's first inhabitants – lived in the interior.

Each of these native groups was affected in different ways when European explorers arrived at their shores and engaged them in the fur trade. The Aleuts were traumatized by the Russian *promyshlenniki* (frontier men) who enslaved them as hunters, but the coastal Indians initially profited from the fur trade – exchanging their furs for metal and tools. Eventually, rum and firearms became popular items of exchange, and native social structures began to unravel. The deadliest European import was disease, and whole villages were wiped out by smallpox and other epidemics.

A wooden cross at Three Saints Bay on Kodiak Island marks the location of Alaska's first permanent European settlement established here by the Russians in 1784.

EUROPEAN EXPLORERS

The 18th century was an era of great naval exploration. Russian explorers – led by the Danish sea captain Vitus Bering – set off from the shores of Siberia to discover what lay to the east. Spanish, French and British ships also ventured into the Pacific's northern waters in search of the elusive Northwest Passage. During this Age of Enlightenment, naval commanders such as Britain's Cook, France's La Perouse and Spain's Malaspina all led scientific expeditions to the New World.

The logbooks of these and other commanders provide a wealth of information on the native cultures that thrived at this time of First Contact. Some natives, upon initially seeing these strangely clad, pale-skinned men, fled into the forest. Others, overcome with curiosity, ran their hands across their visitors' faces to see if darker skin lay beneath a layer of white paint.

Captain Cook speculated that cannibalism was practiced by North Coast natives, but this rumor was dispelled by Captain Vancouver when he wrote that his men, while camped on shore, offered venison to some natives who mistook it for human flesh and made their aversion quite clear, refusing to eat any of it until the British sailors produced a deer carcass to prove that they were not cannibals.

The natives were duly impressed with the sailing ships that magically appeared on the horizon. Captains were honored guests in the homes of village chiefs and, in a show of reciprocal hospitality, ship's tours were often held for high-ranking village members. The ships and their nautical instruments fascinated the natives. One chief, when shown how a telescope worked, asked a naval officer if he could see around a bend in a channel with it and watch for approaching enemy canoes.

The Spanish explored much of the Pacific Northwest in the mid-to-late 1700s but were secretive about their discoveries. When the journals of Captain Cook's final voyage were published in America and Europe in 1783-84, merchant ships began flocking to these northern waters in pursuit of sea otter pelts. Dubbed 'soft gold,' these luxuriant pelts

Britain's* HMS Plumper *lies at anchor in Port Harvey on Johnstone Strait during a 19th-century survey expedition.

fetched a phenomenal price in China. As more merchant ships (from Europe and America) frequented the coast, inevitable misunderstandings erupted in bloodshed. The natives became increasingly wary of white fur traders and, at times, openly hostile. Captain Vancouver's men reported incidents in which they were approached in their open survey boats by canoes filled with weapon-bearing natives. A few shots fired over their heads, however, would prompt the natives to unstring their bow-and-arrows and offer them in trade.

Settlers eventually followed the fur traders, and their arrival changed the coastal landscape. The natives' territorial boundaries became obsolete as homesteaders farmed, logged and mined the land, while Spain, Britain, Russia and America disputed borders and trade monopolies. Spain withdrew from the North Pacific in the late 1700s after a political showdown with Britain over territorial rights. The dispute centered around control of Nootka Sound – a strategic harbor on the west coast of Vancouver Island.

In 1867, Russia withdrew from the North Pacific by selling Alaska to the United States for what now seems like a fire sale price of $7.2 million – about two cents an acre. However, the lucrative fur trade had dwindled and the American people showed little enthusiasm for this large tract of distant land their government had just acquired.

AMERICA'S NEW FRONTIER

The man who masterminded the purchase, U.S. Secretary of State William H. Seward, was ridiculed for his efforts with quips about "Seward's folly." Alaska was dubbed "Seward's icebox" and, for the most part, was neglected by its new owner. The American army and navy were sent to police this vast territory but no civil government was established until 1884 – at the urging of Reverend Sheldon Jackson. A Presbyterian missionary, Jackson travelled throughout Alaska establishing missions to educate the natives and assimilate them into the American way of life. Jackson also supported prohibition in Alaska, to protect the natives from the influence of rum. Liquor licensing was introduced in 1899, however, when the Klondike gold rush proved too much of a match for the prohibitionists.

Gold changed many Americans' perception of Alaska. The first strikes saw prospectors hurry to Wrangell and Sitka in 1872. Juneau was founded almost overnight when gold was discovered in the area in 1880. More strikes followed at Forty Mile River, Yakutat Bay, Lituya Bay, Mastodon Creek and the Kenai Peninsula. Then came the really big one – the Klondike strike on Bonanza Creek in Canada's Yukon. Men and women flocked by the thousands to Skagway for a chance to get rich in the Klondike. The gold fever ended as quickly as it began, with many rushing to Nome to try and cash in on yet another strike.

The 20th century brought continuing social changes to Alaska. Bush planes opened up the rugged interior – formerly the domain of riverboats, pack animals and dogsleds. The first flight up the Inside Passage, from Seattle to Ketchikan, was made in 1922, and 10 years later the first plane to land on an Alaskan glacier touched down on Mt. McKinley's Muldrow Glacier.

In 1942, during World War II, the U.S. Army Corps of Engineers built the Alaska Highway – a supply route safe from the hazards of wartime shipping. In just eight months they constructed a 1,500-mile road from Dawson Creek, in northern British Columbia, through Canada's Yukon to Fairbanks. Alaska was now joined to "the Outside" and the next step was statehood – achieved in 1959, making Alaska the 49th State of the Union.

The discovery of North Slope oil and natural gas deposits in 1968 transformed Alaska's economy. A pipeline was built from Prudhoe Bay on the Beaufort Sea to Valdez on Prince William Sound. Completed in 1977, this 800-mile-long pipeline is half underground and half aboveground where it's supported in a flexible, zigzag pattern to withstand earthquakes.

The city of Anchorage, economic center of the state, now has a population exceeding a quarter of a million, which is 42% of the state's total population, and the majority of Alaskans live in an urban setting. Yet, with a median age of 32.4 years, Alaska continues to attract people of pioneer spirit who are prepared to battle the elements on a day-to-day basis. America's two largest fishing fleets are stationed at Dutch Harbor in the Aleutians and at Kodiak Island. In the early 1980s, a sudden population boom of king crab in the Bering Sea, coupled with a strong demand for this product in Japan and the U.S., turned fishermen not yet out of their twenties into instant millionaires.

The money madness made for some interesting stories. One year, during a protracted strike, hundreds of boats sat moored in Dutch Harbor waiting for a settlement. When the word came, fishermen dashed to their vessels and, during this chaotic mass departure, boats were rammed and skippers accidentally left behind. One frenzied crew forgot to untie the docking lines and had to cut themselves loose. The end came as quickly and mysteriously as it arrived. Old myths die hard though, and each summer college kids flock to Alaska's legendary fishing ports, drawn by tales of lucrative deckhand jobs. The greenhorns often have trouble getting hired as crew and have to settle for work in the canneries.

When the Exxon oil spill of March 1989 threatened the fisheries of Prince William Sound and Kodiak Island, entire fishing fleets stayed home that year to help with clean-up operations. Ironically, this environmental disaster focused world attention on the natural beauty of Prince William Sound. Oil tankers now share these waters each summer with increasing numbers of cruise ships and tour boats bringing people to view the area's beautiful fjords and tidewater glaciers.

Although petroleum taxes and royalties produce about 85 percent of Alaska's general revenue, the state's greatest resource may prove to be

Commercial fishing in Alaska is a billion-dollar industry ranking high above any other American state.

its spectacular scenery. America's 49th state is enjoying a tourism boom right now and, unlike the rush for furs, gold and other natural resources, this one looks like it will last. Mankind cannot deplete the mountains and fjords that took millions of years to create. All we can do is gaze at them in wonder.

A WORD ABOUT PLACE NAMES

Thousands of place names have, over the centuries, been bestowed on the islands, channels and mountains of the Inside Passage and Gulf of Alaska coastline. The natives who first inhabited the coast had their own names in place when European sailing ships began appearing on the horizon in the mid-1700s.

Survey expeditions continued in the 1800s. In Canadian waters these were conducted by the British Royal Navy, while the United States surveyed Alaskan waters after purchasing the territory from Russia in 1867. The Bostonian William Dall was a member of various American survey expeditions from 1865 to 1899, and his name now graces an island in Southeast Alaska, not far from Annette Island which he named for his wife. Dall's romantic streak is further evidenced by his naming Marmiom Island to commemorate a poem by Sir Walter Scott.

Then there was Captain Pender of the British Royal Navy who, while surveying the Canadian Inside Passage in 1864, named a point of land Connis after his Skye Terrier. Alma maters, winning racehorses and wives, mothers and sisters have all been honored with place names along this coastline.

The rules for naming landmarks were never cut and dried. The natives often had more than one name for certain places and when explorers from various countries were busy surveying this coast, it was anyone's guess which name would endure. Some names are misnomers, such as British Columbia's Gulf Islands – named when the Strait of Georgia was incorrectly called the Gulf of Georgia. Others, such as the city of Seattle and the country of Canada, are derivatives of native names. Alaska's name comes from the Aleut word Alyeska, meaning The Great Land.

The last word on place names goes to John Muir, an explorer who harbored a healthy skepticism about the relevance of place names. "People look at what they are told to look at or what has been named," he wrote in *Travels in Alaska*. "Nameless things, however fine, go unnoticed."

GLACIERS

Glaciers are rivers of ice, always in movement. Fed by layers of compacted snow at higher elevations, they flow at varying speeds, depending on a variety of factors such as the height and slope of the mountain collecting the snow. The causes of glacier movement are complex and unique to each glacier, with the center and surface of a glacier moving more rapidly than the sides and bottom, which encounter friction. Decreased snow accumulation or increased melting results in a retreating (or shrinking) glacier. Those still advancing (or expanding) move at speeds varying from several feet daily to sudden surges of up to 300 feet per day. A stationary glacier is one in which its rate of advance and rate of melting are the same.

The Taku Glacier's ice flows steadily seaward from the massive Juneau Icefield where more than a dozen peaks collect snow..

Most glaciers stopped advancing in the mid-1700s and have been retreating ever since. A few are re-advancing and this is often due to a slight change in the local climate – either a drop in temperature or an increase in snowfall. Regardless of whether a glacier is retreating, advancing or stationary, its ice always flows in a downhill direction (due to gravity).

Glaciers carve deep valleys, and when valley glaciers flow together at the base of a mountain, they become a fan-shaped piedmont glacier. An icefield forms when numerous alpine glaciers join together and cover a large land mass with solid ice and snow. A tidewater glacier is a valley glacier that flows right down to the sea and lies at the head of the fjord or inlet it carved while retreating.

When chunks of ice fall from the snout of a tidewater glacier and crash into the sea, the glacier is said to be calving. The causes of glacial calving are still being studied and debated, but one known factor involves ice melting faster when in contact with water versus air. This results in an erosive undercutting of a glacier's snout below the high water mark. Each time the tide drops, an eroded section of the snout loses the water's support and this weakening of the ice may hasten its collapse. Blue ice at the face of a glacier means it's actively calving. The water near a glacier often appears milky turquoise because of fine sediments carried by glacier meltwater.

Although Alaska's glaciers are millions of years old, they flush their ice fairly rapidly, and the chunks we see dropping off the face of a tide-water glacier are usually a few hundred years old. These bergs are much smaller than those discharged from the polar ice caps and they

GLACIER GLOSSARY

BERGY SELTZER – Also called 'ice sizzle', in reference to the crackling or sizzling sound emitted when a melting iceberg is relieved of the intense pressures that formed it and trapped air bubbles are released.

CALVING – The breaking away of ice from the terminus (or snout) of a tidewater glacier.

CIRQUE – A valley head shaped like an amphitheater, its vertical walls eroded by a mountain glacier's source.

CREVASSE – Deep, elongated cracks that form in a glacier's brittle surface due to tensions caused by the glacier's movements. A snowbridge is a layer of snow concealing a crevasse.

DRIFT – The sedimentary deposits of a glacier, including till, which is unsorted drift deposited directly by a glacier.

FIRN – The intermediate stage in the transformation of snow to glacier ice. The compression of snow into dense firn takes about one summer.

MORAINE – Unsorted glacier deposit of rock and gravel that collects, through erosion, along the sides and snout of a glacier.

NEVE – The upper end, or source, of a glacier covered with perennial snow.

ROCK FLOUR – Pulverized rock ground by a glacier to a fine powder.

SERACS - Spires of ice pointing skyward.

SURGING – A sudden rapid movement (up to 300 feet per day) of a glacier, that may or may not involve an advance of the glacier's terminus. Factors causing a surge include the build-up of water pressure beneath the ice. Famous surges include those of Hubbard, a tidewater glacier that advanced hundreds of feet within a few weeks in the summer of 1986.

TERMINUS – Also called the snout or toe, this lower extremity of a glacier can be rounded in shape or form a sheer wall of ice. In the case of tidewater glaciers, the terminus is often several hundred feet in height with much of it submerged in water.

(Above) Icebergs are slippery and can suddenly roll, but some people can't resist climbing aboard for a quick ride.

melt quickly as they drift seaward toward the open waters of the Gulf of Alaska. One of the largest bergs ever recorded in Alaska was about 300 square feet and a hundred feet above the water. It was discovered in May 1977 floating in Icy Bay, which is located on the Gulf of Alaska at the base of the massive Bering Glacier complex.

An iceberg's blue color is the result of compressed ice absorbing light's short wave colors (reds) and reflecting the long wave colors (blues). If a piece of ice is relieved of pressure, air bubbles form and create a porous surface which is rough (like snow) and doesn't allow any light to penetrate, with light coming back as white. When afloat, about five-sixths of a berg is usually submerged. This ratio can vary, depending on the iceberg's shape and the amount of rock debris it might be carrying.

EARTHQUAKES

The coastal belt of the Pacific Ocean is one of the world's most active earthquake zones. This is due to the earth's surface being divided into crustal plates, some of which meet along the edges of the Pacific Ocean. Blocks of rock move along these plate boundaries, passing one another along fault lines (fractures in the earth's crust). Their relative movements can be vertical, horizontal or oblique and are usually measured in inches per year, except when a sudden release of stress along a fault triggers an earthquake.

An earthquake begins with tremors, followed by more violent shocks which gradually diminish. The origin (focus) of a quake is underground or underwater, and the epicenter is a point on the surface

An upthrust rock formation at Taku Harbor in Stephens Passage is evidence of a now-inactive fault of the earth's crust.

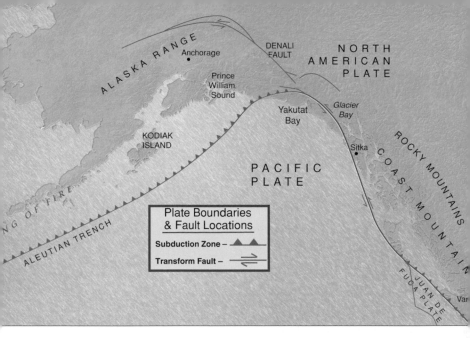

directly above the focus. The magnitude and intensity of an earthquake is determined by the Richter scale, which measures the ground motion to determine the amount of energy released at the quake's origin.

A reading of 4.5 on the Richter scale indicates an earthquake causing slight damage; a reading of 8.5 indicates an earthquake of devastating force. The energy of a quake measuring 8 on the Richter scale is equal to that of a 250-megaton thermo-nuclear bomb. (The atom bomb dropped on Hiroshima in 1945 was .02 megatons.)

The Good Friday earthquake that hit Alaska in 1964 measured between 8.4 and 8.6 on the Richter scale then in use and has since been upgraded to 9.2, the strongest recorded earthquake ever to hit North America. Its epicenter was in northern Prince William Sound and the damage was widespread. A block of the earth's crust tilted, causing parts of the Gulf of Alaska to rise 30 feet and coastal land to sink as much as 10 feet.

TSUNAMIS (TIDAL WAVES)

A tsunami – meaning 'harbor wave' in Japanese – is often referred to as a tidal wave. However, tsunamis are not caused by tidal action (although a high tide can increase their onshore damage) but by sea floor earthquakes or underwater landslides. Such seismic disturbances rarely trigger tsunamis, but when they do – watch out.

Up to several hundred miles in length but with heights of only a few feet, a tsunami can travel thousands of miles across the open ocean at speeds reaching 450 miles per hour. Its movement is undetected by ships at sea, but when it approaches a shelving coastline, it builds into a series of waves of catastrophic proportion. Anywhere from 10 to 40 minutes can pass between crests and the highest wave may occur

Downtown Anchorage, built on glacial silt deposits, was devastated by the 1964 earthquake when sections of streets collapsed.

several hours after the first wave (generally the third to eighth wave crests are the largest). The sudden withdrawal of water from a shoreline could be the trough of an approaching tsunami, so people who venture onto these newly exposed beaches risk being engulfed by a wave's huge crest.

A tsunami warning system is in place for the Pacific Ocean (where almost two-thirds of all tsunamis occur). Countries with gauge stations

Star marks 1964 earthquake's epicenter in Prince William Sound. Shaded area shows crustal uplift (+) and subsidence (-). Curved lines show leading edge of resultant tsunami, generated at 7:36 p.m.

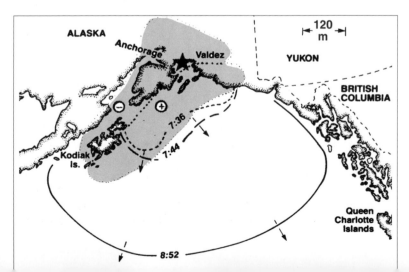

include the United States, Canada, Japan, Chile, New Zealand and the Philippines. Should any of the stations record a drastic change in water elevation, direct telephone contact is made with the warning center located in Honolulu, Hawaii.

The 1964 Alaska earthquake was of such intensity that it sent a series of waves to the far reaches of the Pacific. Waves over 20 feet high swept ashore in Oregon and California, killing 15 people. The Gulf of Alaska ports were hardest hit, with 107 people losing their lives. In 1946, an earthquake in the Aleutians sent 100-foot waves sweeping onto Unimak Island where the lighthouse was destroyed and five people perished. Tsunamis of such magnitude are extremely rare. However, the Alaska Tsunami Warning Center – established at Palmer in 1967 – now provides timely warnings to prevent loss of life from an approaching tsunami. The 2004 Boxing Day tsunami that struck Indonesia and other countries bordering the Indian Ocean was caused by an earthquake off Sumatra that registered 9.0 on the Richter scale. More than 200,000 people perished, many standing on beaches watching the approaching tsunami waves, as no warning system was in place for the Indian Ocean at the time of this calamitous event.

VOLCANOES

There are about 500 active volcanoes on our planet, more than 70 of these located in Alaska. They are part of the Ring of Fire that encircles the Pacific Ocean basin and marks the collision zone of various tectonic plates that comprise the earth's crust. Volcanoes also exist beneath the ocean's surface and are called seamounts. About 100 of these extend from the Gulf of Alaska to the Oregon Coast.

Volcanoes form around an aperture in the earth's crust, through which gases, lava (molten rock) and solid fragments are ejected. A dormant volcano quickly loses its conical shape to erosion, so any mountain that is cone-shaped can be considered a potentially active volcano.

A volcano's crater is formed when the cone collapses during an eruption. Steam vents often cover a crater floor or the collapsed summit may fill with glacial meltwater. The crater lake atop Mount Katmai on the Alaska Peninsula is a unique robin's-egg blue, due to glacial silt and sulphur in the water which remains ice-free for most of the year because of volcanic heat.

The Alaska Peninsula contains 15 active volcanoes, its most famous being Mount Katmai which erupted in June 1912 through a vent in its base. One of the greatest volcanic eruptions in recorded history, it was twice the size of Krakatoa, which killed 35,000 Indonesians in 1883, and ten times the force of Washington State's Mount Saint Helens which erupted twice in 1980 and killed 60 people. Because of Katmai's remote location, no humans were killed, but the residents of Kodiak (90 miles away) were rained with ash so thick that for two days a person couldn't see a lit lantern held at arm's length. Acid rain fell 2,000 miles away in Vancouver, Canada, where laundry hanging on clotheslines disintegrated. An entire valley was filled with burning ash that spewed from Mount Katmai. In total, the volcanic eruption blanketed 40 square miles with ash that was 700 feet deep in places.The 1992 eruption of Mount Spurr, near Anchorage, was merely a hiccup in comparison, sending a giant cloud of ash into the upper atmosphere that disrupted air traffic in Canada and the northern United States for three days.

When a jet plane flies into volcanic ash, the finely ground rock is sandblasted onto the aircraft, clogging its engines and degrading its wing surfaces. One of the most graphic examples of this occurred in December 1989 when a jumbo jet flew into a mass of ash the day after Mount Redoubt, near Anchorage, began erupting. All four engines quit. The pilot tried to restart the engines, unsuccessfully, seven or eight times before two of them finally kicked in, followed by the other two. The plane landed safely at Anchorage, but this and other similar incidents prompted the Civil Aviation Organization to establish a world-wide network of Volcanic Ash Advisory Centers. The one in Anchorage is responsible for Alaska, analyzing information it receives from satellites, volcano observatories and weather agencies to forecast movements of ash clouds and alert airlines and air-traffic control centers of potential danger.

Alaska's chain of volcanoes extends westward along the Alaska Peninsula and Aleutian Islands. Pavlof Volcano, near the tip of the Peninsula, erupted in 1996, and Mount Cleveland Volcano, on the uninhabited Aleutian island of Chuginadak, erupted in 2001. The Aleutians are a string of volcanic islands standing on the edge of the

Volcanic ash from Mount Katmai's 1912 eruption still lies on the nearby mountains of Geographic Harbor.

Aleutian Trench. This ocean trench is a subduction zone in which the Pacific plate is descending beneath the North American plate, and the waters along this trench are thousands of feet deeper than the nearby ocean bottom.

Far away from the Aleutian Trench is Mount Edgecumbe – a solitary volcano located near Sitka. This volcano has been inactive for the last 200 years, although in 1974 the residents of Sitka wondered if another eruption was imminent when black smoke was seen rising from the volcano's caldera. The smoke, however, was coming from a pile of burning tires placed there by an April Fool's Day prankster.

AURORA BOREALIS (NORTHERN LIGHTS)

A poet would describe the Northern Lights as curtains of shimmering light that flutter across the sky. A scientist would say they are high-speed particles from the sun colliding with the earth's air molecules. Both descriptions are correct.

When charged electrons and protons – released during sunspot activity – drift toward the earth, they are magnetically pulled to the planet's northern and southern latitudes. These charged particles strike gases in the earth's upper atmosphere and turn luminous – ranging from silvery white through the colors of the rainbow. The shimmering effect is caused by the differing intensities of light.

The aurora borealis is most prevalent over the Arctic Circle but can occur throughout the northern latitudes. (Those which occur over the Antarctic Circle and southern latitudes are called the aurora australis.) The Northern Lights appear most often during the spring and fall equinoxes, when the sun crosses the equator and night and day are of equal length. Northern Lights can also occur on dark winter nights and during increased sunspot activity. The last phase of intense sunspot activity was during the late 1950s.

The aurora borealis lights up a northern sky.

Bathers relax in the hot mineral waters of Warm Spring Bay on Baranof Island in southeast Alaska.

HOTSPRINGS

The hot water flowing from a natural spring is the result of ground water seeping to great depths through faults in the earth's crust, where it is heated and recirculated back up to the surface. A soak in a steaming mineral bath is considered by many to be a most therapeutic pastime. Alaskans are fortunate to have about 80 such thermal springs scattered throughout their state. Half of these are located along the volcanic Alaska Peninsula and Aleutian chain, with another concentration of hotsprings in southeast Alaska.

Some of these natural springs are developed, with bath houses built over tubs that collect the flow of spring water. The village of Tenakee Springs on Chichagof Island grew up around its hotsprings. Enclosed by a cement bathhouse with bathing hours for men and women posted on the door, the springs at Tenakee attract plenty of visitors seeking relaxation, including state legislators from Juneau. The Alaska ferry calls at Tenakee Springs, as do fishermen and pleasure boaters looking for a good soak in a hot bath – compliments of Mother Earth's ingenious plumbing system.

MARINE WEATHER

Alaska encompasses a number of climatic zones: maritime along its southern coastlines; continental in its vast interior; arctic along its northern shores. The cruise ship routes remain within the moderate maritime zone, which is dominated by the Pacific Ocean.

Weather systems flow in an easterly direction in the northern hemisphere, so the west coast of North America enjoys the moderating effects of the Pacific Ocean throughout the year. Wet and windy weather prevails along the Pacific coast in winter as storms originating offshore flow into the Gulf of Alaska where its mountain-rimmed coastline acts as a catch basin and precipitation falls as snow at higher elevations. Summer weather in the North Pacific is dominated by a subtropical high which brings reduced precipitation and increased sunshine. Autumn is a transition season as the North Pacific High gradually shrinks and the relatively light breezes of summer are replaced with winter storms generated by the Aleutian Low.

Ocean currents also flow eastward across the Pacific from Asian waters, but the warm Japan Current never reaches the shores of Alaska. This slow-moving current joins the North Pacific Current (a broad, slow, easterly drift), which eventually veers south somewhere off the Oregon or California coast. The Subarctic Current runs parallel with the North Pacific Current and it gradually splits as it approaches the Washington/British Columbia coast, with one branch veering south to become the California Current, and the other veering north to become the Alaska Current. This current flows in a counter-clockwise direction along the Gulf of Alaska coastline and keeps it free of winter ice, except in protected waters.

It can take two to five years for a parcel of water carried by the Subarctic Current to cross the North Pacific. Along the way its temperature is determined not by the current's origin but by the surface water's constant heat exchange with the atmosphere.

This archival shot of Kodiak's harbor, taken before a breakwater was built, shows the smoking waters of a winter storm as it sweeps onshore from the Gulf of Alaska.

WHALES

Of all the wildlife a visitor might see while cruising Alaskan waters, the most thrilling sight is that of a whale surfacing. Called cetaceans and found in all the world's oceans, whales vary greatly in size, from the massive blue whale to the relatively small dolphin and porpoise. These aquatic mammals, which never leave the water at any stage in their lives, are warm blooded, breathe air and produce milk for their young. Their skin is nearly hairless and an insulating layer of blubber keeps their internal body temperatures high. Their nostrils (blowholes) are located on top of their heads to allow breathing while swimming, with the nostril valves closing and lungs compressing during dives. Most whales must surface every 3 to 20 minutes to breathe, although some can remain submerged for up to an hour. Although their eyes are small (to withstand great pressures), whales have good eyesight and excellent hearing, often navigating via echolocation. Their flattened tails with horizontal flukes propel them through the water.

Whales are broken into two major groups: toothed and baleen. Those with teeth, such as the killer whale (orca), eat salmon and other marine mammals. Baleen whales are filter feeders who eat schooling fish, plankton and other small organisms, which they catch by swimming with their mouths wide open. When the whale closes its mouth, it raises its tongue to force the scooped water out the sides where the bristles of its baleen plates trap the food.

HUMPBACK WHALE

The humpback whale, a filter feeder, is frequently sighted in Alaskan waters during the months of June, July and August. Almost one-quarter of the world's estimated 8,000 to 10,000 humpback whales feed in Alaskan waters each summer, and about 500 of these are concentrated in the waters of Southeast Alaska. In winter, most Pacific humpbacks migrate south to breed and calve in the tropical waters off Hawaii and Mexico. December and January are the birthing months, following a 12-month gestation period. Cows give birth to a single calf weighing about a ton and measuring 12 to 15 feet in length. Calves are born without a blubber layer and nurse on their mother's milk which contains 50 percent butter fat.

WHALE WATCHING:

Good areas to sight humpback whales include Frederick Sound and Stephens Passage (south of Juneau), Lynn Canal (north of Juneau) and the waters off Point Adolphus (opposite the entrance to Glacier Bay). One telltale sign to watch for is the appearance of a plume of mist in the distance, which could indicate a pod of whales surfacing. While it's always possible to sight whales (including dolphins and porpoises) from the ship's rail, the surest way to see a humpback whale is by taking a whalewatching boat excursion out of Juneau.

(Opposite) A humpback whale breaches in Alaskan waters. (Far left) Humpbacks blow air bubbles in a column to collect krill.

Adult humpbacks are, on average, 45 feet long and weigh up to 40 tons. Their large flippers provide maneuverability and the pleats on the sides of their mouths can create a pouch large enough to hold six adult humans. When feeding, they blow bubbles beneath schools of fish to create a concentrated cloud which they then lunge at with their mouths wide open. Sea birds, attracted by the water disturbance, feed on shrimp-plike krill and herring which swim to the surface.

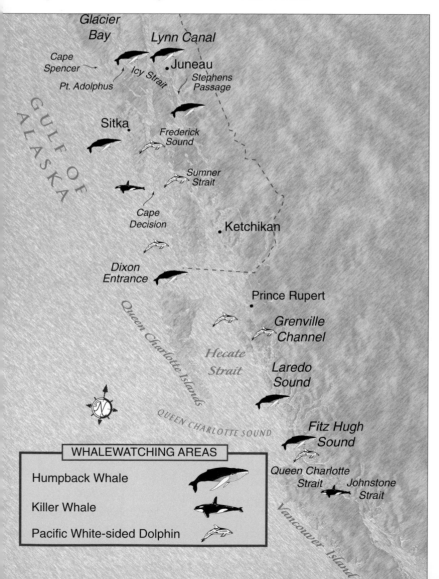

Glacier Bay
Lynn Canal
Cape Spencer
Juneau
Icy Strait
Pt. Adolphus
Stephens Passage
GULF OF ALASKA
Sitka
Frederick Sound
Sumner Strait
Cape Decision
Ketchikan
Dixon Entrance
Queen Charlotte Islands
Prince Rupert
Grenville Channel
Hecate Strait
Laredo Sound
QUEEN CHARLOTTE SOUND
Fitz Hugh Sound
Queen Charlotte Strait
Johnstone Strait
Vancouver Island

WHALEWATCHING AREAS

Humpback Whale

Killer Whale

Pacific White-sided Dolphin

Humpbacks travel in threesomes – a female, her calf and a male escort. The male earns his position as escort. He serenades the female by performing a repeated pattern of sounds (called a song) at depths of 60 feet or more. If this doesn't win her, the male will confront her current escort by smacking him with his fluked tail which packs 8,000 pounds of muscle and, studded with barnacles, is a humpback's most powerful weapon.

Only the males sing and they rarely do this while feeding in Alaska. They do, however, perform their usual acrobatics such as breaching (heaving themselves out of the water), lobtailing and flippering (smacking the water's surface with their tail or flippers). No two humpback tails are alike and scientists identify each whale by the pattern on its flukes which are visible when the whale raises its tail high out of the water before making a deep dive.

KILLER WHALE (ORCA)

Killer whales belong to the dolphin family of toothed whales and for decades they were much feared by humans because of their swift, ferocious attacks on seals and other prey, their mouths holding more than four dozen sharp teeth. Today the social habits of this handsome species are a source of fascination for both scientists and enthusiastic whale watchers.

dorsal fin

saddle patch

Male Orca

Female Orca

Males, which can reach 30 feet in length, live for about 30 years while females, which average 23 feet in length, can live 50 years, sometimes longer. The male is distinguished from the female by his taller, straighter dorsal fin (up to six feet high on mature males). Each sub-group within a pod consists of a mature cow and her progeny of all ages. Females give birth to single calves following a gestation period of 15 months.

A killer whale's most distinguishing features are its prominent dorsal fin and the white marking just behind it, called a saddle patch. Scientists who observe killer whales in the waters of the Pacific Northwest have developed a database in which regularly sighted pods and their members – identified by individual markings – are given reference names. Every killer whale belongs to a pod – the extended family group into which it was born. Each sub-group within a pod consists of a mature cow and her progeny of all ages. Mature males likely mate with females of other pods, but they always return to their own pod and remain with it until death. Pod structures change very slowly, many lasting the lifetime of the cow.

A killer whale's most distinguishing features are its prominent dorsal fin and the white marking just behind it, called a saddle patch.

Resident pods, with up to 50 members, form the largest groups, remaining near established salmon runs along inshore waters. Transient pods form smaller groups and travel a wider area in search for food, preying primarily on marine mammals such as seals and sea lions. Offshore pods are found farther out to sea, well away from coastal waters, and apparently feed on fish.

Killer whales can swim for long distances at a cruising speed of about seven knots, but can accelerate dramatically when attacking prey or leaping from the water (breaching). Resident pods communicate with high-pitched sounds that can be heard on hydrophones. These vocalizations include sonarlike clicks, squeaks and whistles. Transient pods remain silent, so as not to alert potential prey of their presence.

Killer whales are frequently sighted in Johnstone Strait (feeding on salmon) and in the waters off Victoria, but can appear anywhere along the Inside Passage, Prince William Sound and Gulf of Alaska. Their distribution is worldwide.

The beluga, a northern whale, can often be sighted close to shore in Turnagain Arm south of Anchorage.

OTHER WHALES

The smallest baleen whale to frequent Alaskan waters is the minke which reaches lengths of 33 feet. The blue whale, the largest known animal ever to have lived (reaching 100 feet in length), is sometimes sighted during July and August in eastern and northern areas of the Gulf of Alaska. This whale came close to extinction about 50 years ago, but the species has fought back and, although it is still endangered, estimates of its population run as high as 17,000. Blues are protected worldwide.

The gray whale is another large baleen whale, about 40 to 45 feet in length and weighing up to 40 tons. Strongly migratory but a relatively slow swimmer, the gray whale travels near shore on its twice-yearly migration between Mexico's Baja coast and the Beaufort Sea.

The beluga (or white whale) is a small toothed whale. Reaching lengths of 19 feet, the beluga is sometimes called a 'sea canary' for the variety of noises it makes. Travelling in large groups, belugas winter in the Arctic Ocean and in summer enter northern rivers and inlets, such as Turnagain Arm, south of Anchorage in Cook Inlet.

The legendary sperm whale, largest of the toothed whales, is usually blue-black in color and has a blunt snout containing up to a ton of sperm oil (a liquid wax). Males can grow to over 70 feet and their range extends from the Bering Sea to Antarctica. Females, which grow to 30 feet, remain closer to the tropics. Herman Melville based his classic novel *Moby Dick* about the 1822 ramming and sinking of a Nantucket whaling ship by an albino sperm whale.

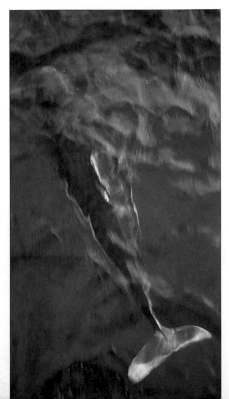

DALL PORPOISE

These speedy mammals are sometimes confused with killer whales because their black-and-white coloring is similar. However, Dall porpoises are much shorter (about seven feet long) and stockier in shape, and their

Dall porpoises skim the water's surface at speeds reaching 30 miles per hour.

dorsal fin is topped with white. They are the world's fastest marine mammals, reaching speeds of 30 miles per hour. Travelling in groups of a half dozen or more, they swim just beneath the surface of the water, kicking up splashes called rooster tails when they leap partially out of the water.

These sociable creatures love to ride the bow wave of a moving vessel and will perform dazzling, crisscross patterns as two pairs race toward the front of the bow, one from either side, only to veer off at the last moment to prevent a collision. Their split-second reflexes and swift speed allow them to dart through the water and turn quickly. They range from the Bering Sea to Baja California.

PACIFIC WHITE-SIDED DOLPHIN

Playful and sociable, these high-spirited dolphins travel in large groups (115 members on average) and are, like the Dall porpoise, attracted to the bow waves of moving vessels. The larger and faster the vessel, the better the surfing as far as a Pacific white-sided dolphin is concerned.

Slightly longer than the Dall porpoise, these dolphins are black with a white belly and a hooked dorsal fin. During the fall mating season, they go crazy with acrobatics – leaping with total abandon in front of large fishboats and cruise ships. Passengers watching from a forward lounge are often treated to the sight of hundreds of dolphins leaping and somersaulting in front of the ship.

Fall sightings can occur in Sumner Strait, Dixon Entrance, Grenville Channel and Queen Charlotte Sound.

Pacific white-sided dolphins are playful and sociable, often seen leaping in the bow wave of a moving vessel.

Sea lions haul out on rocky outcroppings to breed and tend their young. Sea lion populations have declined sharply in recent years.

SEAL & SEA LION

These fin-footed marine mammals have a thick layer of fat beneath their outer, hair-covered skin and spend much of their time in the water. They do, however, leave the water to rest, breed and give birth, but they always remain close to the water's edge. They haul out onto rocky islets, sandbars and ice floes where land predators cannot reach their pups. Sea lions gather in colonies to breed, with mature males assembling harems. Seals and sea lions live for about 30 years and feed on fish.

Harbor seals are commonly seen throughout the Inside Passage and Prince William Sound, often poking their large-eyed faces above the water to take a look around. They fear the transient killer whale and will quickly climb onto the closest rock or shoreline if such a pod is in the area. In one instance, a seal that was being circled by killer whales leaped into a whalewatching vessel to escape its predators.

Steller sea lions are larger than seals, with the males reaching 13 feet in length and weighing up to 2,000 pounds. Seals and sea lions will steal fish from fishermen's nets, and sea lions have been known to pull fishermen into the water from docks and skiffs, but it's illegal to shoot them under the 1972 Marine Mammal Protection Act. The Steller sea lion has, in recent years, suffered a dramatic decline in population – due possibly to an unexplained shortage of forage fish.

Two popular haul-out and pupping sites for seals and sea lions are Benjamin Island in Lynn Canal and Seal Rocks at the entrance to Prince William Sound.

A female harbor seal and her pup rest on a small piece of glacier ice which affords some security from predators.

SEA OTTER

The largest member of the weasel family, a sea otter can reach five feet in length and weigh close to 100 pounds. Although an aquatic mammal, the sea otter is kept warm not by blubber, like other marine mammals, but by its extremely thick fur coat – the most dense of any mammal at 675,000 hairs per square inch.

Sea otters congregate in large groups where they play together in pairs, hugging each other while they roll and perform somersaults in the water. A young otter will ride on its mother's stomach as she floats on her back. Sea otters also eat urchins and other shellfish on their chests, which they break apart with a rock. They're crowd-pleasers with their playful personalities and round, whiskered faces.

Sea otters once ranged from the Aleutians to Baja California, their population about 150,000. Russian fur traders, realizing how quickly these animals were being decimated for their valuable pelts, eventually set quotas to limit harvests, and by the mid-1800s the species was recovering. However, when the U.S. purchased Alaska in 1867, unlimited hunting was again allowed and the total sea otter population was reduced to about 2,000. In 1911 sea otters were given complete protection and they have now returned to numbers approaching their original population.

Sea otters are often sighted along the northern and western shores of Chichagof Island and on sightseeing expeditions out of Sitka. They are also a common sight in Prince William Sound, near Seward in Resurrection Bay, and around Kodiak Island.

RIVER OTTER

River otters, like sea otters, belong to the weasel family. With webbed feet, they are agile both on land and in the water. They run humpbacked because of their long bodies and relatively short legs. Males reach four feet in length and weigh up to 25 pounds. River otters are very sociable and playful. They like to slide headfirst on their bellies down mud banks into the water.

FISH

SALMON

Salmon are at the top of the fish evolutionary ladder and, with a very streamlined body and a powerful tail fin, they are fast, agile swimmers. The meat on all species of salmon is rich in protein, providing an important food source for humans and animals. Many coastal towns and cities owe their existence to this fish, which every year returns in large schools to natal spawning streams along the Pacific coast. There are five

Sea otters spend much of their time floating on their backs – grooming, eating and nursing their young.

species of Pacific salmon caught in Alaskan waters: king (chinook) is the largest; silver (coho) is prized by sportsfishermen; red (sockeye) with its rich red meat, is the highly-valued commercial salmon; pink (humpy) is the most common and an important commercial fish for the canneries; and chum (dog) salmon, when smoked, is a tasty delicacy.

Salmon spawn in fresh water, usually streams, where they spend varying lengths of time depending on the species, before heading out to sea. Some juveniles migrate directly to saltwater while others linger in river estuaries where they grow and adapt to the mix of fresh- and saltwater habitats. Depending on the species, salmon will spend one to seven years in the open ocean before returning to their natal streams to spawn. Salmon struggle against incredible odds to return to the stream of their birth. If a fish makes it past the sport and commercial fisheries, there will be other predators – such as bears and eagles – waiting along stream banks to make a meal of the weary fish. Salmon often have to leap up waterfalls and swim against rushing currents to return to their spawning grounds. Once there, the females dig nests in the gravel and lay their eggs while their male partners release milt which fertilizes the eggs. All Pacific salmon spawn only once – in mid-to-late summer or fall – then die.

Coho (silver) salmon, a favorite catch of sportfishermen, has become seriously depleted in southern waters of the Inside Passage.

Salmon stocks are suffering serious depletions in some areas of the Pacific Northwest. A complex combination of factors is likely to blame, including overfishing and destruction of stream habitat. Salmon are also extremely sensitive to temperature fluctuations, and a recent increase in ocean temperatures, possibly due to global warming, is another likely culprit. Each salmon stock, which is grouped according to its stream of origin, has a specific genetic make-up which has evolved over tens of thousands of years. Sudden environmental changes, whether natural or man-made, threaten a specific stock's ability to adapt and survive.

HALIBUT

While salmon are generally found within 100 feet of the ocean's surface, halibut are always found near the bottom. Salmon is a pink or red meat; halibut is white. This fish is highly valued in Alaska, and around the world, for its delicate taste and texture. Pacific halibut can grow to over eight feet and weigh over 800 pounds. Halibut fishing is generally good near Sitka and Seward where numerous charter operations are available for fishing.

KING CRAB

In 1976, a sudden and inexplicable explosion in the number of harvestable king crab occurred in the Bering Sea. Within months hundreds of young men rushed to cash in on a boom which lasted almost eight years. Some came away millionaires, but many ended up with only memories of exciting years in the tough waters off Kodiak and in the Bering Sea. King crab can weigh up to 15 pounds and measure six feet across from claw to claw. Although the king crab population has declined since the mid-1980s, a large number of crab boats still operate out of Dutch Harbor and Kodiak.

BIRDS

The Inside Passage is part of the Pacific Flyway, a migratory route for millions of birds, and this coastal region's river estuaries and tidal passes provide habitat for a variety of species, with over 400 documented in Alaska and British Columbia. If you're interested in birds, it's well worth bringing a pair of binoculars and a field pocketbook to identify birds along your cruise.

Birds differ dramatically in size, shape and plumage but wing shape is an indication of a bird's survival strategies. Some, like gulls and shearwaters, have long-tapered wings suitable for gliding long distances over water with little effort. Others, like auklets and murres, have short and less efficient wings more suitable for propelling themselves underwater. And some, like eagles and ospreys, have long wide wings to provide additional payload capacity for such maneuvers as snatching salmon out of the water.

The flight of any bird is a marvel to behold. It derives both forward power and upward lift from its wings. As a bird propels itself forward from the motion of wing flapping, a slight vacuum or low pressure area is created above the wing, lifting the body. As the bird picks up speed, the wing and tail feathers fold in to streamline the bird's shape and provide greater flying efficiency. A bird can turn very quickly using movements of its body, such as tilting the head, fanning the wings' secondary feathers, or subtly angling the tail feathers.

For an Alaska-bound traveller one of the best locations to see birdlife is Vancouver's Stanley Park, around Lost Lagoon and Beaver Lake. While cruising the Inside Passage you'll see gulls, herons, sea ducks, bald eagles and cormorants, which often perch on pilings or buoys with their wings outstretched to dry. In the Gulf of Alaska, shearwaters and albatross can be identified by the keen birder, and near Seward you're likely to see large colonies of horned and tufted puffins which thrive by the thousands near the western end of Prince William Sound, along the Kenai Peninsula and around Kodiak Island. The Mendenhall Valley marshlands near Juneau is another prime location to spot many species of birds.

BALD EAGLE

Without a doubt, the bald eagle is one of the most magnificent sights of an Alaskan cruise. With a wingspan of between six and eight feet and weighing 15 pounds or more, the bald eagle is the largest member of the hawk family. The bald eagle gets its name from its distinctive snow-white head. Its bill is yellow and it has a thin, chittering call.

A high-soaring eagle can spot a fish from over a mile away and can dive from the sky at 100 miles per hour. Eagles mate while somersaulting through the air with their talons locked. The female lays one to three eggs in late April and the young birds leave the nest in early fall. Their mortality rate is high, with over 90 per cent failing to survive the first few years of life. Juvenile eagles retain their ragged plumage until the age of five, when they attain the distinctive markings of a mature bald eagle.

Eagles usually build their nests in the tallest tree of their nesting territory (a range of one to five miles) and close to the water. Since eagles mate for life, the couple will return to their nest each year and do minor upgrading, renovations, and the occasional expansion. One excellent opportunity to see a nest is the Eagle Tree on the ground floor of the Alaska State Museum in Juneau. This exhibit includes the nest, eggs and mounted specimens of juvenile and adult eagles.

(Above) Bald eagles use their talons to grab at salmon swimming near the surface.
(Left) Bald eagle's nest is the largest of any bird in North America, built five to eight feet in diameter and two to 10 feet in depth.

Now protected, the bald eagle was once the target of bounty hunters, with over 100,000 killed before the predator control program was repealed in 1952. Today, of North America's total bald eagle population of 75,000, about 35,000 to 45,000 reside year round in Alaska. Although they are birds of prey, using their keen eyesight, swift speed and sharp talons to scoop salmon from the water, eagles are also scavengers and will gather by the hundreds along riverbanks to feed on spawning salmon.

RAVEN

Ravens and crows use their sense of curiosity as a survival technique. Anything dropped or odd in shape or color will be quickly spotted by these black birds, which promptly swoop down to investigate. Ravens are larger than crows and have thicker bills. They are very intelligent, capable of making diverse sounds, and are highly respected in Northwest native cultures, the raven an integral creature of Haida mythology.

SEABIRDS

Unlike eagles, who don't like to get their feathers wet, are the many species of duck. Sea ducks eat intertidal invertebrates (mussels, hermit crabs, snails) and dominate the bird populations in many coastal areas of Alaska. They are robust, noisy and have colorful summer plumage, most notably the Harlequin duck. Sea ducks can be observed near shore while in port, often parading past in single file.

Sub-species include dabbling ducks, who feed on the surface or by dipping their heads and bodies until only their tail protrudes from the water. Dabblers include the well-known mallard, the drake (male) sporting an emerald green head and chestnut chest. Other dabbler species are the teal, northern pintail, wigeon and wood duck.

Diving ducks, as the name implies, completely submerge when feeding. Scoters, goldeneye and bufflehead are diving ducks, as are scaup and harlequin. Mergansers are nicknamed 'sawbills' due to their long, tapering bills lined with sharp 'teeth' for grabbing fish. A mother merganser will carry her brood of newborn chicks on her back as she swims near shore.

Puffins, like murres and auklets, are alcids (a type of seabird) and are able to

Horned puffins, when gathering food for their young, can hold three or four small fish at a time in their large bills.

Seabirds, gulls and eagles hover above a feeding minke whale in Queen Charlotte Strait, along British Columbia's Inside Passage.

swim underwater to great depths using their wings. These birds are not great flyers, however, and are often seen bouncing off wavetops trying to take off. Puffins come ashore only to breed and nest. A boat tour from Seward will take you to some of the largest nesting colonies in Alaska at the entrance to Resurrection Bay.

Shorebirds include sandpipers and the Black Oystercatcher, which has a long orange beak with which it pries open shellfish. The feet of the Pigeon Guillemot are also bright orange and quite a sight when this seabird runs across the surface of the water, gaining speed for take off. Ducks look like water skiers when landing as they dig the heels of their webbed feet into the water. In contrast are the balletic landings of gulls, which flutter their wings like backwinded sails to delicately set themselves down on the water.

Cormorants, which enter the water only to feed, are often seen perched on rocks or buoys, their wings outspread to dry. Loons, on the other hand, remain mostly in the water and come ashore only to nest, for they cannot walk on land and they cannot fly during moult. Swimming is their specialty and their heavily built bodies are designed for diving.

ALBATROSS

Glacier cruise passengers, while traversing the Gulf of Alaska between Yakutat Bay and Prince William Sound, may be fortunate to spot the black-footed albatross. These beautiful gliders spend most of their lives at sea and, for survival, have special adaptations. To meet their freshwater needs, they drink seawater which is filtered and secreted through enlarged nasal glands to remove the salt. These birds, along with shearwaters and petrels, are called "tube-nosed swimmers" because their nostrils are situated in raised tubes on their bill. This gives them a sense of smell so acute they are believed to track fish and squid underwater.

GULL / JAEGER

The long-tailed jaeger is a small gull-like bird renowned for its annual migration from northern Alaska to Southern Hemisphere oceans.

Gulls are buoyant swimmers and strong fliers with well-developed scavenging abilities. Most common are white and light grey glaucous-winged gulls, herring gulls (with black-tipped wings) and mew gulls – smaller birds with cries similar to a child's. Another member of the gull family is the kittiwake, flocks of which feed on tiny krill near tidewater glaciers. The predatory jaeger may be sighted in the northern Yukon and Alaska. Jaegers are known to migrate many thousands of miles.

LAND MAMMALS

BEAR

Of all the land mammals in Alaska, none excite the imagination quite like bears – most particularly the brown bear (Ursus arctos) and the grizzly, a sub-species of the brown bear. The brown bears that inhabit the Alaska coast are especially large because they have an advantage over interior (grizzly) bears – namely large numbers of available salmon spawning in shallow streams. This protein-rich diet combined with a mild climate produces bears that are between eight and nine feet tall (when standing upright) and weigh well over 1,000 pounds. In 1969 a brown bear measuring over ten feet was recorded on Kodiak Island.

The black bear (Ursus americanus) is the most widespread and numerous of North American bears. Although smaller and seemingly more docile than the brown bear, it can

Black bears can be viewed at Neets Bay near Ketchikan.

This brown bear is one of many who arrive at the McNeil River each summer to feed on spawning salmon.

still pose a serious threat when hungry, startled or injured. Black bears forage mainly on berries and occasionally on salmon along the coast. Adult male black bears weigh an average of 500 pounds, are 6 feet long and vary in color from blonde to black, including the rare blue (or glacier) bear, which is found in the Yakutat Bay area along the Gulf of Alaska. Black bears have been known to spend their entire lives within five miles of their birthplace, and a transplanted black bear will travel many miles to return to its home range.

Brown bears are solitary animals, usually avoiding one another, but will exhibit a site-specific tolerance for one another at particularly abundant salmon feeding streams, such as Pack Creek on Admiralty Island (28 air miles south of Juneau) and the McNeil River on Cook Inlet (200 air miles southwest of Anchorage), a site that draws photographers from around the world. Brown bears may also be spotted on the foreshore from ships or ferries travelling through Peril Strait or along Lynn Canal. Brown bears can occasionally be seen along the north shoreline of Chichagof Island near Glacier Bay.

The polar bear (Ursus maritimus) is rarely sighted by the casual traveller to Alaska, for this large white bear (an adult male can reach nine feet in length and weigh up to 1600 pounds) lives mainly on the drifting pack ice. Its hair is extremely dense and its paws have hairy soles for gripping the ice. A fearless and wily hunter, the polar bear will stalk any prey, including humans. Well aware that its black nose gives it away, a polar bear stalking seals will often hold a paw in front of its nose to conceal it.

Bears have an excellent sense of smell and hearing, and can run with bursts of speed reaching 35 mph. Black bears are also good tree climbers and polar bears are exceptional swimmers, crossing 30 miles of water at a time. Bears sleep through most of the winter in dens made in caves or holes in the ground but they do not truly hibernate, for their metabolism remains normal and they may even awake and emerge during warm spells. Polar bears wander all winter, except for pregnant females who dig dens in the snow. Cubs are born in pairs during the winter and remain with their mothers for about a year.

WOLF

Close to extinction in the Lower 48, the gray wolf (also called timber wolf) is thriving in Alaska where it enjoys a high reproductive rate and is protected by strict trapping and hunting regulations (aerial sporthunting of wolves has been banned since 1972). Resembling a German Shepherd dog, the gray wolf stands three feet at the shoulder and weighs about 100 pounds. Wolves usually travel in a pack (family group) which averages five to eight members and they hunt just about everything from moose to mice, wearing down even the swiftest of prey with their ability to run at about 20 mph for many hours. The wolf is of the genus Canis and can be bred with dogs to produce hardy animals for pulling sleds. The coyote is a small, swift wolf and resembles a medium-sized dog. Its cry – mournful high-pitched yelps – is heard early in the evening.

SLED DOGS

Dogs in the north have always been highly valued, both as working animals and as man's best friend. The early gold prospectors relied on dogs for winter transportation, and stealing someone's dog was a serious crime leading to arrest. The Alaskan malamute is one of the oldest arctic sled dogs and is often referred to as a 'husky', although this term actually applies to the purebred Siberian husky. The snowmobile threatened to replace the working dog-sled team, but dog mushing has made a comeback and was named Alaska's official state sport in 1972, with races held in various locales throughout the winter. Each March, the state's famous Iditarod Trail Sled Dog Race is

Sled dogs are working animals as well as beloved pets.

run between Anchorage and Nome. The race, first held in 1973, follows an old dog-team mail route blazed in 1910. Strictly a winter trail of frozen muskeg and river ice, over 1,000 miles in length, it was made famous in 1925 when teams of mushers relayed a life-saving diphtheria serum from Seward to epidemic-threatened Nome.

MOUNTAIN GOAT

This agile animal inhabits mainland mountains, alongside Dall sheep, and is often spotted on windswept ridges and the steep slopes of fjords and inlets. With a body designed for balance (short legs and heavy shoulders), the mountain goat climbs steep rocky terrain on spreadable, padded hoofs. Its double coat of long coarse outer hair over a thick layer of cashmere-quality wool insulates the mountain goat from winter winds as it battles sub-zero temperatures and snow-covered slopes in search of exposed forage. The mountain goat's ability to survive in steep terrain is its main protection from predators.

DALL SHEEP

A white, wild sheep, this animal inhabits Alaska's mountain ranges and alpine meadows. Its current population is about 50,000. Dall sheep graze on grasses and other plants, and climb above the timberline in summer in pursuit of succulent new growth. The ram's horns are heavy and curled, and their growth rings determine the sheep's age.

Mountain goats can scramble up steep mountainsides on spreadable hooves cushioned with skid-proof pads.

DEER

Sitka blacktail deer, caribou and moose all belong to the deer family. Males are called bucks, females are does and babies are fawns, except for moose and caribou, which are called bulls, cows and calves. Deer are strictly plant eaters, with vegetation hard to find in winter. A moose can eat up to 20,000 leaves or weeds a day, often foraging underwater in the bottom of shallow lakes and ponds. Deer have a stomach divided into four chambers for digesting the tough leaves and grasses, allowing the deer to dine and

Dall sheep inhabit much of Alaska.

dash. After retreating to a safe spot, the deer digests its food by returning it to the mouth in small bits, called cud, and chewing this slowly before swallowing it again.

Deer are superb athletes, able to run up to 45 miles per hour, and to dodge boulders and trees without slowing down. By taking long leaps, especially over streams, the deer leaves little scent for predators, such as wolves and cougar, which a deer can outrun. With eyes located on the side of its head, a deer can see movement in every direction except right behind, so it usually has a head start.

The moose is the largest member of the deer family, with mature males standing as high as eight feet at the shoulder and weighing nearly 2,000 pounds. The moose inhabits mixed woods and wetlands. The spread of a bull moose's antlers can measure six feet, and males become very aggressive during the fall mating season. In winter, to avoid deep snow, moose often travel at night along highways and train tracks where they present a serious traffic hazard.

Made of solid bone, antlers are shed every winter and a new set is grown, which is soft and tender and covered with a thin skin called velvet while growing. This velvet is covered with fine short hairs and consists of thousands of blood vessels that carry calcium and other minerals for building strong bones. A young male's first set of antlers are just spikes; the second set branches into points (called tines). Over time, a full set develops that fork into many points and weigh about 80 pounds. Antlers protect males when fighting one another. A large set attracts females and acts as a deterrent to other males who might challenge his position as leader of the herd.

The barren-ground caribou of Alaska's tundra regions have broad hooves which provide support on boggy or snow-covered ground.

Both the male and female caribou grow antlers. On a mature bull, the antlers extend four feet from base to tips. Caribou number more than 300,000 statewide. They often travel in large herds and have been called 'nomads of the north' because they are always on the move in search of food – and thus hard to track. Alaska's interior and the Alaska Peninsula are where these elusive animals roam.

Moose often wander into Alaska towns when they are unable to forage beneath a deep snowpack. One November, a male moose wandered into a yard on the Kenai Peninsula where the owners watched him take off with their children's swing set after his antlers got entangled in the metal structure. After following the animal's trail of shredded blue plastic, state biologists concluded some of the ropes and chains were still tangled in the moose's antlers but the animal would be free of these once it lost its rack for the winter.

Moose are plentiful in Denali National Park and the Kenai Peninsula. In winter, when snow cover restricts their grazing range, they often show up in downtown Anchorage in search of food.

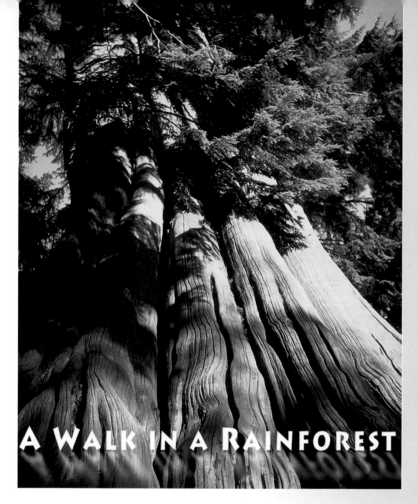

A WALK IN A RAINFOREST

Alaska's coastal rainforests flourish during the long, warm days of summer. Fronted by shoreline meadows of tall grass and leafy alders, these forests contain towering evergreens that can grow over 200 feet tall and live for hundreds of years.

The two common species of conifer found in Southeast Alaska are the Sitka spruce (Alaska's official tree) and the Western hemlock. The Sitka spruce grows quickly (up to three feet per year), reaches an average height of 160 feet and is three to five feet in diameter. Its branches project at an upward angle from its straight trunk, giving the tree a conical crown, and its spiky green needles are a deep green. The tree's strong, lightweight timber is used for boatbuilding, piano sounding boards and, in the early days of aviation, aircraft construction.

The Sitka spruce grows in pure stands or alongside the Western hemlock – a tall, slender tree with branches that droop slightly and with twigs containing two rows of needles that are flat and soft. At an average height of 100 to 150 feet and a diameter of two to four feet, the Western hemlock covers 75 percent of Southeast Alaska's forested area. This tree is tolerant of shade and often sprouts up among the faster-growing Sitka Spruce. Western Hemlock is a major source of pulpwood and lumber.

Another member of the pine family that thrives along the Pacific Northwest coast is the Western red cedar – the giant of the forest with a massive trunk (two to eight feet in diameter) and an average height of 100 to 175 feet. Its shiny needles grow in splayed clusters from the cedar's drooping branches and its aromatic wood is straight grained, durable and resistant to decay – the perfect material for dugout canoes and totem poles, as well as for panels, posts and other outdoor objects. The Western red cedar grows throughout the southern half of the Panhandle and along the Inside Passage.

Carpeting the forest floor are ferns, mosses and flowering plants. In an old-growth forest, toppled trees are reclaimed by mosses and become "nurse" logs to evergreen seedlings. Skunk cabbage is found in wet areas of the forest, near streams and bogs, and is easy to spot with its yellow, tulip-shaped inner leaf and large outer leaves. These leaves are eaten by deer and geese, and were tradtionally used by natives to wrap salmon for baking.

Blueberry and salmonberry bushes are plentiful and are a major food source for bears. Blue lupine, its tall spires thick with pod-like flowers, is a common sight, and brilliant fireweed grows in dense stands on recently-cleared land, its bright rosy-pink petals blooming on stalks that grow four feet high.

Other plants to look for include devil's club, a big, prickly, maple-leafed plant that belongs to the ginseng family, its medicinal properties long ago applied by the natives who would make a tea brewed from the root to cure colds and other ailments. The plant's tough, prickly spines can inflict bad scratches on bare-legged hikers. However, if you stay on

park trails maintained by the Forestry Service, you will have to watch out for nothing more than the odd slug lying on the path. Slugs feed at night on roots and plants and they grow to grand proportions in Alaska, earning such labels as Banana Slug, so named for its yellow-green colour with brown or black spots.

Slime mold is a fungus that grows under the damp leaves and rotting logs of a rainforest. Coral slime looks much like frost covering a log, and scrambled-egg slime

Skunk cabbage, as its name implies, has a pungent odor.

resembles an unappetizing helping of powdered eggs fried sunny side up. A conk is a type of bracket fungus that grows on dead tree trunks. When conks become hard and dry, Alaskans like to snap them off and turn them into decorative ornaments.

A variety of birds and animals live in the forest, including black bears who feed on wildberries in late summer, and Sitka blacktail deer who forage here for food throughout the winter. They thrive in second-growth forests except in areas of high snowfall, where their rate of survival is better in old-growth forests where browse plants grow around toppled trees and the forest's canopy prevents snow from covering the ground.

HIKING TIPS

The wilderness is always close at hand in the Alaskan ports of call, and hiking a maintained trail is a good way to enjoy the great outdoors. The cruise lines usually offer a few organized hikes at each port of call, with guides/naturalists escorting the group. However, it's usually possible to go for an independent hike along trails near town that are easily accessed from the cruise docks.

Detail on these trails is provided in the port-of-call chapters in Part II of this book, but some general tips for hiking include wearing sturdy shoes or boots and a waterproof jacket with a hood because the weather can change quickly. Pack some water and a high-energy snack, and always hike with at least one other person. Also, let someone other than your fellow hiker(s) know where you are going.

When hiking in a forest, be mindful of bears. Make plenty of noise on the trail (an airhorn works well) and be aware that salmon streams and berry patches attract bears. Should you encounter a bear, back away very slowly without making eye contact, which is perceived as aggression by the bear. Never run, unless you can run faster than your hiking companion!

Sunlight filters through the canopy of this northern rainforest.

Thousands of years ago, when the inhabitants of our planet lived in isolated pockets, few locations were more remote than the Aleutian Islands. A string of barren, volcanic islands, the Aleutians dot the open waters west of Alaska where the North Pacific meets the Bering Sea. The Aleuts who lived here were highly skilled at open-ocean hunting. They set out to sea in baidarkas (kayaks made of animal skin) and they used harpoons with poisoned tips to kill whales many times the size of their tiny vessels. Their waterproof clothing was made from strips of sea lion intestine stitched together and their boots were made from sea otter flippers.

When winter came and the hunting season ended, the Aleuts spent much of their time feasting and dancing. They lived in pit dwellings with sod roofs, and their villages extended throughout the Aleutians and along the Alaska Peninsula to the Shumagin Islands.

Sharing many of the Aleut customs, such as matrilineal descent and a similar language, were the Southern Eskimos whose territory bordered the Bering Sea and Gulf of Alaska coastlines, including Kodiak Island and Prince William Sound. They too hunted individually from kayaks and wore wooden visors to protect their eyes from both rain and ocean glare.

Kodiak Island is covered not with forests but tall grasses, and the Alutiiq who first lived here resided in semi-subterranean sod houses. The Chugach Eskimos, living on the forested shores of Prince William Sound, built planked wooden houses.

Alaska's Northern Eskimos, living along the Arctic coastline, built homes to withstand the freezing temperatures of winter. An underground entrance tunnel, which trapped any cold air coming in from outside, led into a semi-subterranean dwelling where seal-oil lamps were used for light and warmth. For clothing, they wore two layers of fur-lined garments. The Northern Eskimos hunted for whale and walrus from umiaks (large, open skin boats) but also used kayaks and, on land, sleds. They often saved Yankee whalers when their ships became trapped in Arctic ice.

The Aleuts and Eskimos believed in reincarnation and in maintaining a positive relationship with animal spirits through special rites performed at the beginning of each hunting season. The blanket toss, in which a person is bounced high in the air off a trampoline made of seal skins and held taut by a circle of onlookers, was traditionally held after a successful whale hunt. Shamans – who could cure illness and foretell the future – were important members of all native groups.

The Athabascans, who lived in the interior of Alaska and Northern Canada, were nomadic tribes who lived by hunting and fishing. Their clothing was often made of moose and caribou hides, and their homes were of various forms – from semi-subterranean log dwellings to dome-shaped tents made of animal skins. In the 18th century, the Athabascans increased their hunting and trapping of fur-bearing animals to supply the flourishing fur trade.

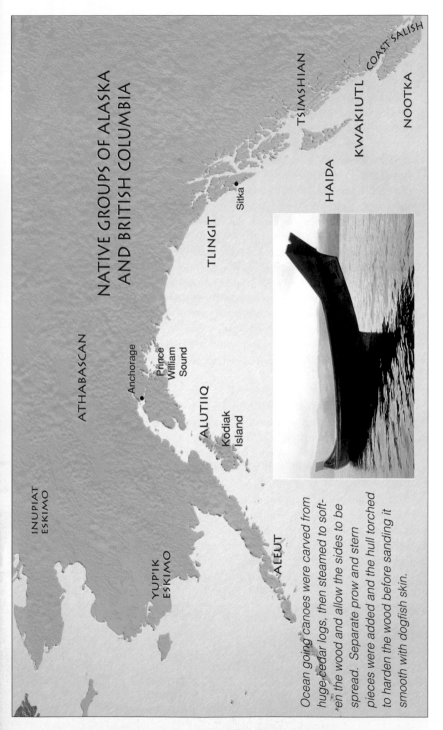

NATIVE GROUPS OF ALASKA
AND BRITISH COLUMBIA

INUPIAT
ESKIMO

YUP'IK
ESKIMO

ATHABASCAN

Anchorage

Prince
William
Sound

ALUTIIQ

Kodiak
Island

ALEUT

TLINGIT

Sitka

TSIMSHIAN

COAST SALISH

HAIDA

KWAKIUTL

NOOTKA

Ocean going canoes were carved from
huge cedar logs, then steamed to soft-
en the wood and allow the sides to be
spread. Separate prow and stern
pieces were added and the hull torched
to harden the wood before sanding it
smooth with dogfish skin.

The natives who inhabited the Inside Passage enjoyed a mild climate in a region where rivers teemed with salmon and foreshores were covered with shellfish. These reliable food sources supported a thriving population who had free time to develop sophisticated art forms. Their ancient civilizations are today recognized as complex social structures that produced monumental works of art.

The pyramids of Egypt were being constructed when permanent settlement of the Inside Passage began about 5,000 years ago. People had already been inhabiting this region for four or five thousand years, following the last retreat of the glaciers, but wild fluctuations in sea levels kept forcing them to relocate. When sea levels finally stabilized, the area's inhabitants began establishing permanent coastal villages. But their building materials, unlike those of the Egyptians, were not of stone but of wood.

Thick stands of cedar, spruce and hemlock provided an abundance of building materials but, just as uncut conifers eventually topple to the ground and slowly rot, so too did the natives' wooden dwellings and monuments. What did survive, however, were their kitchen middens.

A midden is a prehistoric refuse dump of shells and bones. At first glimpse it appears to be a natural beach of crushed shell, when in fact it is an archaeological site containing clues to a lost civilization. The shell, neutralizing the acid in the soil, has preserved ancient tools and artifacts such as antler carvings and stone bowls, engraved with human

The massive corner posts and cross beams of this traditional long house formed a permanent support for cedar planks that could be removed and transported between the clan's winter village and summer fishing camps.

and animal figures. Weapons for hunting and warfare have also been found in middens, as well as skeletal remains and the caches of chiefs.

Middens were formed from empty clam and mussel shells tossed into heaps which, over time, were crushed and compressed into beaches several yards deep. These white beaches were easily spotted by villagers returning after dark in their canoes. Another feature marking ancient village sites is a fish trap – stone barriers designed to trap salmon near shore at low tide. The fish could swim across the trap at high water, but as the tide dropped they could not get past the row of stones blocking their way seaward.

While the Athenians of Ancient Greece were erecting the Parthenon on the Acropolis some 2,500 years ago, a complex and artistically productive civilization was also thriving in the Pacific Northwest. Archaeological digs reveal a society that produced masters at weaving, woodworking and sculpturing. Personal adornments were miniature works of art depicting human, animal and supernatural figures carved from stone, bone, antler and tooth. Petroglyphs were cut into foreshore stones, and pictographs were drawn on rock walls. These images were possibly inspired by shamanism – a belief in supernatural powers – or some may have had a more pragmatic purpose, such as marking a good fishing hole or a territorial boundary.

As the knights of medieval Europe rode off to battle, chiefs and warriors of the Northwest Coast also engaged in warfare, paddling their canoes hundreds of miles into enemy territories. The northern tribes often headed south to raid villages and capture slaves – the lowest rank of a social hierarchy consisting of nobility, commoners and slaves. During this period, mortuary practices shifted from burying the dead in middens to placing their remains in boxes hung from trees or inside small mortuary houses near the village.

Today's visitors to the Inside Passage can enjoy (but not disturb) the area's numerous shell beaches, which are prehistoric kitchen middens from native societies.

Ancient petroglyphs, such as this one at Port Neville on Johnstone Strait, are found throughout the Inside Passage.

The 18th century's Age of Enlightenment, in which the pursuit of knowledge prompted numerous scientific expeditions resulted in Europe's maritime nations sending explorers on voyages of discovery. The inevitable exploration of the North Pacific marked the end of pre-history for its inhabitants.

When European explorers first landed on the Northwest Coast, they encountered various native groups who shared some general traits but spoke different languages and displayed regional differences in their architecture, art and social customs. Coastal Indians ranged from the top of the Alaska Panhandle to the lower reaches of the Inside Passage.

The three northern groups – the Tlingit, Tsimshian and Haida – were highly respected as warriors and artisans. The Haida's cedar dugout canoes were considered top-of-the-line and the Haida would often tow a newly carved canoe across Hecate Strait to the mainland where they would trade it to the Tsimshians for candlefish oil. The Haida, skilled mariners, travelled as far away as present-day San Francisco in these seaworthy craft.

Although their languages were unrelated, the northern groups' social structures were similar. The Tlingit and Haida were divided into two sub-groups (called moieties by anthropologists) which were symbolized by the Eagle and the Raven. The Tsimshian were divided into four sub-groups, termed phratries. Sub-groups were further divided into kinship clans represented by crests (totems) depicting the Frog, Beaver,

Wolf, Grizzly Bear and Killer Whale. Each clan was further subdivided into family households.

Descent was through the female line and a person was not allowed to marry someone from the same moiety or phratry. This intermarriage among sub-groups forged alliances between village chiefs and their heirs. Etiquette and ceremony were fundamental to these structured societies in which power and wealth were manifested in potlatch celebrations of feasting, dancing and gift-giving. Custom dictated that invited guests would repay the host chief's hospitality with a reciprocal potlatch, preparations for which could take years. Totem poles were often raised at a potlatch.

The post-and-beam houses of the northern groups were solidly built. Massive corner posts and cross beams – which sometimes took 300 men to raise – supported the roof and sides made of cedar planking. The main frontal pole and interior poles, elaborately carved, displayed the clan and moiety crests. Sometimes a portal was carved in the lowest figure of a frontal pole to serve as the entrance. Freestanding poles were raised in front of the houses to commemorate an important event, such as a birth, marriage or, most importantly, a death. When a high-ranking chief died, his cremated remains were eventually placed in a niche at the back of a mortuary pole that was raised – with much ceremony – in his honor.

The architecture of the Wakashan groups to the south was slightly different from that of the northern groups. House planks were not permanently attached to the post-and-beam framework, allowing them to be dismantled and towed by canoe to a summer village during the salmon season. The earthen floors were also simpler than the recessed levels of northern homes, but common activities included burning indoor fires and hanging salmon to dry.

Wakashan is a linguistic term and the people of this language group consist of the Kwakwaka'wakw (Kwakiutl), who inhabit much of

The Beaver Clan House at Saxman Village near Ketchikan is an example of Tlingit art and architecture.

British Columbia's central coast, and the Nuu-Chah-Nulth (Nootka), who live on the west coast of Vancouver Island. Because the natives' traditional languages were oral and not written, there is often a variation in the spelling of their words and names. Early explorers, attempting to phonetically record what they were hearing, gave certain groups erroneous names. For instance, the Nuu-chah-nulth were called Nootka by Captain Cook, and for decades the name Kwakiutl was applied to the Kwakwaka'wakw – "those who speak Kwakwala".

The societies of the Wakashan peoples were, like the northern groups, based on kinship. Each clan bore its own hereditary crests such as the killer whale and thunderbird. Ancestral privileges among these groups were more often inherited through the male line than the female, and the right to display certain crests and perform certain songs and dances was passed down through the generations.

Kwakwaka'wakw potlatch festivities were the most flamboyant of all the groups, their theatrical dances performed with elaborate props and costumes, especially masks. They often painted themselves and even altered the shape of their heads by binding them in infancy to make them elongated and thus more beautiful. The Nuu-chah-nulth natives were skilled mariners who hunted whales and other sea mammals in the open waters of the Pacific.

The southernmost group is the Coast Salish, their territory encompassing the modern cities of Vancouver and Seattle. The Coast Salish inhabited flat-roofed houses that were often built in long rows under a common roof and divided by plank partitions, which could be removed for social and ceremonial occasions. At the time of European contact, their social structure was less rigid than the Wakashans or the northern groups, and class distinctions were less evident. Their winter festivities were more contemplative, less devoted to feasting and dancing than to personal acquisition of spirit power. To acquire a guardian spirit meant success at hunting and fishing. Those with the ability to foretell events and cure sickness became shamans and their supernatural powers were highly respected.

Also respected were the souls of other living creatures. In mythic times, it was believed that animals had the ability to transform themselves into humans. Elaborate rituals were conducted at the beginning of each fishing and hunting season to pay homage to the various species which were sought for food and clothing.

Native legends were passed orally from generation to generation. These traditional stories, set in a timeless past, are an expression of the universe's creation and the evolution of humanity. In native mythology, the Raven plays a major role as a supernatural trickster and transformer. The Raven represents curiosity and he continually alters the world provided by the Creator. While stealing, he accidentally released the sun and stars, and when he opened a clamshell he released the first humans.

UNDERSTANDING NATIVE ART

At the time of first contact by European explorers, Northwest native communities were filled with skilled artisans. The explorers engaged in a healthy trade with the natives, acquiring artifacts that were sometimes handcrafted on the spot. In exchange, the natives received European tools which enhanced their woodworking and carving. Glass beads were also a coveted trade item, especially with the Athabascans who used them to decorate their leather garments.

Basket weaving was a skill shared by all the native groups. The women of the coastal Indian tribes wove watertight hats and baskets out of spruce roots and cedar bark. The Athabascans used willow root, and the Southern Eskimos and Aleuts used beach ryegrass.

Another product of native craftsmanship was the bentwood box – made from a single cedar plank that was steamed until soft enough to bend at ninety-degree angles. Three of the corners were, as a result, per-

fectly smooth while the fourth corner was skillfully joined with pegs or spruce root stitches. These boxes held all sorts of items and were often decorated with ornate carvings.

Totem poles, made from the trunks of massive red cedars, were the most monumental of all native art. As the chosen cedar was felled, the cutters looked away while its spirit departed. Master carvers were commissioned to sculpture the pole and, upon its completion, they performed a dance around the base of the pole while it was being raised. A freestanding totem pole survived for about 60 years before the elements took their toll and the weathered pole toppled to the ground. Then, its spirit would depart and the fallen pole was left to return to nature.

Throughout the early years of the fur trade, native groups flourished and their art continued to evolve. But when white missionaries and schoolteachers moved into these regions, native customs were dis-

The sculptured figures of Tlingit totem poles can be viewed at Saxman Village, including works in progress in the carving shed.

Haida dancers re-enact native myths, which were passed orally from generation to generation at potlatch celebrations.

couraged and a unique art form was all but abandoned. Its rebirth came in the late 1960s and gained momentum in the '70s when native artists discovered a new medium – the silkscreen print. The ensuing mass production of native art prompted the general public to take an interest. Each group has its own artistic style but they share basic components. The form line defines the shape of the figure being portrayed. Its flowing outline varies in thickness and is usually painted black, with the figure's secondary features in red.

Black and red are the traditional colors of native art. Red was made from ochre (a clay-like mineral) ground to a powder and turned into a paste with the addition of a binding agent such as oil from salmon eggs. Black came from charcoal, graphite or lignite. With the introduction of commercial paints, artists began experimenting with non-traditional colors; however, much of their work is still done in the original colors. The Kwakwaka'wakw (Kwakiutl) traditionally used more colors than the northern artists, adding green, white and yellow to their palettes.

Another basic component is the ovoid – an oval that is pushed out of shape to fit inside the form lines. An ovoid can represent a face, eyes, major joints or simply fill in empty spaces. The U form is used to help contour the figure, fill in spaces or represent features such as feathers. The S form is also used in a variety of ways, such as joining elements, filling in space or representing part of a leg or arm. The four basic design elements – form lines, ovoids, U forms and S forms – are closely assembled to create other shapes in the spaces between them.

Split figures (mirror images) are also widely used, as are transformation figures (i.e. half human/half animal). The basic elements of a figure are sometimes dismantled and rearranged to fit inside a given shape, such as a blanket, hat or spoon. The key to recognizing the figures portrayed in native art is to learn a few of their dominant features.

For example, a raven has a long, straight beak whereas an eagle has a shorter, hooked beak. The legendary Thunderbird – a crest used only by the most powerful and prestigious chiefs – is always portrayed with outstretched wings and a sharply recurved upper beak. A bear will have flared nostrils, clawed paws and sharp teeth, sometimes with its tongue hanging out. The beaver has two large front teeth and a cross-hatched tail. The wolf is often shown standing on all four legs whereas the bear and beaver are usually sitting upright.

One of the easiest motifs to recognize is the killer whale, frequently portrayed in an arched position with a tall dorsal fin protruding from its back and two saw-like rows of teeth in its mouth. The moon, an exclusive crest of high-ranking Haida chiefs, is round with a face in the centre. The sun is similar to the moon but with long rays projecting from the outer circle. Human figures are also part of native art and those wearing high-crowned hats atop a totem pole are watchmen who can see others approaching. In Kwakwaka'wakw (Kwakiutl) art, the eyes of supernatural beings are hollow and those of animals and people protrude.

Haida drawings and sculptures embody Northwest native art's classical purity. The trademarks of Haida art are a fluid, stylized use of well-defined form lines and a complex intertwining of figures. Poles and other objects are minimally altered by shallow carvings that blend with the basic shape. Heads are often large (especially those portrayed on totem poles) and in print works the blank spaces are seldom left unadorned. Tlingit art is similar to Haida, although the figures on a Tlingit totem pole are more isolated and sculptured. The Tlingit are well known for their Chilkat blankets – woven of goat hair and decorated with clan crests – and for their button blankets on which intricate crests are outlined with thousands of buttons. Tsimshian artists implement many of the traditional northern elements but with slight varia-

This 19th-century Haida drawing by Johnnie Kit-Elswa represents the Raven in the belly of a killer whale.

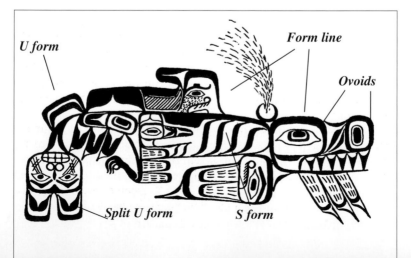

U form

Form line

Ovoids

Split U form   S form

tions, such as detaching certain components from the main figure. Kwakwaka'wakw art is recognized by its variety of colors, abundance of small elements and the protruding beaks, fins and wings that are added to totem poles.

Nuu-chah-nulth (Nootka) art is more flexible than classic northern art, with frequent breaks in the form lines or even the complete absence of form lines. Shapes are often geometrical and fewer design elements, such as ovoids, are used.

Coast Salish natives used no crest system, so their art traditionally depicted animal and human figures rather than clan emblems. They are noted for their excellent weaving and basketry as well as their carved spindle whorls. The Cowichans on Vancouver Island still employ traditional methods when making their famous sweaters.

With a renewed interest in preserving the traditions of native art, another concern has arisen – that of authenticity. By definition, anything created by a native Indian is authentic. However, some of the best native artists are not content to replicate the work of their ancestors but are experimenting with their art's classical components. As the acclaimed Haida artist Robert Davidson says, if an art isn't changing, it's dead. Davidson's professional career as a Haida artist began with his carving miniature totem poles for customers at a Vancouver department store. His work is now displayed in art galleries, and his original prints and sculptures are collectors items.

The late Bill Reid, of Haida and Scots-American ancestry, is credited with reviving West Coast native art and reintroducing it to the world. His major works include *The Black Canoe*, which is the centerpiece of the Canadian embassy in Washington, DC. A second casting, *The Jade Canoe*, stands in the departure hall of Vancouver's International Airport. His *Killer Whale* bronze sits outside the entrance to the Vancouver Aquarium, and his massive yellow cedar carving *The Raven and The First Men* is housed at the University of British Columbia's Museum of Anthropology.

When a Haida embarks on an artistic career, the first step is to become an apprentice – one who copies the art of predecessors. The next stage is that of journeyman – learning the symmetrical and classical forms of Haida art. The next stage is to become a master, which entails experimenting with what has been learned. Finally, those with exceptional talent become artists, their work reflecting both mastery and emotion.

The most recent development in native art is the use of computer graphics. Roy Henry Vickers, a talented Tsimshian artist, has recreated traditional forms on a computer screen. He says that his computer-generated ovoids and U-shapes look no different than those created by his ancestors a thousand years ago. The use of computer technology also provides for long-term storage of totem pole designs on disks.

Fairweather Range

Misty Fjords

PART II

THE VOYAGE AND THE PORTS

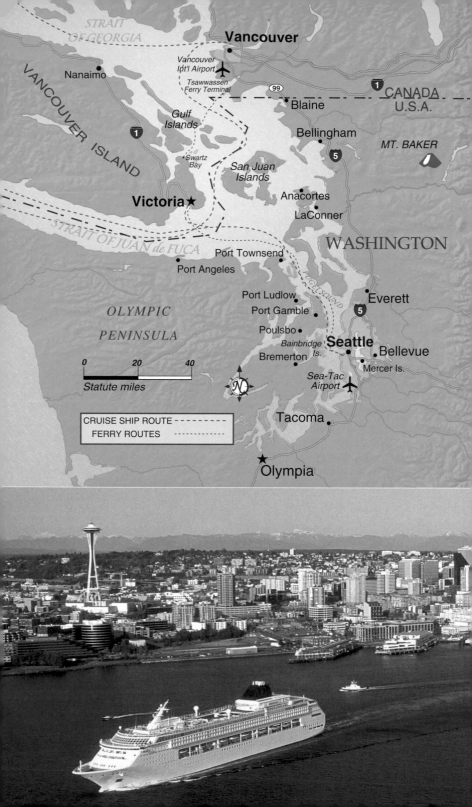

CHAPTER ONE

SEATTLE & VICTORIA

I n times past, seafaring explorers believed the Strait of Juan de Fuca led from the Pacific to the Atlantic. Today this major waterway is a busy marine highway and the southernmost entrance to the Inside Passage. It is also part of the international border running between Canada and the United States. On its north side, on the shores of Vancouver Island, is British Columbia's provincial capital of Victoria. Bounding the south side of the strait is Washington State's Olympic Peninsula, east of which is the dynamic city of Seattle, stretching along the sheltered shores of Puget Sound. Victoria is a convenient port of call for ships heading to and from Seattle, an increasingly popular base port for cruises to Alaska.

SEATTLE

When two ships of Britain's Royal Navy sailed into Puget Sound in the spring of 1792, the expedition's commander was so impressed with the "pleasing landscapes" and "serenity of climate" that his logbook entries read more like those of a travel writer than a sea captain. Yet, with uncanny foresight, Captain George Vancouver's comments were right on the mark. He looked around at the forested shores and saw a potential lumber industry, noting "thousands of the finest spars the world

Alaska-bound Norwegian Sky departs Seattle.

Seattle became a busy shipping port when gold fever sent men and women rushing north to the Klondike in 1897.

produces." He gazed at the future site of Seattle and wrote that the verdant lawns and abundant fertility required "only to be enriched by the industry of man." But it was the esthetic beauty of the area that caused this skilled surveyor to momentarily forget about compass bearings and potential northwest passages. "To describe the beauties of this region," he wrote, "will, on some future occasion, be a very grateful task to the pen of a skilful panegyrist."

Captain Vancouver's prophetic words have been echoed time and again in recent years. Ranked in various surveys as the number one place in America to live, visit, do business and raise children, the city of Seattle has realized its potential. This achievement, however, was a long uphill struggle which began in 1851. In the fall of that year, when the lands around Puget Sound were still part of Oregon Territory, two men from Portland – John Low and Lee Terry – explored Puget Sound and chose Alki Point for a townsite.

When their sawmill venture failed, a group of settlers – led by Arthur Denny, Charles Boren and William Bell – relocated four miles away on the east side of Elliott Bay in what is now Seattle's downtown core. This larger group was joined by Dr. Maynard and a Portland lumberman who came to build a steam sawmill. Land claims were quickly made and a name chosen for their new town. They decided on Sealth (later altered to Seattle), after a chief of the local Duwamp natives.

Their settlement slowly grew into a service and supply centre for nearby mining and logging camps, but the town's fate was still uncertain. Its future hinged on the Northern Pacific Railroad, and land speculators eagerly anticipated that Seattle would be chosen as a western terminus. When Tacoma got the nod over Seattle, her disappointed citizens joined together to build their own railroad. This civic pride and energy became known as the 'Seattle Spirit.'

In 1880, railroad magnate Henry Villard bought the nearby Newcastle Mine, gained control of the Northern Pacific Railroad and, a few years later, a main line finally reached Seattle. This helped the brash young city sustain its growing prosperity, although a depression in the mid-80s caused a downturn and in 1889 a fire wiped out 60 city blocks. But the Seattle Spirit, fueled by immigrants from other parts of the country and Europe, propelled the city forward with dogged determination. Then, on July 17, 1897, the steamer Portland arrived from Alaska with gold prospectors on board. They had struck it rich in the Klondike and the great gold rush began.

Seattle, already shipping freight to Alaskan ports, quickly established itself as the outfitting center and port of departure for prospectors heading north. The city never looked back. Its economy diversified further with the establishment of Boeing Airplane Company in 1917 and, more recently, high-tech industries such as the Microsoft computer software company.

In the 1990s, wealth generated by Microsoft and other computer/dot-com companies propelled an unprecedented building boom in Seattle's downtown as high-tech billionaires redirected millions into civic projects. Seattle's roots, however, have not been lost to the 21st century, and the city's wealthy benefactors also fund the restoration of historic landmarks – tangible reminders of the city's pioneer soul.

GETTING AROUND IN SEATTLE

The cruise ships dock at Pier 66, at the foot of Bell Street, and at Pier 30, which is a short taxi ride to the city's hotel and shopping area. The **Visitor Information Bureau** is located at 7th and Union, in Level 1

A horse-drawn carriage takes visitors on a tour of Pioneer Square.

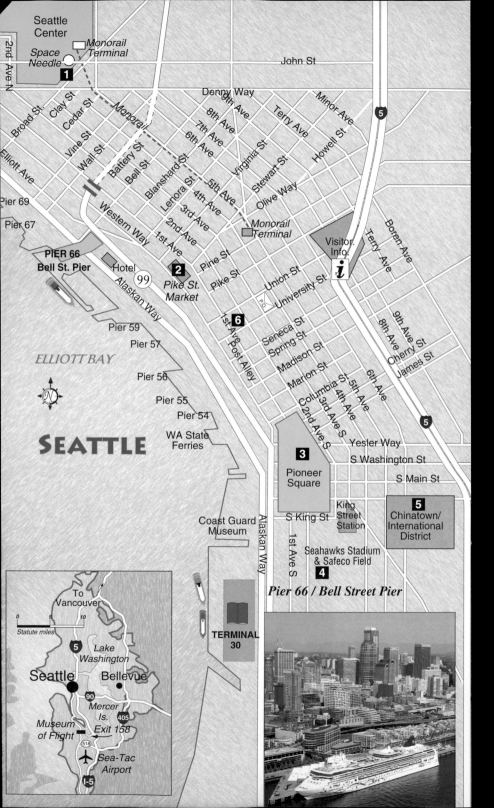

Seattle Center
Space Needle
Monorail Terminal
1

2nd Ave N

John St

Clay St
Broad St
Cedar St
Vine St
Wall St
Elliott Ave
Pier 69
Pier 67

Denny Way
9th Ave
8th Ave
7th Ave
6th Ave
6th Ave
Terry Ave
Minor Ave
Howell St

Battery St
Bell St
Blanchard St
Lenora St
Western Way
Virginia St
Stewart St
Olive Way
4th Ave
5th Ave
3rd Ave
2nd Ave
1st Ave

5

Monorail

Boren Ave
Terry Ave

PIER 66
Bell St. Pier

Hotel
99
Alaskan Way

2
Pike St.
Market

Monorail
Terminal

P.O.

Visitor.
Info.
i

Pine St
Pike St

Union St
University St

9th Ave St
8th Ave St
Cherry St
James St

Pier 59
Pier 57

6

1st Ave/Post Alley

Seneca St
Spring St
Madison St
Marion St

6th Ave

ELLIOTT BAY

Pier 56

Pier 55

Pier 54

Columbia St
3rd Ave
4th Ave
5th Ave

5

WA State
Ferries

2nd Ave S

SEATTLE

3
Pioneer
Square

Yesler Way
S Washington St
S Main St

5
Chinatown/
International
District

Coast Guard
Museum

Alaskan Way

1st Ave S

S King St

King
Street
Station

Seahawks Stadium
& Safeco Field
4

Pier 66 / Bell Street Pier

TERMINAL 30

To
Vancouver

0   5   10
Statute miles

5
Lake
Washington

Seattle   **Bellevue**

90
Mercer
Is.
405
Exit 158

Museum
of Flight

518

Sea-Tac
Airport

I-5

Galleria of the Washington State Convention Center. The downtown Metro buses in the core area – between Battery and South Jackson Streets, and between Sixth Avenue and Alaskan Way – are free from 4 a.m. to 9 p.m. A high-speed monorail whisks passengers between Westlake Center and the Seattle Center, while a more leisurely pace is taken by the tram and trolley cars servicing the waterfront piers and other downtown attractions. Seattlites pride themselves on their eccentricities, so you may notice your taxi driver dressed as if going straight to a Halloween party after work – that's because local cabbies are allowed to wear costumes on the job.

WHERE TO STAY IN SEATTLE

In addition to the reliable chain hotels, Seattle's distinctive establishments include the stately Fairmont Olympic Hotel, built in 1924 in the Italian Renaissance style. The Edgewater, at Pier 67, offers a mountain lodge decor with windows overlooking Elliott Bay. When the Beatles stayed at the Edgewater in 1964 at the height of Beatlemania, a cyclone fence had to be erected around the hotel to keep the fans at bay but this didn't deter those who tried climbing in from the water. In 1992 the Edgewater was used as a location for an episode of TV's *Northern Exposure*, called 'It Happened in Juneau.' Opposite Pier 66, on Alaskan Way, is the Seattle Marriott Waterfront Hotel.

SEATTLE SHOPPING

During the Klondike Gold Rush, prospectors shopped in Seattle for tents, picks, shovels, beans and bacon. Today the outfitting stores supply freeze-dried food and Gore-Tex clothing for outdoor

Terminal 30 is about 15 minutes by cab from downtown.

(Left) The Pike Place Market sells fresh seafood and farm produce. (Below) Waterfront restaurants are a Seattle attraction.

recreationists, and local suppliers provide everything from skis to back-packs. Seattle is a good place to do some pre-Alaska shopping for items such as a wide-brimmed felt hat, rain slicker and binoculars. If high fashion is more your taste, head for Fifth Avenue's shops and malls, such as Westlake Center, Nordstrom and Rainier Square.

NORTHWEST CUISINE

In the mid-1980s, a new culinary trend began in the Pacific Northwest. With its moderate climate, rich soil and access to salt and fresh water, the region enjoys a year-round bounty of fruit, vegetables, meat, poultry and seafood from nearby farms and fishboats. These locally harvested products, enhanced with regional delicacies such as wild mushrooms, are highlighted in Northwest Cuisine.

Preparation may vary but the natural flavor of the ingredients is always the emphasis. To help wash down an oyster in the shell or a steaming bowl of clams, Seattle diners can choose from a growing list

of local wines and brews.

In addition to Seattle's many old-fashioned pubs and specialty coffee bars, there are a number of award-winning restaurants serving Northwest cuisine, such as Fullers (in the Sheraton Seattle), The Painted Table (in the luxurious Alexis Hotel) and, on Fourth Avenue, The Dahlia Lounge (Northwest cuisine with an Asian influence). Also on Fourth is the Assaggio Ristorante, serving excellent Italian cuisine. Seafood lovers might try Chandler's Crabhouse overlooking Lake Union, McCormick & Schmick's in

The Space Needle, built for the 1964 World's Fair, dominates Seattle's modern skyline.

downtown Seattle or Ray's Boathouse on Shilshole Bay where the sea and mountain views are as good as the food.

LOCAL ATTRACTIONS

A good place to enjoy Seattle's beautiful mountains-and-sea setting is from atop the 600-foot **Space Needle 1**, built for the 1962 World's Fair. The observation deck's 360-degree view lets you gaze down at the city built on the hills between Puget Sound and Lake Washington. To the west lie the Olympic Mountains and eastward is the Cascade Range of snowcapped peaks which includes Mount Rainier and Mount Baker. The Space Needle is part of the 74-acre **Seattle Center** which encompasses a theater, opera house, children's museum and science center. Nearby is the **Science Fiction Museum and Hall of Fame**, brainchild of Microsoft co-founder and sci-fi fan Paul Allen, who donated $20 million to build it. The **Experience Music Project**, an interactive rock'n'roll museum, was also funded by Paul Allen to the tune of $250 million. The museum, at the base of the Space Needle, is housed in a modernist red, blue and purple steel-skinned building designed by Frank Gehry.

Six blocks south of the Space Needle is Seattle's waterfront – formerly called 'The Gold Rush Strip' when freighters and passenger liners from Alaska and other American ports docked here. It stretches the length of Alaskan Way, from Pier 70 – a restored wharf now filled with shops and restaurants – down to Pier 52. In between are restaurants, gift shops and tour boat operators offering harbor tours, cruises of the canal locks and trips to Blake Island State Park.

*Pier 66 now houses a
modern complex.*

The **Seattle Aquarium** and **Omnidome Theatre** are located on historic **Pier 59**, and the recently renovated **Bell Street Pier (Pier 66)** is where **Odyssey, The Maritime Discovery Centre** is located. This interactive maritime centre contains four galleries and hands-on exhibits celebrating the city's marine environment, such as taking a simulated kayak ride through Puget Sound. A public rooftop deck, with telescopes, is a good spot to enjoy the harbor views.

Perched on a bluff overlooking the waterfront is the **Pike Place Market 2**. Its cobblestone streets are lined with stalls of fruit, vegetables, seafood, meats, cheeses, coffees, teas and spices. When you tire of strolling the busy aisles, there are three levels of shops and restaurants below the main arcade. The stairs of Pike Place Hillclimb connect the market with the waterfront below. Here pedestrians can hop aboard vintage trolleys which travel up and down Alaskan Way. They stop at various pier attractions, then carry on to Pioneer Square and the International District. Seattle trolley tours can be boarded at the waterfront or downtown booths for a one-hour narrated loop tour of the city's best attractions, with on/off privileges at each stop.

The restored brick buildings of **Pioneer Square 3** stand where settlers' shacks stood before the Great Fire of 1889. Yesler Way, which runs through the middle of Pioneer Square down to the waterfront, was originally a skid road for logs. A guided underground tour follows sidewalks (one storey down) that were abandoned after the Great Fire. The Klondike Gold Rush National Historical Park, hidden away in a storefront at 117 South Main, commemorates Seattle's boomtown days as 'Gateway to the Gold.'

Next to Pioneer Square is the new **Seahawks Football Stadium** and adjacent **Safeco Field 4**, home to the Seattle Mariners baseball club. Due east of the Kingdome is the **International District 5** where Asian restaurants, bazaars and exotic shops are bordered by the Kobe Terrace Park. Guided tours are available of this colorful area rich in Oriental culture.

The **Seattle Art Museum 6**, internationally known for its Native American and modern art of the Pacific Northwest, is located at 100 University Street. On the block just uphill from the Museum is the

Seattle Symphony's concert hall – Benaroya Hall – which opened with a two-week gala celebration in September 1998.

To the north, separated from downtown by the Lake Washington Ship Canal, is the Ballard area – settled by Scandinavian fishermen and loggers. The canal connects Lake Washington with Puget Sound and near its western entrance are the **Chittenden Locks**. Here sightseers can watch fishboats and other vessels being raised or lowered as they travel between fresh and saltwater. Seattle's huge fishing fleet moors at nearby Fisherman's Terminal and each spring hundreds of seiners and gill netters head north to fish the waters of Alaska. The **Woodland Park Zoo**, on Phinney Avenue North, is one of the best zoos in the U.S. with its re-creation of natural habitats.

On the southern outskirts of the city, off Airport Way, is the **Museum of Flight**, a national historic landmark. Built around the Boeing Company's original factory on the edge of Boeing Field (King County Airport) the museum's Great Gallery contains vintage aircraft suspended in simulated flight from the ceiling, which is six storeys high. The Spirit of Washington dinner train will

Entrance to Klondike Gold Rush National Historical Park.

A retired Concorde supersonic jetliner is on permanent display at the Museum of Flight.

take you on a scenic trip around Lake Washington to the Chateau Ste. Michelle Winery situated on the landscaped grounds of Woodinville.

Farther afield, scenic country roads lead into the Cascade Mountains past rocky gorges, plunging falls and pretty alpine villages such as North Bend at the base of Mt. Si, Leavenworth with its charming Bavarian theme, and Roslyn – the fictional Cicely, Alaska of the TV series *Northern Exposure*. Ninety miles south of Seattle is **Mount St. Helen's National Volcanic Monument**, where a new lava dome began forming in fall 2004. With steam billowing from the main crater, officials closed the immediate area to visitors who normally come to hike the trails and witness the devastation caused by the volcano's cataclysmic eruption in May 1980.

To the west of the city, beautiful Puget Sound beckons. The Washington State ferry system (the nation's largest) provides access from downtown Seattle to Bainbridge Island and to Bremerton on the Olympic Peninsula. A loop drive of the Peninsula can include stops at Poulsbo (settled by Norwegians), and the ports of Gamble, Ludlow and Townsend (all 19th-century towns where schooners loaded lumber for shipment to California). Port Angeles, with its mile-long spit called Ediz Hook, is the gateway to Olympic National Park, where attractions include the Sol Duc Hot Springs. Ocean beaches beckon on the Peninsula's west coast, and the state capital of Olympia is situated on Puget Sound's southern shore.

North of Seattle, the Interstate 5 is the quickest land route to Vancouver, Canada – a 3-1/2 hour drive of 140 miles. Time permitting, you can turn off at Conway for a visit to LaConner – a century-old port town with interesting shops and restaurants. Another recommended detour is to turn at Burlington onto the scenic Chuckanut Drive, which hugs the coastline. Chuckanut Drive reconnects with the I-5 at Bellingham – southern terminus of the Alaska State Ferry and an interesting waterfront town with turn-of-the-century buildings. From here Mount Baker is a 60-mile detour east.

A Washington State Ferry plies the waters of Puget Sound with Mount Rainier in the background.

The Fairmont Empress hotel, built by the Canadian Pacific Railway, is a Victoria landmark.

VICTORIA

More than any other Canadian city, Victoria has retained its British colonial heritage. The provincial capital of British Columbia, it is a city of tearooms, English pubs, double-decker buses and flower gardens that bloom year-round in the temperate climate. Victoria began as a fur trading post when the Hudson's Bay Company built a fort here in 1843. British immigrants soon arrived by sailing ship, having rounded Cape Horn with their fine English china and Victorian ideals, ready to carve a piece of the old country out of this new land of rugged wilderness. The city was named in honour of Queen Victoria, Empress of India, whose statue graces the lawns leading to the Legislative Buildings, designed by British architect Francis Rattenbury and completed in 1898. By the end of Queen Victoria's reign in 1901, the city that bears her name was coming into its own. Rattenbury's architectural achievements would soon define the city's Inner Harbour, the sight of which prompted Rudyard Kipling to say that a visit to Victoria was "worth a very long journey" – a sentiment still expressed to this day.

GETTING AROUND

The cruise ships dock at Ogden Point, about a 10-minute taxi ride from downtown Victoria, where most of the major attractions are within walking distance of the Inner Harbour. Passenger ferries dock in Victoria's Inner Harbour and floatplanes also land here. The Victoria International Airport is a 45-minute drive north of the city, as are the car ferry terminals at Sidney and Swartz Bay. The cruise lines offer pre- and post-cruise tours to Victoria. There is an excellent seawalk that starts southeast of the cruise ship dock.

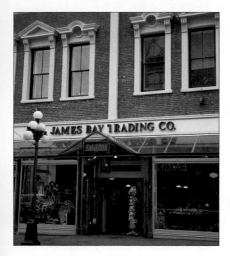

Heritage buildings line Government Street, such as the one above, built in 1869 by a local real-estate magnate and relative of Queen Victoria.

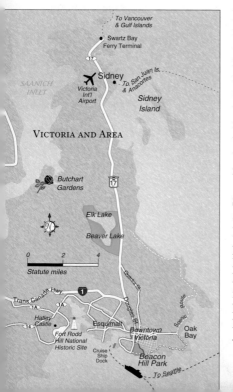

SHOPPING & DINING

For shoppers, some of the best browsing can be done on Government Street where the late Victorian era is preserved in chocolate shops, bookstores, tobacconists and tea merchants. Here you can buy Scottish tweeds and tartans, English bone china, Waterford crystal and Irish linen. Munro's Bookstore and Rogers' Chocolates are worth popping into just for a look at their splendid interiors. On Fort Street is 'Antique Row' and at **Market Square** ⓫, the Olde Town's former hotel and saloon district, the shops front an open-air square. **Fan Tan Alley,** ⓮ said to be the narrowest street in Canada, leads to colorful Chinatown.

For fine dining, **The Fairmont Empress Hotel** serves award-winning cuisine in the Empress Room and a popular curry buffet in its famous Bengal Lounge where colonial decor includes a Bengal tiger skin over the marble fireplace. Tea with sandwiches, pastries and scones is served throughout the afternoon in the hotel's elegant Tea Lobby (reservations for one of the seatings are recommended).

Victoria's inviting pubs include **Swans Brewpub** (at Pandora and Store Streets) where draft ales and lagers are served on its flower-filled patio. The **Snug**, Victoria's oldest English pub, is at the **Oak Bay Beach Hotel** – an English country inn overlooking the Strait of Juan de Fuca. Across the Inner Harbour, in Esquimalt, is the **Olde England Inn** – a Tudor-style mansion where the decor and staff attire are Elizabethan and the menu features traditional English fare. On the hotel grounds is a replica of **Anne Hathaway's Cottage** – birthplace of William Shakespeare's wife – complete with country garden.

CITY SIGHTS

There's no better place to start a tour of downtown Victoria than strolling the Inner Harbour. Replica historic vessels tug at their moorings while small passenger ferries whisk visitors around the harbor. In summer a festive atmosphere ensues when flowers spill from hanging baskets and spectators throng the seawall during various regattas, festivals and outdoor concerts. The harbor's dockside attractions are part of an imperial setting of lawns and lamp posts, overseen by the regal **Fairmont Empress Hotel 1**. This grand hotel, designed by Francis Rattenbury, first opened its doors in 1908 and was built by the Canadian Pacific Railway. The hotel has been restored to its original Edwardian opulence and afternoon tea at The Empress remains a Victoria tradition.

Equally imperial in style and scale are the **Legislative Buildings 2**, designed by Rattenbury and completed in 1898. Rattenbury was in his early twenties when he won a competition to design these buildings. Built of granite and other indigenous materials, this Beaux-Arts structure is a mix of Victorian, Roman and Italian Renaissance styles. At night its classical domes and arches are outlined by thousands of lights.

Rattenbury trained with his uncle in England before moving to Canada where the wide-open spaces of the west suited his grand schemes. His life ended in scandal back in England when his young, second wife and her paramour (the chauffeur) were charged with bludgeoning him to death in 1935. Alma Rattenbury was acquitted, only to

Funky shops and historic buildings are found at Market Square.

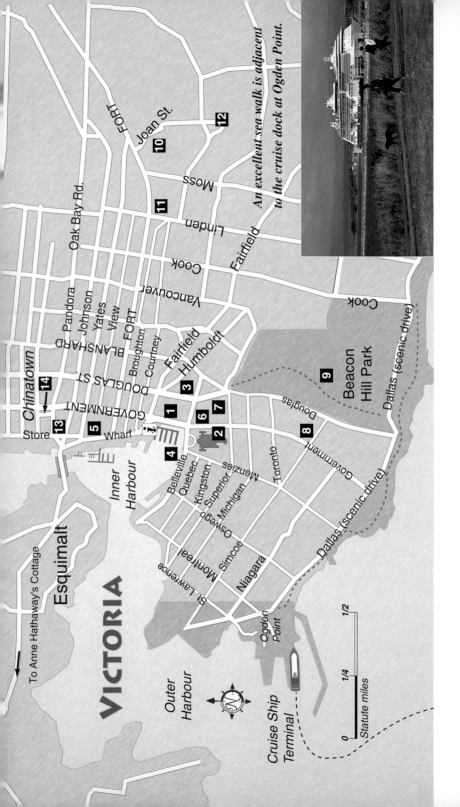

VICTORIA

Esquimalt

To Anne Hathaway's Cottage

Chinatown

Store **13**

Oak Bay Rd.

Pandora
Johnson
Yates
View
Broughton
Courtney

FORT
BLANSHARD
DOUGLAS ST.
GOVERNMENT

14

5 Wharf

i

1

3

Fairfield
Humboldt

6 **7**

2

4

Inner
Harbour

Belleville
Quebec
Kingston
Superior
Michigan
Oswego
Simcoe

Menzies

Toronto

Montreal

St. Lawrence

Niagara

8

Government

Douglas

Beacon
Hill Park **9**

Cook

Dallas (scenic drive)

Dallas (scenic drive)

Ogden
Point

Cruise Ship
Terminal

Outer
Harbour

N

0   1/4   1/2
Statute miles

FORT

Joan St. **10**

Moss **12**

Linden **11**

Cook

Vancouver

Fairfield

*An excellent sea walk is adjacent
to the cruise dock at Ogden Point.*

commit suicide by the side of a river, while George Stoner was sentenced to life imprisonment and later released.

Right behind The Empress, near the bus depot, is the **Crystal Garden 3**. It too was designed by Rattenbury, and this glass-roofed tropical paradise contains exotic flowers, birds and small monkeys. On the south harborfront is yet another Rattenbury design – the former CPR steamship terminal. It now houses the **Royal London Wax Museum 4**, based on the famous Madame Tussaud's.

An the north side of the harbor at the corner of Government and Wharf, is the **Visitor Info Centre**, where you'll find a helpful staff and a selection of maps and brochures. City tours are available by motor coach, double-decker bus and horsedrawn carriage. Local whalewatching tours are also available, with three resident pods of killer whales regularly sighted in the waters off Victoria. Harbor tours can be taken on the small ferry boats operated by Victoria Harbour Ferry, which make regular stops at various points along the waterfronts of the Inner, Upper and Outer Harbours.

Wharf Street leads north of the Inner Harbour, past the original Customs House (1876), to historic **Bastion Square 5**, its narrow streets and restored brick buildings now housing restaurants, shops and art galleries. The original courthouse, at 28 Bastion Square, now houses the **Maritime Museum**. Inside this turreted building, visitors can ride an ornate elevator built in 1900 for an elderly judge. Exhibits include a dugout canoe named Tilikum which was sailed by Captain Voss from Victoria to England. Across the street is the Garrick's Head Pub, which opened for business in 1867.

(Above) The Provincial Legislative Buildings. (Below) Historic buildings line the lanes of Bastion Square.

THE PIG WAR

The Oregon Treaty of 1846 fixed the border between the United States and British Columbia (then a colony of Britain) to lie along the 49th parallel. However, before dipping south of Vancouver Island, the exact placement of the border in local waters remained a contentious issue, with both sides claiming the San Juan Islands.

The dispute came to a head in June 1859 when Lyman Cutler, an American settler on San Juan Island, shot a pig belonging to a Hudson's Bay Company farmer named Charles Griffin, who represented British claims to the island. When Griffin demanded $100 in compensation, Cutler responded "I think there is a better chance for lightning to strike you than for you to get a hundred dollars for that hog!"

Both sides promptly mobilized. The Americans landed a troop of soldiers and Governor Douglas sent two British warships as a show of force. Fortunately, no military action was taken by either side and joint occupation of the island was agreed to, a situation that prevailed until the German emperor Wilhelm I (considered an impartial party) was asked to arbitrate the boundary dispute. He decided the border should run along Haro Strait, making the San Juan Islands an American possession. As for Cutler, he received a small fine for the incident that nearly sparked a war.

Entrance to Bastion Square, site of the original fur trading fort.

Other downtown sights include the **Royal British Columbia Museum 6** which houses an outstanding exhibit on the area's natural and native history. Beside it is Thunderbird Park with an impressive display of totem poles, and behind it is **Helmcken House 7**, one of Victoria's oldest houses, built in 1852 by a pioneer doctor.

A 10-minute stroll away, heading south on Government Street, will take you to **Carr House 8**. Now a museum, this Italianate-style house, built in the 1860s, was the birthplace of Emily Carr (1871-1945), one of Canada's most acclaimed artists. Carr's paintings of native villages and totem poles reflected a style defined by simplified forms and a vivid intensity of color.

Two blocks east on Simcoe Street is Victoria's oldest and cherished municipal park – **Beacon Hill Park** , named for the navigational range markers which sat atop its hill in the 1840s. Today, visitors enjoy the classic English landscape garden while below in the strait a modern beacon marks a dangerous shoal's position outside the harbor entrance.

A mile east of the downtown core, in the upscale Rockland neighborhood, is **Craigdarroch Castle** – built in the late 1800s by the coal baron Robert Dunsmuir, a Scottish immigrant who became British Columbia's wealthiest and most influential businessman, and whose son James became premier of the province in 1900. The four-storey castle, complete with a tower, turrets and French Gothic roofline, is now a museum with the family's original furnishings and artwork on display. Nearby, housed in an 1889 mansion, is the **Art Gallery of Greater Victoria** where works of Emily Carr are exhibited.

A car ferry heads toward the Swartz Bay terminal near Victoria after transiting Active Pass in the pastoral Gulf Islands.

CITY OF GARDENS

Victoria's rocky bluffs and sweeping sea views are tempered by gardens which bloom in early spring when other parts of the country are still in the grip of winter. Daffodils, rhododendron, honeysuckle and hyacinth are just a few of the flowers that thrive in Victoria's temperate climate. A British fondness for gardening is reflected everywhere – streets lined with blossoming cherry trees, lawns bordered by rockeries and rose bushes, and enough public gardens to satisfy any flower aficionado. The gated grounds of **Government House 12** (official residence of the Lieutenant-Governor, the Queen's representative in British Columbia) and **Hatley Castle** in Esquimalt (built by the coal heir James Dunsmuir), are both beautifully maintained and open to the public.

The gardens everyone wants to see, however, are the world-famous **Butchart Gardens**. A 20-minute drive north of Victoria, this 50-acre garden site took root in 1904 when Jennie Butchart decided to clean up the mess her husband left behind when his cement plant excavated a limestone quarry on their estate. Employing workers from the cement company, Mrs. Butchart transformed an eyesore into the Sunken Garden. She spent hours tucking ivy into the rock wall's pockets and crevices while hanging over the sides of the quarry in a bosun's chair. For years the Butcharts welcomed all visitors to their gardens, serving afternoon tea in summer

Visitors from around the world enjoy the magnificent Butchart Gardens near Victoria.

houses scattered about the property until the sheer number of visitors made this impossible. Today more than a million visitors arrive annually to view the grounds which include a Japanese Garden, Rose Garden, Italian Garden, Concert Lawn and Fireworks Viewing Area. At night the gardens are transformed when hundreds of hidden lights illuminate the flowers and fountains.

SIDNEY BY THE SEA

The seaside town of Sidney is a pleasant detour for Victoria visitors heading to or from the B.C. Ferries terminal at Swartz Bay. Just south of the ferry terminal is Canoe Cove where you'll find the cozy Stonehouse Pub tucked in the hillside woods. Continuing south along the highway, you'll come to marina-filled Tsehum Harbour. At its southern end, off Harbour Road, is the rustic Latch Restaurant – built in 1920 as a summer retreat for a former lieutenant-governor of the province. More restaurants and shops await in downtown Sidney, especially on Beacon Avenue which runs through the center of town down to the waterfront where a small whale museum, seaside walkway and more restaurants provide visitors with waterfront views of the San Juan Islands in Washington State.

Ferries ply the waters off Sidney where a string of islands – Canada's Gulf Islands and America's San Juan Islands – dot the horizon. Blessed with a Mediterranean-type climate and picturesque coves, both island groups attract plenty of visitors each summer. Recreational boaters, kayakers, campers, cyclists and nature lovers are all drawn to their shores. The larger islands are accessible by inter-island ferries. Marina resorts and bed-and-breakfast inns provide pleasant accommodations from which to stroll the parks and beaches, browse the art galleries and enjoy the peaceful ambience of these island gems.

Otter Bay, Pender Island

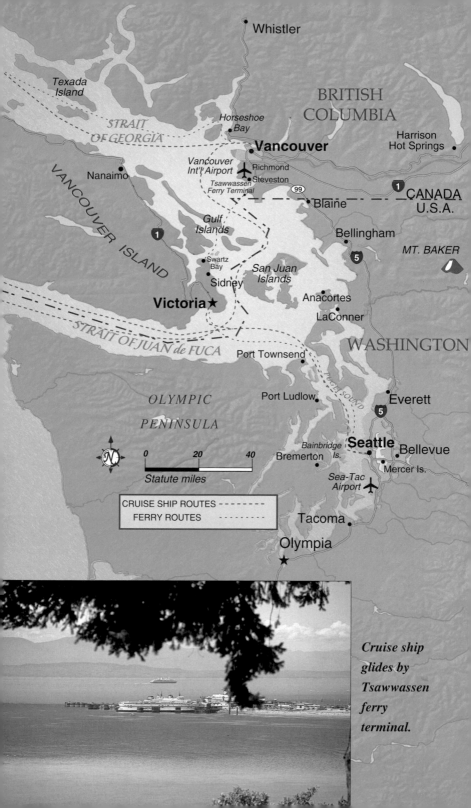

Whistler

BRITISH
COLUMBIA

*Texada
Island*

*STRAIT
OF GEORGIA*

*Horseshoe
Bay*

Vancouver

Harrison
Hot Springs

Nanaimo

*Vancouver
Int'l Airport*   Richmond
Steveson

*Tsawwassen
Ferry Terminal*

99   Blaine

1 CANADA
U.S.A.

VANCOUVER ISLAND

*Gulf
Islands*

Bellingham

5

MT. BAKER

1

*Swartz
Bay*

Sidney

*San Juan
Islands*

Victoria ★

Anacortes

LaConner

STRAIT OF JUAN de FUCA

WASHINGTON

Port Townsend

OLYMPIC

PENINSULA

Port Ludlow

Everett

5

N

0   20   40

Statute miles

*Bainbridge
Is.*

Seattle   Bellevue

Bremerton

Mercer Is.

*Sea-Tac
Airport*

CRUISE SHIP ROUTES ------
FERRY ROUTES ········

Tacoma

Olympia
★

*Cruise ship
glides by
Tsawwassen
ferry
terminal.*

CHAPTER TWO

VANCOUVER
& CANADIAN ROCKIES

Vancouver is a young city set against a magnificent backdrop of coastal mountains and inland sea. Considered Canada's most beautiful city, it is also one of the fastest growing, with an influx of moneyed immigrants from Hong Kong transforming the city's skyline, business climate and local culture.

The city, founded by British settlers in the late 1800s, began as a small lumbering village on the shores of Burrard Inlet and gradually grew into a major shipping port. The 20th century brought continued immigration from other parts of North America, Europe and the rest of the world. This diversity of cultures has transformed Vancouver from provincial town to cosmopolitan city, one that's been described as a cross between an American and European city. Although automobiles clog its busiest streets, the city has retained a vibrant, people-oriented core that is the envy of many a North American city planner trying to contain urban sprawl and car dependence. Hemmed in by mountains and sea, Vancouver's high-density residential areas function as a series of urban villages within easy reach of the downtown office district. An effort has been made to keep cars away from the waterfront and a pedestrian and bicycle seawall now stretches from downtown Vancouver to Pacific Spirit Park, creating a green belt of parks and waterfront attractions that complement the natural beauty surrounding them.

The city of Vancouver, home port for Alaska cruises, has been in a celebratory mood since winning its bid to host the 2010 Winter Olympics. The last time the city basked in international attention was when it held Expo

Stanley Park's Brockton Point stands near the entrance to Vancouver's scenic harbor.

86, a world transportation fair. This event also marked the opening of the Canada Place Cruise Ship Terminal, located in the heart of downtown Vancouver, where it instantly became one of the city's most famous landmarks with its unique five white sails crowning the complex. Originally built to accommodate two cruise ships, it has since been expanded to three berths. A secondary cruise facility, Ballantyne Pier, is located one mile east of Canada Place.

A BRIEF HISTORY OF VANCOUVER

The first people to appreciate Vancouver's natural harbor were the Squamish tribe of Coast Salish natives. Their local villages were well established when, in the summer of 1792, Captain George Vancouver of the British Royal Navy sailed his ship's boats into the harbor to survey the surrounding shores. He was looking for the Northwest Passage, not a good restaurant, so his visit was cursory to say the least.

In seamanlike fashion, he ordered that the boats proceed "under an easy sail" as a welcoming party of natives paddled out to greet these strange-looking visitors. An exchange of goods (salmon for iron) took place on the run as the British survey boats sailed through the First Narrows and the Second Narrows toward the head of mountain-enclosed Burrard Inlet in search of an inland waterway. It was not to be found, so after a night spent camped on shore the British sailors left at dawn.

In his journals Captain Vancouver frequently mentions the lofty barrier of mountains and snow which frustrated his efforts at finding an inland waterway. These coastal mountains, which extend from California to the Aleutian Islands, weren't his only source of frustration. Spain had also dispatched ships to these waters, much to the

Captain George Vancouver commanded one of the most demanding expeditions in naval history when he surveyed the Pacific Northwest's vast and intricate coastline.

surprise of Captain Vancouver who thought he was the first European to venture into what we now call the Inside Passage. The British and Spanish vessels crossed paths off Point Grey and the names English Bay and Spanish Banks commemorate this friendly encounter.

But apart from brief visits by naval ships, the waters off present-day Vancouver remained the domain of the Coast Salish natives who fished here for salmon and harvested shellfish. Merchant ships rarely ventured into the twisting channels of the Inside Passage, choosing to trade for furs with natives whose coastal villages bordered the open Pacific.

Eventually, however, the Hudson's Bay Company forged an over-land route to the west coast where it established Fort Langley on the Fraser River in 1827. But it wasn't until gold was discovered in the Fraser Canyon, 30 years later, that settlers began moving into the area. Gastown, Vancouver's original townsite, was founded in 1867 by a smooth-talking saloon keeper from Yorkshire named John "Gassy Jack" Deighton. Deighton had worked as a riverboat captain on the Fraser River before moving to Burrard Inlet in 1867. He arrived with a barrel of whiskey and promptly built a saloon near the local sawmill. His nickname of 'Gassy Jack' prompted locals to name the new settlement Gastown, although its official name was Granville. The small pioneer town soon consisted of three saloons, one hotel and three stores, all built to cater to the men who worked at the nearby sawmill. Officially registered a few years later as Granville (after Earl Granville, the British Colonial Secretary), Gastown stuck as the name used by locals.

A crowd gathered as the **Empress of India** *– the first CPR liner to arrive in Vancouver – pulled into port on April 28th, 1891.*

In the 1880s, the privately owned Canadian Pacific Railway pushed its tracks through the Rocky Mountains to the west coast. Its termination point was Burrard Inlet, and with the arrival of CPR's first locomotive on May 23, 1886, the newly incorporated city of Vancouver was born, its name chosen by Cornelius Van Horne, chairman of the Canadian Pacific Railway. The young city's first setback came just weeks later when it burned to the ground, but it was quickly rebuilt in anticipation of the transcontinental rail line being extended from the head of Burrard Inlet to the townsite. By the end of the century a booming sawmill industry was supporting a population of over 27,000. The city had an opera house, a museum and horsedrawn coach tours of Stanley Park. Vancouver Harbour had become a busy place. Merchant cargo ships – both the tall-masted and steam-driven variety – brought goods from overseas and loaded shipments of lumber, while CPR's Empress passenger ships offered luxury cruises to the Orient. The Alaska run began with American and Canadian shipping companies filling their extra berths. Then, in the 1950s, Vancouver's Union Steamships offered trips to Alaska aboard converted World War II navy corvettes.

Today Vancouver is one of North America's busiest ports, especially from May to October when the world's leading cruise lines make it their home port for the Alaska run.

From the cricket pitch of Stanley Park, the view is of Coal Harbour and the Canada Place Cruise Ship Terminal where passenger ships bound for Alaska dock throughout the summer.

An aerial view of Vancouver Harbor showing the city center, English Bay with freighters at anchor, and Spanish Banks in the distance.

VANCOUVER'S ROYAL CONNECTION

When Britain's Royal Navy dispatched ships to explore and survey the New World, her officers were called "King George's Men" by the natives they encountered. Fortunately there were a number of King Georges who ruled Britain during this era of naval exploration.

Captain Vancouver was the first European explorer to survey in detail the waters of the Pacific Northwest, from Puget Sound in Washington to Cook Inlet in Alaska. Thus began the proliferation of British place names in and around the City of Vancouver, a trend that continued in the 19th century when Britain extensively surveyed all of her empire's distant coastlines.

At the turn of the last century, Vancouver was an Edwardian outpost of the British Empire. Many of the city's settlers built grand homes containing stained glass windows, potted palms and plush velvet furniture. Summer days were filled with lawn croquet and tennis, lemonade and tea parties on the verandah. Bath houses appeared along English Bay and those who dared wore bathing costumes guaranteed to protect their bodies from sun, sand and prying eyes.

Among Vancouver's early royal visitors were King George VI and Queen Elizabeth (the Queen Mother) who arrived by train in May of 1939. In 1954, on the final day of the British Empire Games. Prince

Philip was among those who witnessed Britain's Roger Bannister and Australia's John Landy break the 4-minute 'miracle' mile in a thrilling finish. In the spring of 1982, Queen Elizabeth II arrived in port on board the Royal Yacht Britannia. Hundreds of Vancouverites sailed out to greet their visiting monarch and escort her into the harbor.

STAYING IN VANCOUVER

Close to where the ships dock in downtown Vancouver is a wide range of accommodations, including several five-diamond hotels. Adjacent to the Canada Place Cruise Terminal is the luxury **Pan Pacific Hotel** and right across the street is **The Fairmont Waterfront**. The Fairmont **Hotel Vancouver**, a city landmark located a few blocks from the cruise terminal on Georgia Street, was built in 1939, but Vancouver's oldest heritage hotel, also on Georgia Street, is the **Hotel Georgia** which opened for business in 1929.

The five-diamond **Four Seasons Hotel** is situated a few blocks south of the harborfront at Howe and Georgia, and the **Wedgewood Hotel** on Hornby (near Robson Square) has been rated Canada's best-value hotel by the readers of *Travel & Leisure* magazine. **The Sutton Place Hotel** (formerly Le Meridien) is located on Burrard Street just south of Robson and is favored by entertainment celebrities when in town, as are the **Pacific Palisades** on Robson Street and the resort-like **Westin Bayshore** near Stanley Park on the waterfront. The **Hyatt Regency,** at Burrard and Georgia, hosted President Clinton when he was in town to meet with Russian leader Boris Yeltsin in April of 1993.

The lobby of the elegant Fairmont Waterfront Hotel, located opposite Canada Place Cruise Ship Terminal.

SHOPPING IN VANCOUVER

Shopping complexes within easy walking distance of the
Canada Place Cruise Terminal include the Sinclair Centre
and The Landing (at the entrance to Gastown), both of which are
restored heritage projects. In the heart of downtown Vancouver, at the
intersection of Georgia and Granville Streets, stand two major department stores – Eaton's and The Bay – and beneath them is a four-block-
long underground shopping mall called Pacific Centre that contains
dozens of stores. Robson is Vancouver's pre-eminent shopping street,
especially the three blocks west of Burrard to Jervis. Lined with fashion
boutiques, coffee houses and restaurants frequented by movie stars and
other celebrities when visiting Vancouver, Robson Street is where
everyone goes to stroll and people-watch. Water Street in Gastown is a
good place to shop for native art; quality works can be bought at
Images for a Canadian Heritage, Inuit Gallery of Vancouver and Hill's
Indian Crafts, which carries authentic Cowichan sweaters. Marion
Scott Gallery on Howe Street is also recommended.

DINING IN VANCOUVER

Just about any cuisine imaginable can be found in Vancouver, includ-
ing West Coast fare. This style of cuisine can be enjoyed at Raincity
Grill on Denman Street, Chartwell in the Four Seasons Hotel, and
Bishop's on West 4th. For seafood, good choices include the Fish
House in Stanley Park and 'C' Restaurant at the foot of Howe on the
False Creek waterfront. Nearby, at Hornby and Pacific, Umberto's Il
Giardino offers fine dining in one of Vancouver's oldest houses, built in
1888. Cin Cin is another popular Italian restaurant, on Robson Street,
and Lumiere on West Broadway is highly recommended for French
cuisine, as is Le Crocodile on Burrard.

GETTING AROUND

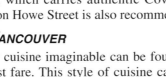

The downtown core is easy to explore on
foot, starting at the Tourist Info Centre
(200 Burrard Street, Waterfront Centre),
where visitors can browse at their leisure
or discuss their travel plans with a staff
member. Maps, brochures, bus and ferry
schedules and other information are all
available. **Canada Place Cruise Ship
Terminal** is located at the north end of
Howe Street in the very heart of downtown Vancouver. It's a city landmark and
instantly recognized for its majestic white

*Restaurants with good views are
numerous in Vancouver.*

(Above) A cruise ship nudges up to Canada Place Cruise Ship Terminal, in downtown Vancouver. (Left) Ballantyne Pier, Vancouver's other cruise terminal, is a refurbished and modernized heritage building.

sails which crown a complex containing the Pan Pacific Hotel, the Prow Restaurant, a Food Fair, promenade shops, and IMAX 3D Theatre. Long-term parking is provided here, and taxis, limousines, public transportation and car rentals are all easily available. The Vancouver International Airport is thirty minutes away, and Seattle a three-and-a-half hour drive.

Vancouver's secondary cruise facility – **Ballantyne Pier** – is located about one mile east of Canada Place at the foot of Heatley Avenue. This terminal received many plaudits when completed in 1923 and it recently underwent a major renovation and expansion to transform it into an ultramodern cruise facility while retaining its original character.

Passengers departing from either terminal will be treated to a unique view of the city's waterfront. On the industrial North Shore are docked freighters loading lumber, wheat, coal and piles of yellow sulphur. To the south stand the office towers and hotels of downtown Vancouver.

These gleaming highrises, fronted by docks and marinas, quickly give way to the lawns and trees of Stanley Park where you may catch a glimpse of the Cricket Grounds. Perched on a foreshore rock is the Girl in a Wetsuit – Vancouver's answer to Copenhagen's Little Mermaid.

As your ship passes under the suspended span of Lions Gate Bridge and heads into English Bay, sailboats can often be seen tacking back and forth among the anchored freighters. Beyond lies the Strait of Georgia and the fabled Inside Passage.

LOCAL ATTRACTIONS

Local tours include one by trolley that begins in Gastown at the Steam Clock and takes in the highlights of Vancouver with 17 stops where passengers can get off and catch another trolley when they are ready to continue their tour.

Harbor boat tours and flightseeing tours by floatplane or helicopter can also be arranged. Vancouver is a very walkable city, its waterfront ringed with seawalls and pathways. Vancouver is also fairly safe, although visitors should avoid the east side of the downtown core and not venture on foot past Carrall Street at night. Car break-ins are a problem, so be careful to park only in well-secured lots and never leave valuables in the trunk.

1 Vancouver Art Gallery – Located at Robson Square, this former court house was designed by British architect Francis Rattenbury, whose other turn-of-the-century designs include Victoria's Legislative Buildings and Empress Hotel. When Vancouver's new Law Courts opened on Robson Street in 1979, Rattenbury's neo-classical court house became Vancouver's art gallery, housing a permanent collection of works by Canadian artist Emily Carr. The building's former role of court house has been used in numerous films including *Accused*, starring Jodie Foster.

The art gallery's main entrance faces Robson Square and the Law Courts. This unusual court house design by Vancouver architect Arthur Erickson is a long, low building with a sloped glass roof and streaming waterfalls. Four blocks south of the Art Gallery on Georgia Street is Library Square. Designed by Moshe Safdie, this modern, coliseum-like structure was modeled on the classical forms of ancient Rome.

Vancouver Art Gallery's main entrance fronts Robson Square, with the stately Hotel Vancouver next door.

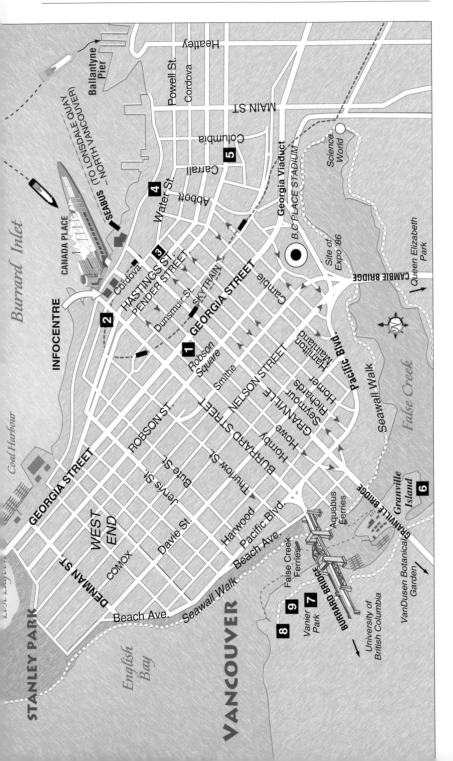

2 **Marine Building** – Vancouver's finest example of art deco architecture, the Marine Building was – and still is – an exceptional building when it opened in 1930 at the corner of Burrard and West Hastings. Its architects described this 25-storey structure as "some great crag rising from the sea, clinging with sea flora and fauna, tinted in sea-green, touched with gold." The building's brass doors open into a muralled lobby where terra cotta panels pay tribute to the days of sail and steam when the Coal Harbour shore-front was a gritty industrial area of mills and rail lines.

3 **The Lookout!** – Take a glass elevator to the top of Harbour Centre Tower where a circular, enclosed viewing deck provides a 360-degree view of Vancouver and its surrounding scenery. American astronaut Neil Armstrong, the first man on the moon, was the guest celebrity at this popular attraction's grand opening in 1977.

4 **Gastown** – The cobblestone streets of Vancouver's original townsite are today lined with shops and restaurants. A statue of Gassy Jack stands in Maple Tree Square, where he first established a hotel in 1867, and at the corner of Water and Cambie Streets is a chiming steam clock, which sounds every quarter of an hour. When the clock was built in 1977 the steam engine constantly malfunctioned, so the clock's auxiliary electrical motor eventually became its sole source of power even though steam billows from the top of the clock – for dramatic effect. Behind Maple Tree Square is Gaoler's Mews, the site of Gastown's first jail and now a cluster of offices. Guided walking tours are available from June through August.

5 **Chinatown** – Vancouver's Chinatown, the second-largest in North America, is filled with

The Marine Building is Vancouver's finest example of Art Deco architecture.

Waterfront condominiums overlook the marinas and seawalk that run along the north shore of False Creek in downtown Vancouver.

restaurants, shops and pagoda phone booths. One of Vancouver's oldest districts and declared a historical site in 1971, it has suffered recently from a reputation for being unsafe after dark. This should not dissuade daytime visitors, however, from visiting the Dr. Sun Yat-Sen Classical Chinese Garden, the first authentic full-sized classical Chinese garden built outside of China. Surrounded by high white walls, this garden is an oasis of tranquillity, its courtyards duplicating the private Ming Dynasty. Next door is the Chinese Cultural Centre, which conducts walking tours of Chinatown.

6 Granville Island / False Creek – False Creek bustles with year-round activity, its shores lined with marinas and overlooked by waterfront parks and condominium towers. Kayakers and scullers share its waters with barge-towing tugboats and recreational boats of all sizes. And throughout the day and early evening, the blue-colored False Creek Ferries and the multi-colored Aquabus ferries criss-cross False Creek, carrying foot passengers to Granville Island and other creekside attractions, including TELUSphere (formerly Science World) – a science centre housed in a silver geodesic dome at the head of False Creek.

Granville Island is the centerpiece of False Creek. An artisans' enclave with an art college and craft studios, Granville Island is home to one of North America's most successful public markets, where locals shopping for fresh produce and cut flowers mix with visitors strolling past the crafts stalls, absorbing the atmosphere and perhaps pausing to buy a freshly baked croissant or a box of Belgian chocolates. The island

A great way to get around False Creek, and see the city from the water, is by the mini-ferries running from Granville Island.

also contains a community center, tennis courts and a children's water-park, in addition to boutiques, restaurants and live theater. The visitor information center, providing maps and other information, is located opposite the Public Market.

7 **Vanier Park** – This scenic waterfront park with views across English Bay to the West End, can be reached on foot from Granville Island via the seawall, or from downtown Vancouver by boarding one of the False Creek Ferries at the foot of Thurlow on Sunset Beach. A popular park with dog walkers, kite flyers and model boat owners who gather at its ornamental lake on Sunday mornings, Vanier Park is also where you will find several museums.

8 **Vancouver's Maritime Museum** houses the historic St. Roch, an Arctic supply and patrol vessel that was the first to navigate the North West Passage from west to east in 1940-42 and is now a national historic site. Outside the museum is Heritage Harbour where traditional wooden vessels are moored and visiting tall ships dock. Nearby is a complex housing the **9** **Vancouver Museum and Pacific Space Centre**, which features the H.R. MacMillan Planetarium beneath its white circular roof.

Floathomes line the False Creek waterfront in downtown Vancouver.

Prospect Point

Restaurant

LIONS GATE
BRIDGE

Siwash
Rock

Park/
Picnic area

Good
walks here

STANLEY PARK

Hollow Tree

Park Trails ------

Third
Beach

Beaver
Lake

Ducks &
geese here

Miniature
Railroad

Girl in a
Wet Suit

Sequoia
Restaurant

Children's
Zoo

Vancouver
Aquarium

Brockton
Point
Light

Police

Gardens

Lost
Lagoon

Ducks, geese &
swans here

Park
Entrance

Totem
Poles

Second
Beach

Pool/
Playground

Fish House
Restaurant

Vancouver
Rowing Club

PARK

CHILCO

DENMAN

ROBSON

GEORGIA

0   1/4   1/2

Statute miles

NELSON

English Bay
Beach

BEACH

DAVIE

JERVIS

BUTE

PENDER

HASTINGS

CORDOVA

STANLEY PARK

The largest urban park in Canada originated as a 1,000-acre military reserve in the mid-1800s. A 12-pound muzzle loader installed near Brockton Point became a time check for local fishermen when it would fire each Sunday at 6 p.m. Today it booms across the water each evening at nine o'clock.

A free shuttle bus operates in the park throughout the summer, departing from the lower parking lot and making frequent stops along its half-hour circuit of the park. Horse-drawn tram rides are also available, and bicycles and rollerblade skates can be rented near the entrance to the park. Attractions within the park include the Rose Garden and the Vancouver Aquarium Marine Science Centre, Canada's largest marine mammal rescue and rehabilitation centre, which is home to Steller sea lions, beluga whales and sea otters rescued from the *Exxon Valdez* oil spill that struck Alaska's Prince William Sound in 1989.

The park's layout is based on the planning principles of American landscape architect Frederick Law Olmsted, who designed New York City's Central Park. Vehicular traffic is one way and counterclockwise. Upon entering Stanley Park from Georgia Street, the road paralleling the seawall veers to the right and traces the shores of Coal Harbour where you will see the Vancouver Rowing Club, the Royal Vancouver Yacht Club and Deadman's Island, which was a traditional burial ground of the Coast Salish natives who lived in the area when British colonists first arrived.

As you approach the park's most easterly point of land – Brockton Point – you will pass (on your left) a display of Northwest Coast native totem poles where there is ample parking to stop and enjoy the setting. After rounding Brockton Point, doing a 180-degree turn and doubling back, you pass the cricket grounds and Brockton Oval to the left. A bit further along is Lumbermen's Arch (to

Thunderbird sits atop this Kwakiutl totem pole, one of several on display near Brockton Point.

(Above) North coast totem poles overlook the cricket pitch near Brockton Oval. (Left) Bill Reid's Killer Whale sculpture rests outside the entrance to the Vancouver Aquarium.

your left) and sitting nearby on a rock in the harbor is *The Girl in a Wetsuit*. Frequently compared to Copenhagen's Little Mermaid, this bronze sculpture is the work of Elek Imredy, who came to Vancouver from Budapest, Hungary, in 1957, following an uprising in his homeland. Just beyond Lions Gate Bridge is Prospect Point – a popular viewing site overlooking the bridge and the location of a good casual restaurant. Several other restaurants are located in the park, including the elegant and highly recommended the Sequoia Grill overlooking English Bay, the Fish House located near the southwest entrance of the park and take-out food stands at Third Beach and Second Beach.

QUEEN ELIZABETH PARK

Second only to Stanley Park as a park attraction, Queen Elizabeth Park's 130 acres of gardens and grounds provide beautiful views of the city skyline and mountain backdrop. On a reclaimed quarry site, the park's landscaping is a pleasing mix of native and exotic trees and shrubs, with seasonal floral displays. Seasons in the Park Restaurant, with views overlooking the park, specializes in fresh seafood and Pacific Northwest cuisine. Located within the park is the MacMillan Bloedel Conservatory, a 'garden under glass' containing 500 varieties of tropical and sub-tropical plants, and some 60 tropical bird species.

MUSEUM OF ANTHROPOLOGY

The MOA, located on the University of British Columbia campus, houses one of the world's finest displays of Northwest Coast native art and the largest collection of works by internationally acclaimed Haida artist Bill Reid, including his famous cedar sculpture 'The Raven and the First Men' which depicts the Haida people's creation myth in which Raven opens a clamshell and releases the first Haida people. The building itself, an award-winning design by Vancouver architect Arthur Erickson, is set on an ocean bluff overlooking the Strait of Georgia. The Great Hall, a concrete structure of soaring glass inspired by the traditional post-and-beam construction of native longhouses, forms a stunning venue for the museum's collection of totem poles, canoes and feast dishes, carved in the different styles of the various native groups. The Masterpiece Gallery displays intricately handcrafted works in silver, gold and argillite. Outside on the grounds stands a replica of a Haida coastal village, consisting of two longhouses and 10 totem poles.

NORTH OF THE CITY

Vancouver's North Shore is reached via the Lions Gate Bridge – built in1938 by the Guinness brewing family of Dublin, Ireland to provide access to their new North Shore subdivision called British Properties. This suspension bridge was named for The Lions – twin mountain peaks visible from the bridge. Its span is outlined at night by a string of lights which were a gift from the Guinness family to commemorate the city's 100th birthday in 1986.

A cruise ship departing Vancouver passes beneath the suspended span of Lions Gate Bridge.

GROUSE MOUNTAIN

Only 15 minutes by road from downtown Vancouver, a ride up Grouse Mountain is one of the easiest ways to experience British Columbia's famous mountain scenery. The Sky Ride, which departs every 15 minutes from 9 a.m. to 10 p.m. is one of North America's largest aerial tramway systems, whisking passengers 3,700 feet (1,100m) above sea level to a mountain plateau. There you can enjoy panoramic views of the city, sea and mountain. In summer, the Peak Chair can be ridden to the 4,100-foot summit for an even more spectacular 360-degree view. Facilities on Grouse Mountain include three restaurants and numerous hiking trails.

CAPILANO SUSPENSION BRIDGE

The world's longest and highest suspension bridge spans the Capilano River at a height of 230 feet. Swaying 25 storeys above a river gorge is a thrilling experience, but not for someone who's afraid of heights! The wood-and-wire bridge, 450 feet across, may feel rickety but its multi-strand pre-stressed cables are encased in 13 tons of concrete at either end. The original bridge was made of hemp rope and wood, and was built in 1889 by a Scotsman named George Grant Mackay with the help

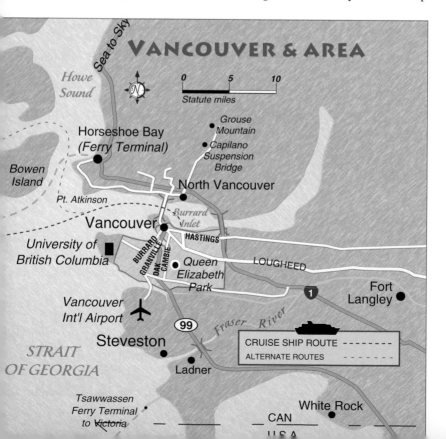

of a local native and his brother. Using a team of horses, they dragged the heavy rope cables across the canyon, secured them to tree trunks and pulled them taut. A more secure bridge, of wire construction and anchored in concrete, was built in 1903 and then replaced in 1914. The current bridge was built in 1956. The Nature Park contains forest trails and a dramatic waterfall.

WHISTLER

If time permits, consider a trip by road, rail or air to the alpine village of **Whistler**, located 75 miles north of Vancouver. View fabulous scenery all the way along the Sea to Sky highway or the rail route that leads to this year-round resort surrounded by snowy peaks, mountain lakes and valley trails. Outdoor activities include hiking, fishing and river rafting, while golf enthusiasts can choose from four championship courses. The European-style Whistler Village features pedestrian streets lined with sidewalk cafes, specialty shops and art galleries.

SOUTH OF VANCOUVER

STEVESTON

The historic fishing village of Steveston, located at the mouth of the Fraser River's South Arm, was once the heart of British Columbia's fishing industry. When its Gulf of Georgia Cannery opened in 1894, it was the largest in the province, employing up to 10,000 workers during the busy salmon season. The century-old cannery was recognized as a national historic site in 1979 and was officially reopened as a museum on its 100th anniversary, in June 1994, allowing visitors the opportunity to see what the west coast fishing and canning industries were once like.

(Above) Capilano Suspension Bridge. (Below) Whistler will be hosting ski events at the 2010 Winter Olympics.

Steveston, once the heart of British Columbia's fishing industry, is home to the century-old Gulf of Georgia Cannery which was declared a national historic site in 1979 and is now a museum.

(Opposite page) The dramatic Sea to Sky Highway hugs the coastline of Howe Sound.
(Left) Whistler Village is the social hub of this year-round alpine resort.
(Below) The Grouse Mountain aerial tramway whisks visitors to a mountain plateau with panoramic views of city, sea and mountains.

Nearby shops and seafood restaurants overlooking the harbor make Steveston a pleasant place to spend an afternoon. There is an excellent park adjacent to the town affording good views of the Fraser River.

CANADIAN ROCKIES

Among the array of land tours that can be combined with an Alaska cruise beginning and/or ending in Vancouver, an enduring favorite is the trip by road or rail to Western Canada's Rocky Mountains. Famous worldwide for their beauty, the national parks of Banff and Jasper, along with Yoho and Kootenay, encompass 7,800 square miles and three mountain ranges.

The Rocky Mountains form the continent's Great Divide, separating rivers that flow into the Atlantic and Arctic oceans from those draining to the Pacific. The challenging terrain of these parks was opened up to

THE FAMOUS SS BEAVER

The *S.S. Beaver* was a famous steamship employed by the Hudson's Bay Company during the fur trade. She also served as a survey ship, freighter, passenger vessel and tugboat. Today, a replica of the ship takes passengers on sightseeing and dinner cruises. The original Beaver met its end in 1888 at the entrance to Vancouver Harbour when the departing ship was gripped not by tidal rips and back eddies but by a sense of panic in her crew when they discovered their liquor supply had been left behind in port. They turned the ship sharply around and grounded her.

The paddle wheel Beaver, the first steamship on the North Pacific, ran aground off Prospect Point in 1888. A few years later the luxurious new CPR liner Empress of India is shown leaving port after stopping at Vancouver on her maiden voyage.

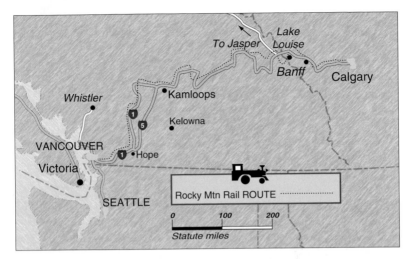

tourists more than a century ago with the construction of a transcontinental railroad, followed by hotels and lodges to accommodate them. As Cornelius Van Horne, vice president of the Canadian Pacific Railway (CPR) declared, "If we can't export the scenery, we will import the tourists."

Such splendid scenery was a formidable challenge to those who first explored this vast region of mountain ranges. Skill, courage and back breaking work opened up this once-inhospitable land, bounded as it is to the east where the Rocky Mountains, standing on the edge of the Great Plain, presented a physical barrier to any westward route to the Pacific. Aided by native guides familiar with mountain passes, the early fur traders tackled the region's steep gorges and raging rivers, at times inching their way along canyon walls on rope ladders while sure-footed mountain goats no doubt nonchalantly watched the proceedings from rock ledges.

Today, millions of visitors travel in comfort along the routes forged by these daring men. A transcontinental railroad was completed in the late 1800s, later joined by the adjacent Trans-Canada highway. Today a leisurely rail journey can be enjoyed along winding tracks that cling to mountainsides and plunge through tunnels. For those who prefer to travel by motor coach or car, the highway is equally scenic, with the option of pulling over at scenic viewpoints or points of interest.

There are many highlights along this route, widely touted as one of the world's most scenic, including pristine Emerald Lake with views of the Burgess Shale, and Takakkaw Falls – one of the highest waterfalls in Canada, its water plunging from a crevice with such force that a distant viewing platform remains in perpetual drizzle.

The Great Divide is at Kicking Horse Pass, and the nearby Spiral Tunnels were built in 1907 to reduce the rail line's steep grade descending from the Continental Divide. Further west, outside the Rocky

Rocky Mountaineer Railtours along the Bow River.

Mountain National Parks, is Craigellachie – named for a rock near Banffshire, Scotland (which symbolizes a call to battle) and the spot where the 'Last Spike' was driven into Canada's transcontinental railway on November 7, 1885, joining the country from ocean to ocean.

The heart of the Rocky Mountain National Parks is Banff, the oldest and most visited of the four parks. In 1883, after some railway workers chanced upon the Cave and Basin hotsprings, an area was set aside as park reserve and, in 1887, Canada's first national park was established. Initially called Rocky Mountains Park, the name was later changed to Banff National Park in honor of Banffshire, Scotland, the hometown of the CPR's Lord Strathcona. Jasper National Park was established in 1907 when a second, more northerly rail line was built. The townsites of Banff and Jasper quickly became service centers for railway workers and park visitors.

Both towns contain lovely stone churches, log buildings and gracious hotel resorts. Banff's most famous man-made landmark is the baronial Banff Springs Hotel. Resembling a Scottish castle, this magnificent hotel was built by the Canadian Pacific Railway and has hosted European and Hollywood royalty. Nature, however, receives top billing and today's movie stars must follow much stricter guidelines than did Robert Mitchum and Marilyn Monroe when *The River of No Return* was filmed in Jasper National Park in 1953. No one objected then to their chopping down a huge pine tree in one of the movie's scenes, but when filming takes place today a park warden is always on hand to ensure park rules are followed.

The parks' natural habitat ranges from sub-alpine meadows filled with wildflowers to valley slopes covered with stands of Douglas fir. The parks are home to 56 species of wildlife. Moose, elk, mountain

Cairn at Craigellachie marks where the CPR's last spike was driven.

goats, bighorn sheep and deer are often seen by park visitors – most frequently in the early morning or evening. Less frequently sighted are the bears, cougars and wolves that roam the parks. Gondola rides provide sweeping views of forested valleys and snowcapped peaks.

Summer weather in the Rockies is pleasantly warm with occasional hot spells. On any given day throughout the summer, the parking lot at Lake Louise in Banff National Park is filled with cars bearing license plates from across North America. Described by some people as "the most beautiful place on earth," turquoise-hued Lake Louise is a soothing sight. Lawns and flowers border the lakefront, in genteel contrast to the rugged mountain backdrop which is dominated by the impressive Victoria Glacier. Chateau Lake Louise, resembling a European villa, offers its visitors a picture-window view of the lake's alpine setting.

The highway connecting Banff and Jasper is called the Icefields Parkway, and it snakes through the highest, most rugged mountains in the Canadian Rockies. They form the Great Divide – the continent's backbone – and contain the Columbia Icefield which covers 125 square miles, including the Athabasca Glacier which terminates right beside the Parkway. Snowcoach tours prompt many travellers to pause in their journey and take a ride on a glacier.

The town of Jasper is smaller than Banff, but the park itself is larger. It too contains a famous railway-built resort called the Jasper Park Lodge which overlooks Lac Beauvert and glacier-clad Mount Edith Cavell. The highway west of Jasper National Park affords eastbound travellers a spectacular view of Mount Robson – highest peak in the Rockies. If westbound, be sure to look back at its dramatic face.

The famous Banff Springs Hotel stands on the slopes of the Bow River Valley in the Canadian Rockies.

The majority of tours to the Rockies run between Vancouver and Calgary, by road or by rail. The scenery ranges from cascading water-falls to the arid ranchland and vineyards of British Columbia's interior. The rail line and highway skirt the edge of the Fraser River canyon where, at its narrowest point, is a deep gorge called Hell's Gate. The Fraser River drains a watershed the size of Britain and the whitewater rushing through Hell's Gate can be viewed by an aerial tramway that descends 500 feet down to water level.

The city of Calgary, situated in the rolling foothills of Canada's Rocky Mountains, enjoys a location of remarkable contrast. The west-ern horizon is dominated by the snowcapped peaks and timbered slopes of the rugged Rockies. To the east, stretching as far as the eye can see, is a vast grass-covered plain where herds of buffalo once roamed. This is cattle country, and Calgary's cowboy heritage is proudly displayed throughout the city, its western hospitality symbolized by a white Stetson, the wide-brimmed hat long favored by cowboys. Each summer the city hosts a rodeo extravaganza called the Calgary Stampede and the roof of the city's sports arena is shaped like a giant saddle.

The city began as a fort, built at the confluence of the Bow and Elbow Rivers in 1875 by the North West Mounted Police to maintain law and order among the region's whiskey traders and buffalo hunters. They named it Fort Calgary after a bay on the Isle of Mull, Scotland. A few years later the CPR built a station in Calgary and, in the space of a century, this railway town grew into a major metropolis that hosted the 1988 Winter Olympics. The administrative center of Alberta's oil and gas industry, Calgary is also a transportation gateway for Banff National Park, just an hour away by road.

An outward-bound cruise ship glides past Vancouver's Stanley Park.

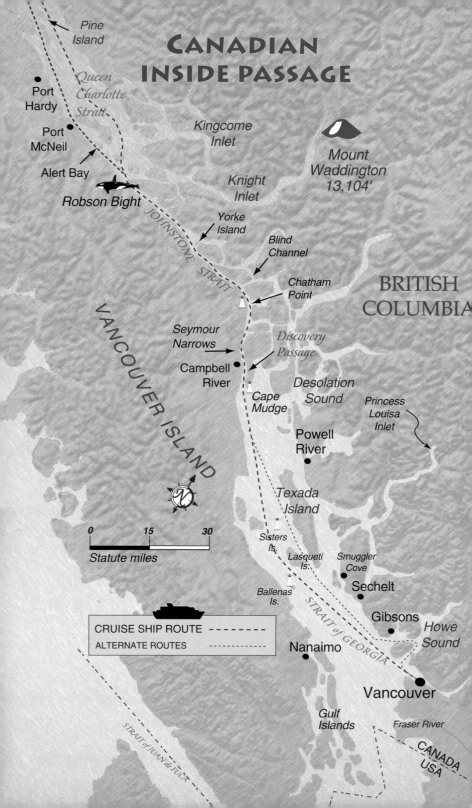

CANADIAN INSIDE PASSAGE

Pine Island

Queen Charlotte Strait

Port Hardy

Port McNeil

Alert Bay

Robson Bight

Kingcome Inlet

Knight Inlet

Mount Waddington 13,104'

JOHNSTONE STRAIT

Yorke Island

Blind Channel

Chatham Point

BRITISH COLUMBIA

Seymour Narrows

Discovery Passage

Campbell River

Cape Mudge

Desolation Sound

Princess Louisa Inlet

Powell River

VANCOUVER ISLAND

N

0   15   30
Statute miles

Texada Island

Sisters Is.

Lasqueti Is.

Smuggler Cove

Sechelt

Ballenas Is.

STRAIT OF GEORGIA

Gibsons

Howe Sound

Nanaimo

CRUISE SHIP ROUTE - - - - - -
ALTERNATE ROUTES ·········

Vancouver

Gulf Islands

Fraser River

STRAIT of JUAN de FUCA

CANADA
USA

CANADA'S INSIDE PASSAGE
Vancouver to Prince Rupert

There are many scenic waterways in this world, but there is only one Inside Passage. Stretching northward from Puget Sound in Washington State to Glacier Bay in Southeast Alaska, this vast and intricate coastline of winding channels and forested islands is unsurpassed in beauty and accessibility for cruisers. The Canadian portion of the Inside Passage spans 500 nautical miles, from the southern tip of Vancouver Island to the exposed waters of Dixon Entrance where the border runs between British Columbia and Alaska.

Cruise ships departing from Vancouver head northward up the Strait of Georgia, a major body of water that is busy with commercial traffic, including car ferries, freighters, fishing boats, tugs with barges and, from May through September, cruise ships. The southern Strait of Georgia is dominated by the Fraser River's outflow, especially from May to early August, when the freshet is running. This green, silt-laden freshwater is run-off from mainland mountains that flows into the Fraser River and eventually drains into the Strait of Georgia.

A northbound cruise ship approaches Texada Island on a quiet evening in the Strait of Georgia.

The mighty Fraser River flows past the fishing village of Steveston which hosted an international Tall Ship gathering in 2002.

The Fraser River is British Columbia's most important watershed. It originates in the Rocky Mountains, at Yellowhead Pass, and meanders for nearly 900 miles before emptying into the Strait of Georgia. Along the way, the Fraser's tributaries drain a watershed encompassing nearly one-third of the province. Its basin, which supports half of the province's agricultural land, is home to two of every three B.C. residents. Thousands of waterfowl nest annually on the river's delta and migrating salmon return regularly to the mouth of the Fraser, which contains North America's chief spawning grounds for the Pacific salmon.

Rising in the west, opposite the mouth of the Fraser River, is a single, mountainous island which protects the southern waters of Canada's Inside Passage. Named for the British sea captain who first circumnavigated it, **Vancouver Island** extends almost 300 miles from the Strait of Juan de Fuca up to Queen Charlotte Sound. Its rugged west coast buffers the Inside Passage from rain, wind and waves but there's one thing it can't stop from reaching these protected waters – the tide.

Controlled by the gravitational pull of the moon and to a lesser degree the sun, a rising tide rushes with cyclical predictability around both ends of Vancouver Island and pours into the straits and channels of the Inside Passage. When this onslaught of water is compressed through narrow passes and channels, bottlenecks occur. But, unlike car traffic which comes to a standstill in such circumstances, water does the opposite – it turns into churning rapids complete with whirlpools, back eddies and rip tides.

The numerous channels that weave through the islands clogging the Inside Passage between Vancouver Island and the mainland are all affected by tidal currents. Mariners pay special attention to the area's tide tables (published annually by the Canadian Hydrographic Service) in order to reach a pass when the water is slack and presents no danger. Even large cruise ships try to time their transit of **Seymour Narrows** – one of the most impressive tidal passes of the Inside Passage – to coincide with slack water.

Upon leaving Vancouver Harbour to commence a northbound cruise, cruise ships will sometimes take an unexpected detour into the scenic waterways of **Howe Sound**. This is not just to provide passengers with a lovely porthole view during dinner, but to delay the ship's arrival at Seymour Narrows. The side trip ensures a safe passage through the Narrows – especially if a large tide is running.

Until recently, Howe Sound was the world's largest log booming ground and recreational boats often tied to these log booms, their skippers hammering a couple of 'dogs' (metal eye hooks) into the outer log for attaching the mooring lines. The only drawback to docking at a log boom was the possibility of a tug arriving in the middle of the night to tow the 'dock' away, complete with attached boats. These log booms featured prominently in the popular TV show *The Beachcombers* which ran for 370 episodes and gained an international audience. Most logs are now sorted and stored on dry land.

The Sunshine Coast, which stretches from Howe Sound to Desolation Sound, has been attracting visitors since the late 1800s when steamships began running excursions to summer resorts along

Howe Sound is a popular retreat for weekend boaters from Vancouver with numerous small islands and coves.

this scenic section of coastline. One of the prettiest anchorages is **Smuggler Cove**. It's now a marine park but during Prohibition in the 1920s it was a storage area for bootleg whiskey that was smuggled by boat into the U.S.A. American yachtsmen who visited Smuggler Cove in those days had a favorite song which went like this:

Four and twenty Yankees feeling rather dry,
Sailed into Canada to have a drink of rye,
When the rye was open they all began to sing,
God bless America, but God Save the King!

The Sunshine Coast is today renowned for its scenic cruising which includes **Princess Louisa Inlet** – one of Canada's most spectacular fjords. Three steep-sided reaches twist inland past hanging waterfalls before culminating at Princess Louisa Inlet where the Chatterbox Falls, fed by glaciers and lakes, plunge 1,800 feet down granite cliffs into the still water. Erle Stanley Gardner, the American writer who created Perry Mason, wrote in his *Log of a Landlubber* that he didn't need to see the rest of the world after seeing Princess Louisa Inlet. "One views the scenery with bared head and choking feeling of the throat," he wrote. "It is more than beautiful. It is sacred."

The natives called the inlet Suivoolot, meaning warm and sunny. When James (Mac) Macdonald, a Nevada prospector, laid eyes on 'The Princess' in 1919 he instantly succumbed to her charms, obtained land by the falls and built a log cabin. After years of welcoming maritime travellers to his very own Yosemite Valley and fjords of Norway, Mac turned this prized property over to the newly formed Princess Louisa

With Vancouver Island in the distance, a northbound sailboat runs with an evening breeze up the Strait of Georgia.

International Society to preserve the inlet "as God created it, unspoiled by the hand of man" so that "all may enjoy its peace and beauty." The Society has chapters in Renton, Washington, and Victoria, British Columbia, and functions in cooperation with BC Parks to maintain the floats, wharves and picnic shelter.

Texada Island is a large island lying in the middle of the Strait of Georgia, often passed by northbound cruise ships as the summer sun is setting to the northwest. It was on Texada that a large whiskey still produced the bootleg liquor that reached thirsty Americans via Smuggler Cove. Before that, in the 1870s, whaling was a profitable enterprise with processing operations set up in Blubber Bay at the island's northern tip. Over the years, Texada has also been mined for gold, copper, iron ore and limestone. The next island over, called **Lasqueti**, is home to domestic and wild sheep which wander the rugged hillsides and cliff-edged shorelines. In rocky coves oysters grow in abundance, the commercially farmed ones shipped to gourmet restaurants in faraway cities. The pace of life on Lasqueti is tranquil and the island residents carefully guard their isolation. No car ferry calls at Lasqueti, so motor vehicles and other large items must be brought in by barge.

A small passenger ferry connects Lasqueti with French Creek on Vancouver Island. From here the Island Highway stretches in both directions along the eastern shores of Vancouver Island. To the south is the city of **Nanaimo**, founded in the 1850s by the Hudson's Bay Company when coal deposits were found in the area. The wooden military bastion is now a museum overlooking the harbor where Nanaimo's

Smuggler Cove is one of hundreds of small-boat anchorages hidden behind islands along British Columbia's Inside Passage.

Annual World Championship Nanaimo-to-Vancouver Bathtub Race is held each July. Year-round bungy jumping takes place from the world's first specially designed bungy bridges. They span a 140-foot gorge of the Nanaimo River where the water is 40 feet deep and – as they say – you really don't have to worry about hitting bottom.

In the waters just north of Nanaimo is a military test range called Area **Whiskey Golf** which, during the Cold War, gained an ominous reputation. Tales circulating through waterfront pubs ranged from the believable to the bizarre, including one that the mountain behind the military base at Nanoose Bay had been hollowed out to hold nuclear submarines. In actual fact, the range is strictly a testing facility, under the command of Canadian military personnel who watch over Area Whiskey Golf from Winchelsea Island Control. The test site, established in 1967, is owned and operated by the Canadian government. It was chosen because its bottom topography is perfectly suited for technical acoustic testings, and most of the tests are conducted by Canadian and American surface ships and submarines. Whenever Whiskey Golf is being used for testing non-explosive torpedoes, sonobuoys or sonars, vessels are not allowed to pass through the "active" portion of this restricted area and any boats caught wandering through the restricted zone are escorted to safer waters. Public safety is the reason for this no-trespassing policy, and even a killer whale passing through will result in a test being cancelled.

Recreational boaters passing through Whiskey Golf are often heading to **Desolation Sound Marine Park** at the north end of Georgia Strait. This wilderness park is one of the most popular in the area with beautiful stream-fed anchorages, mountain lakes and cascading falls.

The wine is poured, the sun is warm and there's plenty of time to relax on deck and enjoy the passing scenery before dinner.

There is little tidal current in the Desolation Sound area, so the water is warm for swimming in summer.

The same cannot be said of the waters in **Discovery Passage** (part of the cruise ship route), where tidal currents are extremely swift. When the tide floods around each end of Vancouver Island, it meets somewhere between Cape Lazo and **Cape Mudge** at the southern entrance to Discovery Passage. Turbulence generated by these opposing tides can worsen into steep, confused seas when a strong southeasterly wind blows against currents flowing out of Discovery Passage. In 1927 a ship loaded with provisions was bound for Alaska when it got caught in a snowstorm and foundered in the waters off Cape Mudge. The residents of Quadra Island wasted no time exercising salvage rights on the beached ship and Christmas that year was especially festive.

The Cape Mudge lighthouse was erected in 1898 when vessels began streaming up Discovery Passage on their way to the Klondike gold fields. Salmon also stream up and down Discovery Passage and sportfishing lodges can be spotted on either side of the channel. In the 1920s, a boatbuilder named Ned Painter and his wife June began renting wooden rowboats at the mouth of the Campbell River. This modest operation evolved from fishing camp to cottage resort to the opening of Painter's Lodge in 1938. This historic resort (which burned in 1985 and was replaced with a modern facility) achieved worldwide fame as a sportfishing retreat and attracted many a celebrity to Campbell River, including Bing Crosby and Bob Hope. April Point Lodge on Quadra Island, established in 1945 by the Peterson family of San Francisco, also became a popular retreat. This tradition continues today, with multi-million-dollar yachts cruising these waters each summer.

Cruise West's Spirit of '98 sails past the entrance to Desolation Sound, a popular destination for recreational boats.

At the mill town of **Campbell River**, residents are often up at dawn in the summer to do a bit of fishing before heading to work. Sportfishing is a tradition here, dating back to 1924 when the Tyee Club was established. It was inspired by Sir Richard Musgrave who, in 1896, was Campbell River's first sportfisherman. Fishing from a dugout canoe with native guides, he afterwards wrote an article for Field magazine in which he praised their simple but skillful method of catching chinook salmon weighing up to 70 pounds. The rules for inclusion in the prestigious Tyee Club are that the fish must weigh more than 30 pounds and be caught in the Tyee Pool, from a rowing boat, using an artificial lure with only a single hook. Simply rowing a boat in these current-ridden waters is a challenge, let alone catching one of these famous Tyee salmon.

Not all sportfishermen come to Campbell River to fish the Tyee Pool. Many are after one of the trophy-sized chinook that gather in swirling back eddies near Seymour Narrows. The salmon caught in Discovery Passage are returning from the open ocean to their spawning rivers. Scientists speculate that outflow from the Fraser, a major river just south of Vancouver, reaches all the way up Discovery Passage to the northern end of Johnstone Strait where it ebbs into the Pacific. This outflow, although minimal and highly-diluted by the time it reaches the open ocean, is still substantial enough for returning salmon to 'smell' its source. That is why anywhere from 10 to 80 per cent of riverbound sockeye salmon will make a diversion down Johnstone Strait instead of entering the Inside Passage via Juan de Fuca Strait.

Salmon like the cold, swift-flowing waters that race down the east side of Vancouver Island, and experienced fishing guides learn how to read the tides and currents in their area to figure out where the best fish-

Carnival Spirit cruises past Campbell River along Discovery Passage.

ing is each day. Mariners also read the tide tables but their goal is to avoid contrary currents, especially at the narrowest part of Discovery Passage, called **Seymour Narrows**.

Ripple Rock, a two-headed pinnacle rock in the middle of the Narrows, used to lie just nine feet below the water's surface at low tide. It caused the sinking of more than 100 vessels before its top was blown off in 1958. Explosives were inserted into the core of Ripple Rock via an underwater tunnel that connected with Maud Island. When the world's largest non-atomic explosion was over, the top of Ripple Rock lay a safe 45 feet below chart datum.

Even with that hazard removed, Seymour Narrows can generate more than 13 knots of mid-channel current on a large tide. When this jet-like stream rubs against the nearly motionless peripheral waters, it produces a line of whirlpools down

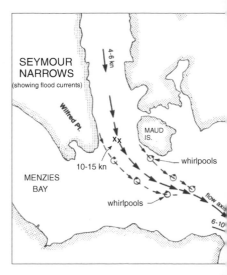

A rising tide is squeezed through Seymour Narrows, creating swift currents and churning whirlpools. Twin X's mark the location of Ripple Rock.

The top of dreaded Ripple Rock, in the middle of Seymour Narrows, was finally blown off on April 5, 1958.

Challenging Seymour Narrows, where currents can reach 16 miles per hour, is the major pass for all Alaska-bound cruise ships.

both sides of the pass. Most passengers will be spared this impressive sight because captains usually time their ship's transit of the Narrows to coincide with calm waters.

It's worth stepping out on deck to watch as your ship glides under the power line spanning Seymour Narrows. The vertical clearance used to be 161 feet – just high enough for cruise liners to pass beneath it at high water. Then, in 1995, Royal Caribbean Cruises positioned its new megaship *Legend of the Seas* on an Inside Passage itinerary and the hydro line had to raised by about 20 feet. The perspective when looking skyward from a ship's deck makes the wires appear unnervingly close to a ship's superstructure.

Chatham Point marks the intersection of Discovery Passage with **Johnstone Strait** – the most direct route through the Inside Passage and the one used by commercial traffic. Smaller boats often take the 'back route,' winding their way through the Discovery Islands. This was the route taken by Lieutenant James Johnstone in 1792 when he led one of Captain Vancouver's survey parties in search of a northwest passage. These survey expeditions were carried out in open boats while the ships remained anchored in one spot. Officers would head each boat party, and crewmen would draw on the oars from dawn until dusk and sometimes well into the night. Stowed in the boats were two weeks' provisions, survey instruments, muskets for shooting game, and trinkets for trade with the natives. These expeditions were not pleasant jaunts. The climate then was wetter and cooler than it is today, and the men

The cruise ships round picturesque Chatham Point when entering or leaving Johnstone Strait.

were constantly drenched by rain. They often ran low on food when an expedition took longer than anticipated so, to supplement their provisions, they hunted, fished and bartered with natives. At night they camped on shore while the men on watch cooked the next day's food over open fires. If the forest above the highwater mark was impenetrable, they were forced to sleep in the boats. This was something the men detested and some preferred to take their chances on shore. On one occasion, when swamped by a rising tide, an oarsman was so tired he didn't wake up and was floating away when roused by his companions.

Johnstone, a talented young officer, was pushing his survey party to its limit as they made their way north. They tried in vain to row through one set of rapids and had to haul the boat through with ropes. Some natives were watching all this activity from shore and lent a hand.

Johnstone's first clue to the existence of Vancouver Island came with the tide. While he and his men were sleeping on shore one night, they were unexpectedly swamped by a tide that was rising instead of falling. This meant the tide was coming in through a northern entrance and this revelation diverted Johnstone's attention from tracing the continental shoreline to locating a seaward passage at the top of Vancouver Island. His crew rowed all the way to **Pine Island** for an unobstructed view of the open waters of the Pacific Ocean. Johnstone and his men were exhausted and hungry by the time they backtracked 130 miles to the ships at anchor in Desolation Sound. But they had found a navigable channel to the Pacific Ocean.

Johnstone Strait is now a marine highway travelled by ships, tugs and fishboats. Much of the forested land viewed from your ship is Crown Land (owned by the provincial government) and tree farm licenses are granted to private forestry companies which harvest the timber. Considerable controversy surrounds a common logging practice called clearcutting and the British Columbia government has drafted a forest practices code outlawing clearcuts in sensitive areas such as wildlife habitats and salmon streams.

A century ago, logging was done by hand. Men would fell a tree with axes while standing on spring boards wedged into tree trunks. The timber was hauled out by oxen along skid trails to the local mill. In 1889, the Union Steamship Company was established to service remote coastal settlements, many of which were built on floats and could move from one sheltered cove to another. Initially these logging camps were a collection of bunkhouses, cookshacks and equipment sheds, but with the growing number of women in the camps – hired to

A hiker on the Blind Channel forest trails gazes at a cedar snag left standing by hand loggers at the turn of the 19th century.

cook or accompanying their husbands – tidy floathomes became a common sight. Picket fences, split from cedar, would prevent small children from falling in the water, and some floats were large enough to hold a garden. If the collection of floats included a large empty one, this would serve as a communal tennis court or baseball diamond. One logging camp evolved into a floating village with a store, community hall, post office and school.

Those built on land included **Blind Channel** on West Thurlow Island, where a sawmill was built in 1910. The community became a center for nearby logging camps, with a hotel and dock built to accommodate the Union Steamship boats that called with freight and passengers. A one-room schoolhouse at Blind Channel served the area, and children not living on West Thurlow Island were rowed to school by their mothers. By 1918 the population at Blind Channel had soared to 120 with a cannery and shingle mill in operation. The mill's boiler usually had enough steam left at the end of the day to power a generator that lit up everyone's home with a recent invention called the light bulb. A gas engine provided auxiliary power on Saturday nights when the dance hall was lit. Loggers from nearby camps would descend on Blind Channel and forget their worries as they kicked up their heels and "skidded the ladies across the floor."

World War II brought changes to the British Columbia coast. Following Japan's attack on Pearl Harbor, blackouts went into effect and the coast darkened. Lighthouses were covered, vessels travelling at night couldn't use running lights and no weather reports were issued. People of Japanese descent living on the coast were relocated to the

Numerous floating villages served the logging community in the early part of the last century. Sullivan Bay, below, is one of the few left.

(Above) Yorke Island guns guarded Johnstone Strait from enemy invasion during World War II.
(Below) Ammunition bunkers were buried deep underground.

interior and their fishing vessels were impounded. To protect against Japanese invasion, flying boat stations were established and a reserve unit of fishermen within the Royal Canadian Navy – dubbed the Gumboot Navy – was formed to patrol the coast. **Yorke Island**, at the junction of Johnstone Strait and Sunderland Channel, became a military outpost designed to detect and destroy any enemy ships approaching Vancouver from the north with its searchlight and 6" turret guns. Yorke Island never came under attack and the last firing practice took place on August 10, 1945. The troops were coming home, the Gumboot Navy had disbanded and the British Columbia coast, like the rest of the world, entered a new era.

A shortage of skilled tree fallers on the coast during the war years spurred the development of gasoline-powered saws. Following the war, improved machinery, centralization of sawmilling operations and the use of floatplanes to fly logging crews in and out of camps, all contributed to the decline of coastal logging communities. Once a working coast, its scenic waterways began attracting recreational boaters and, eventually, eco-tourists who fly to the area's remote wilderness lodges.

![Map of Johnstone Strait showing HANSON ISLAND, HARBLEDOWN ISLAND, BARONET PASSAGE, Growler Cove, WEST CRACROFT ISLAND, JOHNSTONE STRAIT, VANCOUVER ISLAND, Travel Pattern of Whales, and Robson Bight Ecological Reserve]

Johnstone Strait has become famous for its population of resident killer whales, which feed here on salmon and are frequently sighted in the vicinity of **Robson Bight**. In 1982 this bight was protected as an ecological reserve to prevent vessels from entering and disturbing the killer whales that linger here to rub against rounded pebbles in the bight's rocky shallows. The nearby boardwalk village of Telegraph Cove, founded in 1912 as a one-room telegraph station, has become a popular base for whale-watching tours in Johnstone Strait, while serious students of whale behaviour set up camp on a bluff of West Cracroft Island, directly opposite Robson Bight. The whales often travel between Johnstone Strait and Blackfish Sound via Blackney Passage, which is the route taken by northbound cruise ships, and the Pacific Killer Whale Foundation monitors underwater whale vocalizations from Hanson Island.

Southbound cruise ships often follow Broughton Strait past **Alert Bay** on Cormorant Island (named for the British naval survey ships *Alert* and *Cormorant*). In 1870, the 'Namgis moved their main village to this location after white settlers established a store and saltery here. A sawmill was soon built, as well as a hospital, residential school and salmon cannery.

Killer whales inhabit Johnstone Strait
from spring through fall.

A dugout canoe bobs on its moorings in front of the U'mista
Cultural Centre at Alert Bay.

Natives from other villages also moved to Alert Bay and it became a
major port for the commercial fishery. The fishing village remains a
cultural and commercial centre of the Kwakwaka'wakw.

At one end of town, along the waterfront, is the 'Namgis Burial
Grounds where the first of its 17 totem poles was raised in the late 19th
century. One of these poles was carved in 1970 by Henry Hunt and
Tony Hunt at the Royal British Columbia Museum in Victoria. This
pole is a memorial to Mungo Martin of Fort Rupert who was a high-
ranking chief, renowned carver and respected leader, the first to openly
host a potlatch when its prohibition ended.

At the other end of town is the **U'mista Cultural Centre**, a modern
museum built in the traditional plank-and-beam style. Inside is a collection of elaborate masks, rattles and whistles that were used at
Kwakwaka'wakw potlatch celebrations of feasting, dancing and gift
giving. Many of these items were seized by the Canadian government
following a mass arrest at Village Island in 1921, then returned in 1979
to be housed in the U'mista Cultural Centre.

A 10-minute hike up the hillside behind the museum, along residential streets, takes visitors to the Big House, originally built in 1963
(replaced in 1999 following a fire) and modeled on the traditional residences of the Kwakwaka'wakw. A community centre, it is primarily

used for potlatches. Standing nearby is the world's tallest totem pole, which is 173' high. Raised in 1973, the pole displays the crests of the various Kwakwaka'wakw tribes and is crowned with Sun Man, crest of the Quatsino. This pole has become a point of interest for passing cruise ships which glide slowly past Cormorant Island before entering Johnstone Strait.

At the western end of Broughton Strait is the logging town of **Port McNeill**, named for a Boston-born captain hired by the Hudson's Bay Company during the fur trade. Immediately inland are the rivers, lakes and forests of the Nimpkish Valley. An ecological reserve in the lower portion of the Nimpkish River now protects a stand of some of the tallest Douglas firs in Canada. Logging and over-fishing have depleted the Nimpkish system – once one of the coast's most productive salmon rivers – but the sportfishing is still good in the waters off Port McNeill.

Across the water from Port McNeill, on Malcolm Island, is the fishing port of Sointula (a Finnish word meaning harmony) which was founded at the turn of the last century by pioneer farmers from Finland who wanted to create a utopia of co-operative, rural living in a scenic, seaside setting. They were granted government land and although the commune collapsed in 1905, many of the settlers remained.

(Right) Totem poles at the 'Namgis Burial Grounds. (Below) Welcome sign at Alert Bay harbor.

Ketchikan

DIXON ENTRANCE

USA
CAN

*U.S. pilots are picked up
in this area for Ketchikan
bound ships.*

*Cruise ships stop briefly
in this area to pick up or
drop off Canadian pilots.*

Dundas
Is.

Green
Island

Khutzeymateen
Inlet

Triple
Island

Metlakatla
**Prince
Rupert**

Tyee

*Porcher
Is.*

QUEEN

CHARLOTTE

ISLANDS

Bonilla
Island

Grenville
Channel

*Captain
Cove*

HECATE

BANKS
ISLAND

Pitt
Island

STRAIT

*Campania
Island*

Butedale

*Princess
Royal Island
(Great Bear Rainforest)*

Anthony
Island (Ninstints)

*Aristazabal
Island*

Boat
Bluff
Light

*Cruise ships
coming
from Seattle*

*Laredo
Sound*

Ivory Is.

PACIFIC OCEAN

Bella
Bella

•Namu

0   25   50

Statute miles

*Queen
Charlotte
Sound*

*Calvert
Island*

*Fitz Hugh
Sound*

Triangle
Island

Egg
Is.

Pine
Is.

Queen Charlotte Strait

CRUISE SHIP ROUTE - - - - -
ALTERNATE ROUTES – · – · –

Port
Hardy

*Malcolm
Island*

Port
McNeill

PORT HARDY

The lighthouse at Pulteney Point on Malcolm Island is one of numerous lighthouses built after gold was discovered on the Klondike in 1896 and steamship traffic increased dramatically as prospectors rushed north along the Inside Passage. A network of lighthouses, buoys and beacons helped keep many, but not all, vessels off the rocks. When a steamer ran aground in 1916 off Scarlett Point, the lighthouse keeper who rowed out to retrieve the crew was greeted by the ship's captain. "I know all the rocks around here. And this," he said, gesturing to the one that had just ripped a hole in his keel, "is one of them."

The steamships of a century ago have been replaced with cruise liners, and also plying these waters are passenger/car ferries. Those of the Alaska Marine Highway travel the Inside Passage between Alaska and Bellingham, Washington, while the BC Ferry Corporation provides service to British Columbia's north coast out of Port Hardy. **Port Hardy** marks the end of the road and the beginning of the marine highway that winds north through the coastal waters of British Columbia and Alaska. Visitors to Port Hardy can enjoy a stroll past Fisherman's Wharf and Market Street with its many shops and the local museum which features Edward Curtis's epic film *Land of the War Canoe*.

A self-taught photographer from Seattle, Washington, Curtis was determined to make a photographic record of North American aboriginal people, devoting three decades of his life to producing a 20-volume collection of photographs and a film about the Kwakwaka'wakw, *In the Land of the Head Hunters*, which premiered in New York in 1914 and has been renamed *Land of the War Canoe*. George Hunt, an

The fishing and forestry town of Port Hardy is a favorite destination for yachts and ferry travellers venturing along the Inside Passage.

ethnographer whose father was a Hudson's Bay Company factor at Fort Rupert (near Port Hardy) and whose mother was a Tlingit from Alaska, was of major assistance to Curtis. Hunt also assisted the German anthropologist Franz Boas, who visited Fort Rupert in 1894 to gather artifacts and information.

Port Hardy still receives its share of high-profile visitors, such as the group of dignitaries that arrived by private plane in July 2004. The party included former U.S. president George Bush Sr. and former British prime minister John Major, who joined British Columbia billionaire Jimmy Pattison on board his 135-foot yacht awaiting them at the local wharf.

The open waters of Queen Charlotte Strait lie off Port Hardy, where remnant ocean swells roll in from Queen Charlotte Sound and sweep onto shorelines or shudder into spray when interrupted by rocky islets. Pine Island stands like a lonely sentinel at the Strait's western entrance, bearing the full brunt of Queen Charlotte Sound's winter storms, one of which the author Jack London experienced and later described in his classic adventure tale *The Call of the Wild*, when the ship carrying "Buck" crosses Queen Charlotte Sound during a bad blow.

Until 1907, when a lighthouse was erected, Pine Island's only visitors were the seabirds who nest here, including the Rhinoceros Auklet. These nocturnal seabirds tend to make ungraceful landings when flying back from sea after dark. Veering in for a landing, they often hit a tree and fall with a thud to the ground, which is where they burrow anyway. In February 1967, hurricane-force winds drove a 50-foot wave onto Pine Island, demolishing outbuildings, washing away fuel tanks, and surging right up to the front steps of the lightkeepers' house. Mr. and

A purse seiner sets its net in the fertile waters of Fitz Hugh Sound near the old cannery town of Namu.

Mrs. Brown, their two daughters and the assistant lightkeeper all scrambled to higher ground where they huddled around a campfire for the rest of the night. The lighthouse was rebuilt on higher ground, and Pine Island is today a pilot station where cruise ships pause to embark or disembark Canadian pilots.

Ships that are tracing the inner channels of British Columbia's north coast will have pilots on board, while those transiting the open waters of Hecate Strait will not. The inner route is along **Fitz Hugh Sound** – a long, wide channel that hugs the mainland coast and is shielded by islands from the open ocean. On the mainland shore of Fitz Hugh Sound is the historic cannery town of Namu, its boardwalks leading past weatherbeaten buildings supported on pilings. Namu in its heyday was a bustling place during the salmon season, when tins of salmon rolled off the assembly lines and were shipped to markets in North America and abroad. The nearby Koeye River attracts grizzly bears in summer with its large salmon runs. Also accessed off Fitz Hugh Sound is **Hakai Recreation Area** – the largest marine park on the British Columbia coast, its myriad scrub-forested islands and waterways providing boaters with sheltered anchorages and access to miles of ocean beaches untouched by development. Most of the park is wilderness, although floating fish camps do operate in these waters each summer.

Ships following Fitz Hugh Sound will often proceed along Lama Pass and cruise past the Heiltsuk community of **Bella Bella** on Campbell Island. In summer of 1993, this remote village hosted a week-long festival and its population doubled when people from 30 different native groups converged on Bella Bella.

(Above) A halibut caught in Hakai Recreation Area is weighed up. (Below) The resident lightkeepers at Egg Island.

Many arrived in traditional dugout canoes they had paddled from as far away as Washington State.

Just north of Bella Bella is **Dryad Point Lighthouse**. Ship passengers are treated to a close look as the ship makes a tight turn around this point. The lighthouse, like many others along the Inside Passage, was established during the Gold Rush when a flood of steamships began using this route to the Klondike.

The lighthouse on **Ivory Island**, at the other end of Seaforth Channel, was built a year earlier – in 1898. Farther along the meandering maze of interconnecting waterways is **Boat Bluff Lighthouse**. This

scenic lighthouse overlooks Sarah Passage and sits on an island inhabited by wolves. One former keeper, fearing for the safety of his small children, asked for a transfer from this lighthouse.

The natives were always wary and respectful of wolves. In her *Klee Wyck* stories the artist Emily Carr writes of an elder who, upon seeing her about to enter a forest, "ran and pulled me back, shaking his head and scolding me...The Indians forbade their children to go into the

Red-and-white lighthouses dot the winding Inside Passage made famous by the Klondike Gold Rush when steamships took prospectors to Skagway. (Left) Dryad Point Lighthouse near Bella Bella, built in 1899. (Below) Boat Bluff Lighthouse at Sarah Passage.

forest, not even into its edge. I was to them a child, ignorant about the wild things which they knew so well."

Wild things are found throughout the Inside Passage of British Columbia, and a huge tract of northern coastal land has come to be known as the "Great Bear Rainforest." Lying within this remote and relatively uninhabited area is **Princess Royal Island,** home to a rare type of black bear called a kermode. A genetic mutation has given this black bear a fur coat that is not black, brown or cinnamon – but pure white. These rare bears are not easy to find in the old-growth forest of an island the size of Princess Royal, but biologists with the Valhalla Wilderness Society have been conducting research here since 1990 to determine the bears' population and habitat. The Society has proposed that a kermode sanctuary be established on Princess Royal Island to save the white 'spirit' bears that live here and, in 2001, a logging moratorium was imposed by the provincial government. However, the fate of this bear sanctuary remains uncertain, which is why a Canadian schoolboy named Simon Jackson decided to found the Spirit Bear Youth Coalition. His impassioned activism sparked Hollywood's interest and the independent production of an animated feature film called *The Spirit Bear,* its profits helping to preserve the kermodes' habitat.

The narrow reaches of **Princess Royal Channel** are lined on either side with cliff-hanging waterfalls that vary from single strands to tumbling cascades. Halfway along this watery corridor a small island splits the channel. Ships often steer to the south of **Work Island**, affording passengers a full view of the abandoned cannery at **Butedale** on Princess Royal Island. To the right of the weatherbeaten cannery is a spectacular waterfall.

An Alaska-bound tug and barge heads up Princess Royal Channel.

Of all the channels of sheer cliff and clinging cedar that comprise the Inside Passage, none is more impressive than **Grenville Channel** – squeezed between the mainland and Pitt Island. Not only do the precipitous sides of this channel rise from watery depths of 1,600 feet to forested heights of 3,500 feet, they form such a narrow corridor that large ships entering from the south look like they're going to get stuck in the first bend. This is of course an optical illusion, but the channel is, at its narrowest point, only a fifth of a mile wide.

Large ships often bypass Grenville and Princess Royal Channels, following instead a more direct route along Principe and Laredo Channels past **Campania Island**, which is a striking sight with its high barren mountains and dome-shaped summit. More and more ships are bypassing the north coast's inner channels and travelling entirely along Hecate Strait, a wide body of water separating the mainland islands from the **Queen Charlotte Islands** – homeland of the Haida. These islands are the peaks of a submerged volcanic ridge of the continental shelf. When the last Ice Age glaciers advanced, parts of this 175-mile long archipelago were left untouched, which is why the islands contain species of plants and animals found nowhere else in the world. Others that thrive here are rare, such as a type of moss found only in the Himalayas and Scotland.

Helping to preserve the unique biology of these 'Canadian Galapagos' is their isolated location. For centuries the only seafarers who plied the shallow, choppy waters of Hecate Strait were the Haida.

The abandoned Haida village of Ninstints, in the Queen Charlotte Islands (Gwaii Haanas), is a World Heritage Site.

Travelling in canoes carved out of cedar logs, these skilled mariners established villages throughout what they called Gwaii Haanas, meaning Islands of Wonder. The southern islands are a wilderness park reserve and are reached only by boat or floatplane. Visitors can wander in solitude through moss-carpeted forests of spruce and cedar, the toppled ones now 'nurse' logs to seedlings which sprout from their trunks.

Near the southern tip of the archipelago is **Anthony Island**, a small island exposed to the Pacific. On it stands the abandoned village of **Ninstints** which was declared a World Heritage Site in 1981. The village is named for a wealthy chief who was head of the Kunghit Haida when they had settlements throughout the southern islands. Some of the totem poles are still standing at Ninstints, where they overlook a lagoon protected by an islet. In summer Haida caretakers live in a nearby cabin and keep these cedar monuments – now bleached by the elements – free of moss to prevent further rotting.

BC Ferries connects the northernmost island of the Queen Charlottes – Graham Island – with the mainland. A car ferry sails between Skidegate and **Prince Rupert**, which is the northern terminus for passengers riding the *Queen of the North* through the Inside Passage. The Alaska state ferry also docks in Prince Rupert.

PRINCE RUPERT

Prince Rupert is located at the mouth of the Skeena River on Kaien Island – a native name meaning Foam on Water – and the townsite was once a gathering place for the Tsimshian and Haida. It eventually

The new cruise-port facilities at Prince Rupert.

became a gathering place for white men when they realized the location's potential as a deep-sea port. Railway magnate Charles Hays, general manager of the Grand Trunk Pacific Railway, envisioned a shipping port here that would rival Vancouver and Seattle with its boast of being a day or two closer in shipping time to the Orient.

A competition was held in 1906 to choose a namesake for the new port. The winner, chosen from history, was Prince Rupert – a cousin of Britain's King Charles II and first governor of the Hudson's Bay Company. The first sod was turned in 1908, followed by a hydrographic survey of the harbor and its approaches so that lighthouses and navigational beacons could be installed to guide steamships arriving at night or in fog. All that remained to establish Prince Rupert as a major port was construction of a rail line by the Grand Trunk Pacific Railway.

Charles Hays, the man who masterminded the founding of Prince Rupert, set off for England to raise investment capital for completion of his railway's western terminus. He decided to do some networking on the return trip and chose the ill-fated maiden voyage of the *Titanic*. His life (and vision for Prince Rupert) was lost along with 1,500 other lives when the "unsinkable" British liner sideswiped an iceberg and sank in the North Atlantic.

A railway terminus was completed a few years later but fishing became the town's main industry.With the outbreak of World War II, Prince Rupert received an economic boost as thousands of American troops passed through on their way to the Aleutians and the Pacific. The port also handled freight and equipment for construction of the

One of the best locations to see grizzly bears is near Prince Rupert at the Khutzeymateen bear sanctuary.

Alaska Highway.

Today Prince Rupert is a major port handling overseas shipments of coal, pulp and grain, in addition to traditional fishing, canning and processing. Local attractions include Mariners' Park, the Museum of Northern B.C. and gondola rides to the top of Mount Hays. The cruise quay is located at historic Cow Bay, named for the first herd of dairy cows that arrived in 1906 and swam ashore. Amid the waterfront shops and restaurants is Smiles Seafood Cafe, a town landmark since 1934. During World War II, Smiles stayed open 24 hours a day to serve Canadian and American troops stationed in Prince Rupert. The cafe's famous halibut and chips are still a favorite with locals and visitors.

Shore excursions offered in Prince Rupert include a tour of the nearby North Pacific Cannery, built in 1889 and now a museum, as well as a scenic train ride on the North Coast Explorer. Whalewatching boat tours are also available, as are floatplane trips to the Khutzeymateen River valley north of Prince Rupert, the site of Canada's first grizzly bear sanctuary. Grizzlies will gather in close proximity to one another only if there is an easy food source, such as a spawning salmon stream, as exists at the head of this uninhabited inlet where the dense concentration of grizzly bears (about 60) prompted the British Columbia provincial government, in 1994, to protect 110,000 acres of the valley. Each summer, the grizzlies emerge from the mountains and gather on the banks of the Khutzeymateen River to gorge on pink salmon.

Small cruise ships can visit remote inlets and bays, such as Captain Cove (near Prince Rupert) shown below.

CHAPTER FOUR

KETCHIKAN
& Misty Fjords National Monument

Mariners have dominated the evolution of the Inside Passage. First they plied its waters in dugout canoes, then in square-rigged sailing ships. They conducted arduous surveys and drew detailed charts of its routes and hazards for future mariners. They delivered people and materials to far-flung ports, pioneers who forged a livelihood from this raw and beautiful land. Roads now connect some of these towns and cities to the rest of North America, as does air travel. But ships still provide a major link and mariners continue to dominate coastal Alaska, where the land is inextricably tied to the sea.

Many of us live far removed from a maritime world and quickly lose our bearings out on the water. Distances become hard to gauge and the many channels and islands passing by our porthole are hard to differentiate. Now and then we might ask ourselves, "Where are we?"

Fortunately the trained mariners on the ship's bridge know exactly where we are. Not only is the officer on watch an experienced navigator, he has at his side a local pilot who is familiar with these waters and highly trained at piloting ships through the intricate waterways of the Inside Passage.

At **Dixon Entrance** there is a changing of the guard, for this open body of water is also the border between Canada and Alaska. Depending on the ship's exact route, two Canadian pilots embark or disembark on the south side of Dixon Entrance and two American pilots do likewise on its north side.

Green Island Lighthouse lies on the Canadian side of Dixon Entrance – the international boundary between Canada and Alaska.

(Above) Aerial view of downtown Ketchikan. (Below) Salmon swim in great numbers up Ketchikan Creek.

The border, lying as it does on water, is not as easy to pinpoint as one on land. It runs from Cape Muzon to the entrance of Pearse Canal, then follows Portland Canal to its head. Called the A-B Line, this border was set in 1903 but it has, over the years, been a source of controversy. Fishboats caught on the wrong side of the Line are often seized and charged with illegal fishing.

Meanwhile, marine traffic carries on as usual, as does life at the head of Portland Canal where the Alaskan village of **Hyder** (population 89) on the American side of the Line is located two miles west of the Canadian town of **Stewart** (population 858). Connected to the rest of mainland British Columbia by a spur of the Cassiar Highway and to the Alaska Marine Highway by once-a-week ferry service from Ketchikan, these two communities share their facilities. The airstrip, school, hospital and police station are in Stewart while the seaplane base, fire hall and post office are in Hyder. Both places have a few inns, restaurants and shops as well as sightseeing tours. The nearby hills are no longer mined for their gold, silver and copper, but their scenic beauty endures.

Hyder sits on the edge of the **Misty Fjords National Monument**, a 2.3-million-acre wilderness preserve – accessible only by boat or plane – which lies within the 17-million-acre **Tongass National Forest**. This huge tract of forested land encompasses 90% of Southeast Alaska and was created in 1907 by President Theodore Roosevelt. An outdoorsman and preservationist, Roosevelt wanted to save the forests and mountains of America from profiteers. The demand for lumber was strong as railroads were built and new towns were constructed across the American West. Minnesota and Wisconsin had already been stripped of their timber stands when Roosevelt camped with the famous naturalist John Muir at Yosemite in 1903, and this experience convinced him of the need for wilderness protection.

About one-third of Tongass National Forest is designated wilderness. The rest is managed as a working forest, with logging and mining in operation alongside wilderness recreation and fishery management. Timber harvesting is limited and little replanting is required due to the area's temperate climate and abundance of rainfall.

This abundant moisture does not go unnoticed in **Ketchikan**, where a Liquid Sunshine Gauge is proudly displayed on the cruise ship dock. This gauge measures the inches of rain the town receives annually – an impressive 150 inches on average. If the sun is shining when your ship pulls into Ketchikan, consider yourself lucky.

During the steamship days, Ketchikan was dubbed 'Alaska's First City' because it was the first Alaskan port of call to receive mail and supplies from the south. Ketchikan is still the first stop for Alaska State Ferries arriving from Bellingham and Prince Rupert. The town stretches along the west shore of Revillagigedo Island at the base of Deer Mountain and is reached only by sea or air. An airport lies opposite on Gravina Island and the narrow channel in between – called Tongass Narrows – is busy with boats and floatplanes.

Near the dockside info center is the famous Liquid Sunshine Gauge.

Ketchikan began with a saltery in 1883, followed by a cannery a few years later. As more canneries were built, a boardwalk town sprung up along the waterfront straddling Ketchikan Creek – a major spawning river for salmon. In 1903 the new sawmill began making boxes for the cases of salmon being shipped out of local canneries and by the 1930s – the industry's heyday – more than a dozen canneries were packing two million cases of salmon annually.

Ketchikan was a rowdy town where local fishermen, miners and loggers spent much of their free time drinking, gambling and visiting the madams of Creek Street, whose houses were built on pilings and connected by boardwalks. Business didn't slow during Prohibition when bootleg whiskey was smuggled into Ketchikan. It was delivered by skiff at high tide and lifted through trap doors in the madams' floors.

Ketchikan's lumber industry flourished during World War II, its mills providing Sitka spruce – a strong and lightweight wood – for the construction of fighter planes. In the 1950s Ketchikan's wood products industry overtook its declining salmon industry, which nearly collapsed in the '70s due to overfishing. Only two canneries are currently in operation but a few million pounds of fresh seafood are now airfreighted annually. The Deer Mountain Hatchery, built on Ketchikan Creek in 1954, currently releases 300,000 salmon a year.

Mining is another local industry. Gold was discovered in the area in 1897 and copper shortly after on nearby Prince of Wales Island. Another thriving industry in Ketchikan is tourism. In addition to its turn-of-the-century boardwalk streets and buildings, the town has become a showpiece for Tlingit culture, with totem poles and other

Dock facilities at Ketchikan are excellent with room for passengers boarding tour buses and providing easy access to downtown.

Ketchikan's population almost doubles when cruise ships fill the docks and the streets bustle with cruise passengers.

native art on display at local museums, parks and nearby villages. The name Ketchikan is based on a Tlingit word which, loosely translated, means 'thundering wings of an eagle', and the Tongass National Forest is named after a Tlingit clan. The island on which Ketchikan sits was named by Captain Vancouver in 1793 for Spain's Viceroy to Mexico whose title was Count of Revilla Gigedo.

Ketchikan's numerous church spires serve as perches for eagles attracted to the salmon in Ketchikan Creek, at the mouth of which residents often gather on a summer evening for a bit of fishing off the Stedman Street Bridge. This is also a popular swimming hole for kids who like to leap into the water from Creek Street's wooden balconies.

With 8,000 residents, Ketchikan has a good selection of banks, restaurants and stores, including numerous jewelers and gift shops located near the cruise pier. A popular port of call, this lively town embraces visitors today with the same exuberance it applied to salmon fishing at the turn of the century. When your ship pulls into port, Ketchikan is open for business.

LOCAL ATTRACTIONS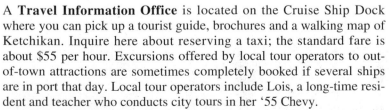

A **Travel Information Office** is located on the Cruise Ship Dock where you can pick up a tourist guide, brochures and a walking map of Ketchikan. Inquire here about reserving a taxi; the standard fare is about $55 per hour. Excursions offered by local tour operators to out-of-town attractions are sometimes completely booked if several ships are in port that day. Local tour operators include Lois, a long-time resident and teacher who conducts city tours in her '55 Chevy.

They're lumberjacks and they're ok! The lumberjack show is pure fun for the spectators who cheer for their respective teams.

A popular local attraction is the Great Alaskan Lumberjack Show, held in an open-air amphitheater on the waterfront **1**. This site is where the Ketchikan Spruce Mill, one of the largest in the world, stood until it shut down in the 1970s. The lumberjack show features skilled woodsmen pitted against one another in log rolling, pole climbing and other competitive events.

A WALKING TOUR OF DOWNTOWN

Many of Ketchikan's attractions are best seen on foot and a stroll along its streets, even in the rain, is a pleasant way to acquaint yourself with the town.

Follow the waterfront promenade to Mill Street which leads to the **Southeast Alaska Discovery Center 2**. Built in the cannery style, this modern center contains impressive exhibits on the area's natural environment, wildlife and native heritage. Nearby is **Whale Park 3** where flower gardens and benches create an inviting setting for Ketchikan's historic Knox Brothers Clock and a replica of the Chief Kyan Totem Pole, carved by Stanley Marsden in 1964. It was first erected beside Ketchikan Creek where the Tlingit Chief Kyan held rights to a summer fish camp. Kitty-corner to Whale Park, on Mission Street, is **4 St. John's Episcopal Church** – built in 1903 and the oldest standing church in Ketchikan, its interior built with red cedar. The **Seamen's Center** was built a year later as a hospital and is now a gathering place for marine workers.

Ketchikan's rowdy past is preserved in the boardwalk buildings of Creek Street.

From Whale Park you can see the pink-colored **U.S. Forest Service building** 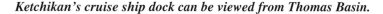 which contains displays and information on the Tongass National Forest. Standing opposite the Forest Service building is the **Chief Johnson Totem Pole** 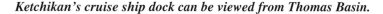, carved by Tlingit artist Israel Shotridge and raised in 1989. It's an exact replica of the original pole raised in 1901 by Chief Johnson, which is now housed in the Totem Heritage Center.

Follow Stedman Street to the bridge spanning the mouth of **Ketchikan Creek**. Look down and you might see salmon milling about in the water while they adjust to fresh water before beginning their uphill swim to their spawning grounds.

Carry on along Stedman, past picturesque **Thomas Basin** with its small boat marinas. In the early part of this century, before a breakwater was built, the basin's long tidal flats were used as a baseball park. The game was called when a rising tide started flooding the outfield. On the far side of Thomas Basin is a wood-plank street built over the water. Called **Thomas Street** ◼, its historic buildings were once part of the New England Fish Co. cannery. A viewing walkway extends to the end of the breakwater.

Retrace your steps along Thomas and Stedman Streets, past The New York Hotel & Cafe, to Ketchikan's famous **Creek Street** ◼. This former red-light district is now a respectable part of town and a major tourist attraction. This boardwalk set on pilings, takes you along the shores of Ketchikan Creek, past shops and a museum called Dolly's House. Dolly was the town's most successful madam and her house has been preserved, complete with furnishings and other memorabilia.

About halfway along Creek Street is a tramway car that whisks passengers (for a small charge) up the hill to the **Ted Ferry Civic Center**

Ketchikan's cruise ship dock can be viewed from Thomas Basin.

A replica of the Chief Johnson Totem Pole stands at the base of the tramway near Creek Street.

9. Here you have a sweeping view of downtown Ketchikan and Tongass Narrows.

Back down on Creek Street, pause at the footbridge where again you may see salmon heading upstream. On the other side of the bridge is the **Tongass Historical Museum and Public Library 10**. Here you can view exhibits depicting Ketchikan's earlier days. Standing outside is the Raven Stealing the Sun Totem Pole by Tahltan-Tlingit Dempsey Bob.

Dock Street leads from the Museum back down to Front Street. On the way you will pass the foot of Edmond Street, which is a long set of wooden stairs going up the hillside. A stroll along Front Street takes you past the historic **Gilmore Hotel 11** (on the National Historic Register) to the tunnel under Knob Hill.

The tunnel was built in 1954 so that historic homes on Knob Hill could be preserved. Had a road been built, part of the hill would have been blasted away and the houses demolished. Many stories are told to visitors regarding this tunnel's construction, the best one being that federal funds were available at the time for building a bomb shelter, so Ketchikan built one with two entrances and a road running through it.

If you carry on along Front Street, you'll reach **Harborview Park 12** overlooking Ketchikan's main boat basin. Benches here provide both a resting spot and a view of the busy harbor's fishboat and floatplane activity.

AN EXTENDED WALKING TOUR

Ketchikan is built on the slopes of Deer Mountain, so to see more of the local sights on foot involves a bit of climbing. Recommended is a hike up Front Street's steps to Cedar Street where you can overlook the waterfront. Take the Main Street stairs back down to Pine Street. At the corner stands the **Monrean House**  – built in 1904 for one of the town's leading businessmen. Preserving the Queen Anne style so popular at the turn of the century, this house is on the National Register of Historic Places. Continue along Main Street, turn left at Grant and at the next block turn right on Edmond. Now you're at the top of the long wooden staircase leading down to Dock Street.

At the bottom of the stairs, turn left on Dock Street, then left again on Bawden. Stay with Bawden until you reach Park Avenue, which veers to the right. Follow Park along Ketchikan Creek to the **Deer Mountain Hatchery** which backs onto a peaceful park containing ornamental ponds once used by the town's first hatchery.

The heritage homes of Knob Hill straddle the Water Street Tunnel.

A footbridge leads between the hatchery and the **Totem Heritage Center** which houses a major collection of authentic totem poles. Outside on the grounds is a self-guided nature path.

A good hike can be taken up Deer Mountain for a splendid view of the island. Follow Fair Street (at the top of Deermont Street) to Ketchikan Lakes Road which leads to the Deer Mountain Parking Lot Trailhead. The trail, which is about 3 miles long and ascends 3,000 feet, is suitable for moderately experienced hikers, and the first overlook is just one mile from the trailhead.

OUT-OF-TOWN EXCURSIONS

There is no shortage of shore excursions to take while in Ketchikan, and if you plan ahead there should be time for both a walking tour of downtown (including the shopping area) and an out-of-town excursion.

Tlingit heritage is strong in the Ketchikan area and eight miles north of town is a former village site now called **Totem Bight State Park**. A

SAXMAN VILLAGE

One of Ketchikan's most popular attractions is Saxman Village, located two miles south of town. A $2 shuttle called The Bus runs every half hour between the cruise dock (near Tongass Hardware) and the village where a collection of totem poles is on public display. Should you wish to take a tour, this can be booked through your cruise line. This popular shore excursion involves a motor coach ride to the village for a two-hour visit immersed in Tlingit culture. Your hosts are descendants of those who lived at Cape Fox and Fort Tongass until the late 1880s, when they were persuaded by Presbyterian missionaries to relocate to this site. Founded in 1894, the village was named for school teacher Samuel Saxman.

In the 1930s, the people of Saxman returned to their original village sites to retrieve the totem poles they had left behind. New poles have been carved since then and they stand in a semi-circle overlooking Tongass Narrows. Guests arriving at Saxman are treated to the live enactment of a Tlingit legend and are ushered into the Clan House, built of red cedar and displaying the Beaver crest on its carved corner poles. In keeping with a traditional potlatch, the Cape Fox Dancers perform a series of dances, then invite members of the audience to join them. Upon leaving, each guest is given a small packet of trading beads – in keeping with potlatch customs.

Outside the Beaver Clan House, a guide explains the stories behind the totem poles displayed in the park. After a visit to the gift shop, the tour concludes in the Carving Center, where the art of totem carving is explained. Anyone interested in native culture will find this tour both enlightening and entertaining.

Wearing traditional regalia, a young Tlingit performs a potlatch dance in the Beaver Clan House.

*(Above) **The ceremonial clan house at Totem Bight State Park.** (Below) **A Tlingit totem pole stands tall outside the Cape Fox clan house.***

short trail through the forest opens into an old campsite containing a collection of authentic totem poles and a ceremonial clan house.

Flightseeing excursions are popular in Ketchikan, providing an eagle's eye view of the region's steeply treed slopes, mountain lakes, hanging waterfalls and winding fjords that were carved long ago by retreating glaciers. You may even spot some wildlife – mountain goats, bear and moose on shore; killer whales, seals and sea lions in the surrounding channels.

Ketchikan is right next door to the **Misty Fjords National Monument** – a wilderness reserve created in 1978 and, at 2.3 million acres, almost four times the size of Rhode Island. Weather checks are made every hour but planes still fly in overcast weather; the fjords are said to be their most beautiful when mist rises off the water and wisps of cloud cling to the mountaintops.

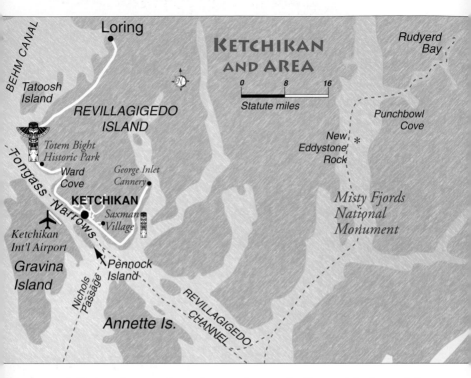

A flightseeing tour lasts about an hour and offers aerial views of the **Behm Canal**, which is about a hundred miles long and wraps right round Revillagigedo Island. Pillar-shaped New Eddystone Rock – a volcanic plug – juts 234 feet skyward from the middle of the canal's eastern arm. Also in the Behm Canal (but outside the National Monument) is the U.S. Navy's submarine testing facility, which is located in these remote waters to escape marine traffic noise. The submarines being tested are so quiet that navy scientists need an equally silent location to plant their rows of hydrophones and record the rhythms of the subs as they race past. Data collected from these underwater tests is analysed and used to make the submarines even quieter.

The silence of these watery canyons is demonstrated when your plane lands on an alpine lake or one of the inlet's upper reaches and the pilot shuts off his engine. You can climb onto one of the plane's pontoons and listen to the subtle sounds of a mountain wilderness.

Highlights of the Monument are: **Rudyerd Bay** – a spectacular, steep-sided fjord; **Punchbowl Cove** – a dramatic cove of sheer cliffs; **Big Goat Lake** – an alpine lake containing a waterfall that plunges almost 1,000 feet; **Nooya Lake** – left behind by a melting valley glacier; and **Granite Basin** – where bare rock ridges separate a row of deep-blue alpine lakes. Some ships' itineraries include a detour up Behm Canal to Rudyerd Bay and Punchbowl Cove.

T H E   B E A V E R

One of the most common sights in Alaska – and especially in Ketchikan – is the floatplane. Used as an important link between coastal villages, remote logging camps and main ports, the floatplane has served Alaska since the 1930s. However, it was the introduction of the Beaver aircraft just after the Second World War that made short-haul air connections in Southeast Alaska inexpensive and, most importantly, safe.

BEAVER MK 1

Engine: 450 hp
Pratt & Whitney
Wing Span: 48 ft.
Length: 30 ft.
Weight: 3000 lb
Performance –
Maximum Speed: 160 mph
Cruising Speed: 130 mph
Rate of Climb: 1,020 ft/min
Service Ceiling: 18,000 feet

Developed by De Havilland Canada, the Beaver was designed to handle payloads over 1,000 pounds, and to take off and land in tight places, whether on land, ice, snow or water. The plane went on to become one of the most successful and long-lived designs in aviation history, with over 1,600 built. Of the 1,000 still operating most are working along the British Columbia and Alaska coast.

Beaver floatplanes line up like taxi cabs along Ketchikan's waterfront. The Beaver has been the bush-plane of choice for 50 years.

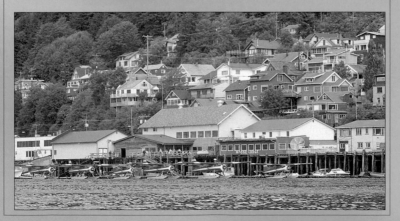

(Above) Hanging waterfalls ribbon the rock walls of Misty Fjords' watery canyons. (Below) A floatplane lands on an alpine lake in Granite Basin north of Punchbowl Cove.

Other guided tours available during your stop in Ketchikan include sportfishing, kayaking and canoeing on a mountain lake. Beginners are welcome and wet weather gear is sometimes provided. Wear warm clothing in layers – the outer layer should be waterproof. Rainforest hikes with naturalists as guides are also offered, as are bear-watching excursions to **Neets Bay** and Traitors Cove, where black bears gather to feed on salmon. These outlying wilderness sites are usually reached by float plane, although some entail boarding a motor coach, then transferring to a tour boat to visit outlying resorts and canneries

Loring, in the western arm of the Behm Canal, was a cannery site from 1885 to 1930, and pieces of the wrecked side-paddle steamer *Ancon* can be seen here at low tide. The steamer used to deliver mail, freight and passengers to Loring until one day in 1889 when an overly enthusiastic cannery worker cast off the departing ship's dock lines before an officer was ready at the controls. The steamer drifted onto a reef where it holed and sank with no loss of life – except maybe the cannery worker's!

When Captain Vancouver's two ships were anchored in 1793 at Port Stewart, on the other side of the Behm Canal, they were visited by Tlingits from the Stikine River and Haidas from Kasaan. The British sailors, who had been attacked by some Tlingits in **Traitors Cove**, watched with apprehension when it looked as though a fight was going to break out between the two native groups. Peace prevailed, however, after an exchange of words between their leaders. On board one of the British ships was a Tlingit who told Captain Vancouver he wanted to sail with him to England, then promptly changed his mind when he saw a British crewman being whipped.

The salmon hatchery in Neets Bay attracts black bears to the nearby creek where passengers can watch them feeding from July through September.

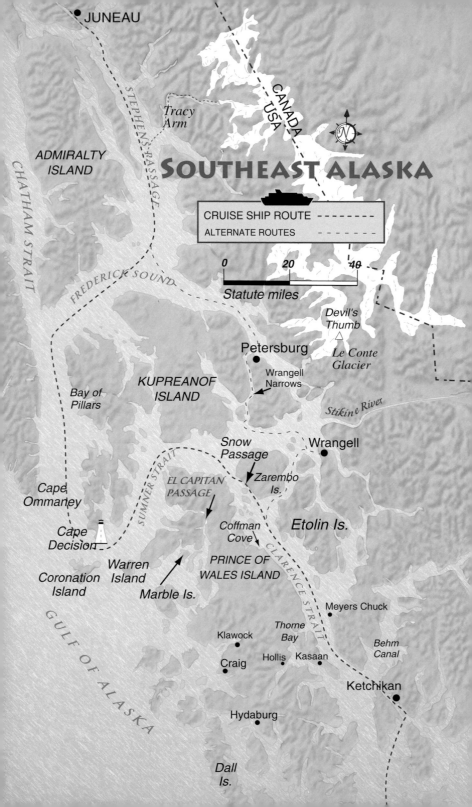

CHAPTER FIVE

PIONEER PORTS

L and is scarce in Alaska – private land, that is. Of the state's massive land area covering 365 million acres, less than one per cent is in private hands.

For almost a century Alaska's single landowner was the U.S. Government. Statehood was granted in 1959, but the complex and controversial process of land allocation is ongoing. Millions of acres lie within national parks and wilderness refuges and, in 1971, the Alaska Native Claims Settlement Act – involving 44 million acres – was passed. Until 1995, under the state's Homestead Program a person with one year's residency in Alaska was able to acquire from 40 to 160 acres (depending on its land-use classification) but had to survey, occupy and improve the land in certain ways within set time periods in order to receive title. Today, remote recreational cabin sites on state land can be staked under legislation passed in 1997.

In Southeast Alaska the land is either national park or part of the Tongass National Forest. Developed property in towns such as Ketchikan is scarce and expensive, with house prices considerably higher than the national average. Yet, in spite of Alaska's land-use restrictions, the lure of the north still beckons. In 1984, the ABC television program 20/20 featured the remote Alaskan village of **Coffman Cove**. Afterwards the residents of this tiny logging community, located on the northeast side of **Prince of Wales Island**, were deluged with

The fishing community of Port Protection has no roads but plenty of trees for building boardwalks. Shown below is the local school.

mail from viewers who wanted to move there. The show's portrayal of Coffman Cove's wholesome lifestyle – fresh air, clean water and freedom from urban crime – appealed to many Americans living in the Lower 48. Yet Alaskans who live in outlying ports similar to Coffman Cove don't harbor any illusions about their lifestyle. Living in isolation is not for everyone. The work is often seasonal and incomes are sporadic. The winters can be long, dark and wet. Supplies must be shipped or flown into port, there are few conveniences and, for many, a trip south each winter is mandatory to their mental health. Still, most say they wouldn't live anywhere else.

Alaska breeds a hardiness in people. Early pioneers came to fish the waters, mine and log the land. Margaret Bell Wiks, well known for her children's books about Alaska's early days, was of pioneering stock. Her Scottish grandparents – James and Margaret Millar – arrived in Alaska in 1879 and established salteries on Prince of Wales Island. Their daughter Florence married a fellow named James Bell who raced his sloop against a steamer – from Puget Sound to Alaska – and won.

The Bells' daughter Margaret was born in December 1898. She was delivered by her Scottish grandmother while the doctor rested in bed. He had suffered a heart attack when the sailboat bringing him to **Thorne Bay** was caught in a storm. Margaret weighed only three pounds at birth and spent the first few weeks of her life in a shoebox on the door of an opened oven. Despite her tentative start, Margaret lived for 91 years.

Millar Street in Ketchikan is named for the family, as is the town of **Craig** on Prince of Wales Island. Craig was one of Margaret's uncles and he ran a cannery there in the early 1900s. With a present population of 1,200, Craig is home port to a substantial fishing fleet and has become the service centre for Prince of Wales – the largest island in Southeast Alaska. The island is indented with inlets and coves, many of which were fishing camps for the Haida and Tlingit before the arrival of white settlers. **Klawock** was originally a Tlingit summer village, and

Alaska's state ferries – called the Alaska Marine Highway – provide a transportation link between remote villages and coastal towns.

Hydaburg was established in 1911 when several Haida villages in the vicinity joined together. About 300 years ago Haida living in the Queen Charlotte Islands (Haida Gwaii) extended the northern boundary of their territory to encompass the southern half of Prince of Wales Island. Then their numbers, like those of other native groups, dwindled when European-imported diseases such as smallpox wiped out entire families and clans along the coast. Many villages were abandoned as survivors coalesced at central locations.

A state ferry runs between Ketchikan and Prince of Wales Island. It pulls into **Hollis**, a former mining and logging town, and each summer more and more visitors come to the island for its superb sportfishing and wildlife viewing. Extensive logging has taken place on Prince of Wales Island and logging roads connect most settlements with the Hollis ferry terminal. But the communities of **Point Baker** and **Port Protection**, at the north end of the island, don't want to be connected. When the forest service proposed extending the road system to include them, a ruckus ensued, with environmental organizations getting involved. The 88 residents of these two fishing ports were quite happy in their isolation. They get about in skiffs and out-of-town visitors arrive by boat or floatplane. In Port Protection, boardwalks lead past homes and the local school. A general store overlooks the fuel dock, and the men and women who live here troll for salmon in **Sumner Strait,** satisfied with a moderate day's catch.

Most cruise ships pass through Sumner Strait on their way to or from Ketchikan. Whales and dolphins also use this major channel. Its southern end is open to the Gulf of Alaska and marked by **Cape Decision** – a rocky bluff atop which sits an unmanned lighthouse.When cruise ships round Cape Decision, mountainous Coronation Island and nearby **Warren Island** lie to seaward. Both are wilderness reserves, where seabirds nest on rocky cliffs and bears feed in the streams. Tall stands of spruce inland give way to bent trees along the islands' windward shores, exposed to the wind and open sea.

In 1793 a September storm forced Captain Vancouver's two ships to seek shelter in Port Protection before heading

The boardwalk streets never get crowded in Port Protection.

out to sea. That summer their survey boats had covered hundreds of miles of shoreline, including the channels that lead to the mouth of the great **Stikine River**. This river delta is one of the most productive estuaries in Southeast Alaska. Its tidal flats attract half a million migrating seabirds each year and the silt it deposits in adjacent Dry Strait prevents vessels of any size from navigating that channel.

Before the arrival of European explorers and fur traders, Tlingit natives had established a major village at the mouth of the Stikine under a series of leaders named Chief Shakes. As the fur trade heated up, the 400-mile-long Stikine River turned into a conveyor belt for furs, with Chief Shakes and his people reaping the profits as middlemen.

The Russian-American Company built a fort at the mouth of the Stikine in 1833 to prevent Britain's Hudson's Bay Company from gaining a foothold in Russian territory. The HBC's main competition was from American merchant ships, so it began hiring American skippers (veterans of the coastal trade) to shadow the Boston ships and outbid the Yankee traders, who were known as 'Boston men' because almost all of them were from that port. As their profits dwindled, the Boston men gradually withdrew from the fur trade and turned their sights on whaling. Their withdrawal also meant a loss of supply ships for the Russians at Sitka. They had no alternative but to turn to the British who had offered to supply the Russian outpost with surplus food from their forts' surrounding farms. So, in return for a reliable food source, the Russians granted the British exclusive access to coastal waters bordering the mainland. The HBC moved into Saint Dionysius Redoubt and changed its name to Fort Stikine. A brisk trade continued between local Tlingit clans and the British, who offered cloth and woolen Hudson's Bay blankets in exchange for furs.

The fur trade eventually dwindled and the British fort had been abandoned by the time a prospector named Buck Choquette discovered gold on the Stikine River in 1861. Men rushed upriver by steamer to Buck's Bar to pan for gold. A second

The American schooner **Lady Washington,** *a replica shown here at Vancouver's Maritime Museum, was commanded by 'Boston men' during the fur trade.*

strike was made farther upriver at Cassiar in 1874. Fort Stikine was now called **Wrangell**, named for Baron Von Wrangell, a former manager of the Russian-American Company, who had ordered the fort's initial construction.

When the famous naturalist John Muir of California arrived at Wrangell by steamer in July 1879, about 1,800 miners and prospectors had already passed through that spring en route to the Cassiar gold mines. This was Muir's first visit to Alaska and his initial impression of Wrangell was that "no mining hamlet in the placer gulches of California, nor any backwoods village I ever saw, approached it in picturesque, devil-may-care abandon." Muir did concede that despite the town's haphazard collection of houses built on swampy ground, Wrangell was a tranquil place. There were no noisy brawls in the streets and the weather was mild.

Muir himself was a bit of a curiosity. The townspeople wondered what he was up to wandering about the forest, examining plants and trees with no apparent objective. One resident observed Muir "on his knees, looking at a stump as if he expected to find gold in it."

A Presbyterian mission was established in Wrangell, where Muir met Dr. Sheldon Jackson (a missionary who would become widely known in Southeast Alaska) and Reverend Samuel Hall Young, who became Muir's lifelong friend. In his book *Travels in Alaska*, Muir describes Young as an adventurous evangelist. Of course, anyone who associated with Muir had no choice but to embrace adventure.

On the first climb Young made with Muir, the young missionary dislocated both arms when he slipped near the top of Glenora Peak and found himself hanging from a crumbling precipice on the edge of a thousand-foot drop. Muir saved his new climbing companion and it was the beginning of a close friendship.

During his stay at Wrangell, Muir also met the current Chief Shakes of the Stikine tribe who invited Muir and the missionaries to a potlatch. The floor of the great chief's house was "strewn with fresh hemlock boughs" while "bunches of showy wild flowers adorned the walls" wrote Muir in *Travels in Alaska*, who enjoyed the rhythmic stamping of feet and clapping of hands and described the chief dancer's headdress as being filled with feathers. With each jerk of his head, he "scattered great quantities of downy feathers like a snowstorm as blessings on everybody." Theatrical imitations of several animals were performed so convincingly that when "the door of the big house was suddenly thrown open and in bounced a bear," they were all quite startled until they realized it was a man wearing a bear skin. Gifts were handed out at the end of the potlatch and Muir, adopted by the tribe, was given the Tlingit name of Ancoutahan ('adopted chief') which would protect him in his travels. Other tribes wouldn't risk harming him for fear of retaliation from the powerful Stikines.

WRANGELL (POP. 2,150)

The Stikine village visited by John Muir in 1879 was situated on a small island known as **Shakes Island** and a replica of that tribal house is now a major tourist attraction. It was built in the traditional manner, without nails but by using adzes to shape and join the posts, beams and planks. Muir was so impressed with the Tlingit workmanship he stated that "with the same tools, not one in a thousand of our skilled mechanics could do as good work." The original interior houseposts of the clan house, which were brought from a previous village, are now housed in the Wrangell Museum. Replica poles grace the inside and outside of the tribal house and the clan's bear crest frames the entrance.

Other carved poles about town include a replica of the Three Frogs Totem, designed to shame the neighboring Kiksadi clan (whose crest was the frog) into repaying a debt. Bear Up The Mountain pole tells the story of a grizzly bear (his prints shown climbing up the pole) who led the Shakes clan to safety when threatened by a great flood. Totem poles of the Kiksadi clan are displayed in a small park on Front Street where false-fronted wooden buildings preserve the town's pioneer heritage.

On Church Street is the oldest protestant church in Alaska, the First Presbyterian Church. It was founded in 1879 and, twice damaged by fire, has been extensively renovated. A large, red neon cross was erected in 1939 and serves as a navigational light for local mariners.

Outside the **public library**, located on 2nd Street, are two totem poles as well as some petroglyphs carved on rocks in the grass. Several petroglyphs can also be viewed in the **Wrangell Museum** next door

A replica of a Tlinglit tribal house stands on Shakes Island in Wrangell. The clan's bear crest frames the door.

and even more petroglyphs are found (after some searching) on the beach a half mile north of the **ferry terminal**. At low tide, about 40 rock engravings of prehistoric images – animals and human faces – are exposed. People are allowed to take rubbings of them and museum staff are happy to explain how this is best done.

Northwest of Wrangell, opposite the south end of Sergief Island, is Garnet Ledge. Its red transparent mineral was mined in 1915 by Alaska Garnet & Manufacturing Company – apparently the world's first all-women corporation. The ledge is now the property of the children of Wrangell (adults need a permit to remove garnets) and youngsters here spend part of their summer holidays selling these local gems to visitors.

North of Wrangell, lies **Wrangell Narrows** – an important water-way in Southeast Alaska which is used by fishboats, tugs, small cruise ships and the Alaska State Ferry. This long, narrow channel (20 miles in length and, at places, only 300 feet in width) is squeezed between two islands and well marked with over 60 navigational aids. Wrangell Narrows has been dubbed Christmas Tree Lane for its nightly blinking of red and green lights. The narrows are very scenic, winding past log cabins and fishing lodges nestled at the foot of treed slopes.

PETERSBURG (POP. 3,150)

At the north end of Wrangell Narrows, on Mitkof Island, is the scenic fishing port of **Petersburg**. Founded by Norwegian immigrants at the turn of the century, the town's site was chosen for its natural harbor and dramatic backdrop of glacier-draped mountains which reminded Peter Buschmann of the fjords back home. He moved here in 1897 and began fishing for salmon and halibut.

Low tide on Hammer Slough reveals the pilings supporting the homes and planked sidewalks.

'Peter's Burg' grew quickly as fellow Norwegians joined Buschmann and, utilizing the ample timber supply, began building a neatly planned Scandinavian community. Buschmann was manager of the Icy Straits Packing Company, which constructed a sawmill, wharf, warehouses, bunkhouses, store and cannery. Fish packing was a year-round operation with salmon caught each summer, halibut and herring in the spring, crab over the winter and shrimp throughout the year. The pack ice was supplied by the nearby Le Conte Glacier.

Unlike some of the goldmining towns of this era, there was no boom and bust cycle in Petersburg. The people here were industrious, community minded and proud of their Scandinavian heritage. They decorated their neat wooden homes with traditional rosemaling (fanciful floral designs painted in bright colors) and built a Sons of Norway Hall in 1912 for Saturday night socials. Many a Petersburg fisherman met his future wife at one of these dances.

Norwegian Independence Day is celebrated annually with a Little Norway Festival held on the weekend nearest May 17th. Residents of Petersburg dress in traditional costume, prepare lavish smorgasbords and dance to Norwegian folk music. As part of the festivities, a replica Viking ship called *Valhalla* (built in 1976 for the nation's bicentennial) is launched by local fishermen dressed as fierce Norsemen.

Petersburg Attractions: Town maps and brochures are available at the Chamber of Commerce **Information Center**, located in the Harbor Master Office overlooking North Harbor. The Valhalla is on display beside the **Sons of Norway Hall** at the entrance to Hammer Slough, which is built on pilings. Hammer Slough's plank streets and brightly colored buildings are a favorite

Petersburg has retained its Norwegian ancestry with such attractions as the historic Sons of Norway Hall and a replica Viking ship.

subject for local artists and their paintings are displayed in the town's shop windows.

Historic **Sing Yee Alley** is named for a local businessman, and the **Clausen Museum** provides insight into Alaska's fishing industry as well as Petersburg's past. Steamers used to deliver freight from the south, and whalers on their way north would pull into Petersburg to stock up with coal. In the Dirty Thirties, farmers from the Dakota Dustbowl came to try their hand at fishing, quickly learning how to lasso icebergs in Frederick Sound and tow them into port for crushed ice. At **Eagle's Roost Park**, just past the cannery plant along Nordic Drive, the women of Petersburg used to gather (before fishboats carried radios) and watch anxiously for their husbands and sons returning from the fishing grounds. Today this is a good vantage for watching both the marine traffic in Wrangell Narrows and the eagles roosting in the spruce trees.

Another good spot to view Wrangell Narrows is at **Papke's Landing** – located along Mitkof Highway which runs parallel with the Narrows. An old-timer named Herman Papke lived here in a cabin and would phone the Petersburg switchboard when he saw a steamer coming up the narrows so that the townspeople could be ready on the dock to greet it. Other sights along **Mitkof Highway** are the Falls Creek Fish Ladder and Blind Slough, where trumpeter swans spend the winter.

Glaciers of the Stikine Icefield drain into Frederick Sound and nearby **Le Conte Glacier** is the southernmost active tidewater glacier in Alaska. Visible from Petersburg, it has retreated two to three miles since it was first charted in 1887. The glacier stabilized in the early 1980s and in recent years appears to be advancing again. Besides producing ice for Petersburg's fish packing plants, Le Conte played a starring role (alongside Richard Burton) in the 1960 film *Ice Palace*. Looming above Le Conte Glacier is **Devil's Thumb** peak – a majestic sight with its pyramid-like peak jutting through the ice and snow.

Glacier-clad mountains provide a dramatic backdrop for Petersburg.

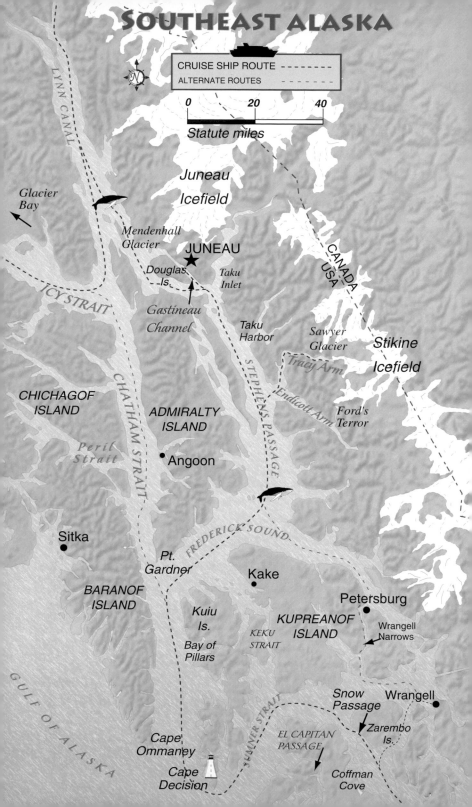

CHAPTER SIX

JUNEAU
& TRACY ARM

T he mainland mountains of southeastern Alaska are dominated by two massive ice fields. Down rugged slopes and steep valleys flow glaciers, some of which reach tidewater. These water-lapped walls of ice hide at the heads of various fjords between Wrangell and Juneau, but there are clues to their whereabouts. Crystalline ice chunks – some as big as bungalows – can be seen floating down various inlets and channels of the Inside Passage.

The Canada/U.S. border runs through the middle of these icefields and is marked by mountains which poke their craggy peaks through thick layers of ice and snow. On the Alaska side of this lonely border, the combined area of these two icefields is more than 2,500 square miles. The southerly Stikine Icefield drains its glacial meltwater into the fjords and inlets of Frederick Sound and Stephens Passage. These two bodies of water join at the top of Kupreanof Island where they form a major marine intersection with 138-mile-long Chatham Strait – the most extensive of Southeast Alaska's channels. Because of Chatham Strait's long fetch and exposure to the Gulf of Alaska, the seas off Point Gardner can be steep and choppy in a winter storm. This is of little concern to the cruise ships that glide past this point throughout the summer, but was of great concern to the native guides who were paddling a canoe across these waters in October 1879.

The man who had chartered their canoe was **John Muir**, the famous and fearless naturalist who was determined to see as many glaciers as possible on his first visit to Alaska. His new friend, the Presbyterian missionary Samuel Hall Young, came along to spread the gospel while the irrepressible Muir preached his own 'glacial gospel' to anyone who cared to listen. The canoe's crew were, in Muir's words: "Toyatte, a grand old Stickeen nobleman, who was made captain, not only because he owned the canoe, but for his skill in woodcraft and seamanship; Kadachan, the son of a Chilcat chief; John, a Stickeen, who acted as interpreter; and Sitka Charley."

Their departure from Wrangell was not a happy scene. There were, as Muir said, a few domestic difficulties. Toyatte's wife wept bitterly for fear he would be killed by his ene-

John Muir

(Above) A humpback whale feeds in Stephens Passage. (Below) A Cruise West captain discusses glacial ice in Tracy Arm.

mies and Kadachan's mother accused Mr. Young of talking her son into going on a dangerous voyage among unfriendly tribes. "If my son comes not back," she said, "on you will be his blood, and you shall pay." Needless to say, no one wished them a bon voyage.

The crew's main concern was crossing Frederick Sound so late in the season and they spoke of it repeatedly as they headed north up **Keku Strait**, a winding, intricate channel used only by small craft. Toyatte was having sleepless nights in anticipation of Frederick Sound but the wind was calm when they crossed this "broad water" and their canoe "tossed like a bubble on the swells coming in from the ocean."

They rounded Point Gardner without incident and proceeded up Chatham Strait along the west side of **Admiralty Island,** which was granted monument status in 1978. Two years later, close to 95 percent of the island's 1,500 square miles became a designated wilderness area called Kotznoowoo – the island's Tlingit name meaning 'Fortress of the Bears.' The Tlingit village of Angoon and some mining interests at the north end of the island lie outside the monument, but the rest of this forested land belongs to the numerous brown bears and Sitka blacktail deer who live here.

The Forest Service manages a bear viewing sanctuary at Pack Creek in the **Seymour Canal**, on the east side of Admiralty Island, and visitor permits control the number of people throughout the latter part of the summer to view the salmon-feeding brown bears from either a spit or a tower farther up the creek. Seymour Canal also supports a high concentration of bald eagles, also attracted to the plentiful salmon.

STEPHENS PASSAGE & TRACY ARM

The cruise ships traverse Stephens Passage on their way to or from Juneau, and a daylight trip along this waterway is filled with natural wonders. Shimmering icefields grace the mainland mountains, floating ice sculptures drift down the wide channel and humpback whales blow puffs of mist into the air as they feed near the water's surface. At night, when the air is still, the thunderclap sound of their tails smacking the water can be heard in distant bays.

Halfway along Stephens Passage lies a dramatic inlet containing two fjords – Endicott Arm and **Tracy Arm**. They each branch into the mainland mountains for a distance of 25 miles before reaching the retreating glaciers that carved them. Muir explored both these arms in the summer of 1880, when they were not yet named or even shown on Captain Vancouver's chart – a copy of which Muir used as a guide. Vancouver's chart did show **Holkham Bay** at the entrance to the two fjords, and Muir refers to this bay as Sum Dum – the Tlingit name for the glacier-covered mountain overlooking it.

A gold mining camp was located beside the large stream into which the Sum Dum Glacier drains. Some prospectors had discovered placer gold in the glacier's moraine and were panning the stream gravels for gold that had been washed downstream from the mountain's orebodies. But Muir was interested not in gold but in the movement of glaciers, while his crew just wanted to save their canoe from being crushed by the ice that clogged Endicott Arm.

(Above) A seal rests on the pack ice in front of Sawyer Glacier in Tracy Arm (below).

They carefully picked their way through the thick ice to the head of the fjord, spotting along the way flocks of wild goats high on the mountain ledges. After 14-1/2 hours of paddling, Muir and his native guides reached the terminus of North Dawes Glacier where they camped for the night on a rock shelf. Next morning they investigated a canyon of water that was later named **Ford's Terror** for a man who, in 1889, rowed through its narrow entrance at slack tide. The water was as still as a pond when he rowed in. Then the tide started running and he was trapped inside for six hours, while his boat was pushed about by swift currents and battered by chunks of ice.

Muir also explored **Tracy Arm**, tracing the fjord to **Sawyer Glacier** at its head. It took a full day to reach the tidewater glacier, and that night Muir pitched his tent on a boulder-covered shore while his guides remained in the canoe to prevent it from being crushed by drifting ice. Whenever a large chunk of ice drops into the water, it sends waves fanning outward until they hit the steep-sided shores of the fjord and rebound. When these rebounding waves collide with the initial waves, they create erratic seas that set the ice pack into motion. Small vessels must be careful not to get too close to a glacier that is actively discharging ice in case they get caught in a churning ice pack. Harbor seals raise their pups on these icepacks, which are relatively safe from predators. When a wave surges through an icepack, seals lounging on the floes will slowly rise with the swell as if nonchalantly enjoying the ride.

Tracy Arm is less than a mile wide throughout most of its length, its cliff walls rising skyward 2,000 feet. Clinging to the schist and granite rock are moss, scrub and spruce trees. Hanging falls plunge down these steep sides into waters a 1,000 feet deep and milky green in color, due to suspended sediments carried in glacial runoff. An advancing tidewa-

Taku Inlet

ter glacier will push a mound of debris in front of its snout. This moraine shoal protects the glacier's terminus from deep tidal water, but when a glacier begins to retreat, it leaves behind a submerged ridge of sediment. The shallow bars at the mouths of Tracy Arm and Endicott Arm are the end moraines of their glaciers, and mariners entering either fjord use navigational markers to safely pilot their vessels through the gap in the bar.

North of Tracy Arm, at the top of Stephens Passage, is another glacier to be reckoned with. Taku Glacier pushed its terminus (end moraine) well into **Taku Inlet** in the late 1800s when the glacier – fed by its substantial snow accumulation area – advanced four miles. Taku is the largest glacier of the massive **Juneau Icefield**, North America's fifth-largest icefield, covering over 1,500 square miles of land. Most of the Juneau Icefield's glaciers have been retreating since the mid-1700s except for Taku. This tidewater glacier is currently stable, neither advancing nor retreating, and its end moraine prevents any calving, which hastens a tidewater glacier's retreat.

An arm of Taku Glacier called Hole in the Wall also flows into Taku Inlet. This tributary was formed in 1940 when part of the glacier jumped the valley wall and found its own way down to the sea. If Taku Glacier resumed pushing its way across Taku Inlet, it could eventually block the Taku River (which drains into the inlet) and form a glacier-dammed lake, but this would take at least a century. The Taku River valley has been considered a potential highway route linking the city of Juneau with the interior road systems of British Columbia. But uncertainty about Taku Glacier's behavior makes construction of a road here a risky proposition.

A cruise ship departing Juneau heads down Gastineau Channel.

JUNEAU

When Captain Vancouver explored the waters around Juneau, he was seeking a northwest passage, only to be turned back time and again by inlets choked with ice. The Little Ice Age was just ending, and even **Gastineau Channel** – upon the shores of which Juneau would eventually be founded – was clogged with ice. A mere century later, the ice had retreated and men now came looking for gold. And they found it.

Gastineau Channel lies along a fault (a fracture in the earth's crust) and when ice covered this entire area it ground away the weakened bedrock of the Gastineau fault. These sediments, both coarse and fine-grained, ended up as surface material covering much of the Juneau-Douglas area. In 1880, on the south shore of Gastineau Channel, gold particles were discovered on the beach. The following year Pierre "French Pete" Eurrusard sold his lode claim to John Treadwell. A mine was built and the Treadwell mining complex eventually became the largest in the world, extracting more than $70 million worth of gold out of the metamorphosed rock.

Meanwhile, on the other side of the Gastineau Channel, two down-and-out prospectors named Richard Harris and Joe Juneau were looking for gold in Silverbow Basin. They had been hired by a German mining engineer named George Pilz of Sitka, who was offering a reward of 100 Hudson's Bay blankets to anyone who could show them where a substantial deposit of gold-bearing ore existed. In October 1880, a Tlingit named Kowee led Juneau and Harris up Gold Creek to Quartz Gulch – so named by Harris when he saw the quartz veins of

A Juneau street mural opposite Marine Park reflects the area's Tlingit history.

this metamorphic rock. They contained more brilliant streaks of gold than he had ever before seen in one gulch.

Claims were quickly staked and within a year the number of prospectors camped in shacks on Gastineau Channel near Gold Creek was large enough to form a small town. The prospectors, who found nuggets as big as beans, eventually cleaned out the placer gold and mining companies took over, tunnelling into mountainsides to extract underground deposits. Between 1881 and World War II, the Juneau Gold Belt yielded 6.7 million ounces of gold and 3.1 million ounces of silver. The Juneau Gold Belt extends south of Juneau to Holkham Bay where the Sumdum Mine eventually produced close to half a million dollars in gold and silver before closing in 1903. The last of three major mines in the Juneau area closed in 1944 but some mining continues today at Green's Creek Mine on the north tip of Admiralty Island.

The streets of downtown Juneau are lined with gold rush era buildings now housing shops and local businesses.

At the turn of the century, Alaska's state capital was moved from Sitka to Juneau. Whaling and fur trading – once thriving industries at Sitka – were on the way out; gold rushes were in. In addition to its lucrative gold mining operations, Juneau was on the steamer route to the gold-rich Klondike in Canada's Yukon territory.

In 1906 the governor's office was transferred from Sitka to Juneau, and six years later the governor's mansion was built. Construction of the capitol building was completed in 1930 and Alaska was granted statehood in 1959. Juneau has remained the capital despite complaints that the city is not accessible by road and that a location near the major population centers of Anchorage and Fairbanks would make more sense. Government jobs – at the city, state and federal levels – provide 50 percent of Juneau's employment, so whenever a 'move-the-capital' campaign surfaces, the resisting residents of Juneau make their stand on the issue perfectly clear.

Juneau, with a population of 31,000, is the largest city in Southeast Alaska, and home port to one of the state's largest fishing fleets with over a thousand boats docking here year round. The mining industry is also showing signs of revival, but tourism is the leading private-sector industry in Juneau. Each summer half a million cruise passengers visit Juneau, a major port of call for ships sailing the Inside Passage. They pull into Gastineau Channel, which is impassable by large vessels at its north end due to the Mendenhall Bar.

Despite Juneau's urbanization, wilderness remains right at the town's doorstep. **Black bears** frequently show up in the downtown area where they risk being hit by motorists. There was a happy ending for one bear who came to town. An orphaned cub, she fended for herself in

Juneau's trolley car heads along Franklin Street to the cruise pier.

the woods near Bartlett Memorial Hospital. Then one day she admitted herself to the hospital by climbing onto a trash receptacle outside the Emergency entrance. "Bartlett" was quickly flown to Bear Country USA in South Dakota, leaving behind one of Juneau's best bear tales.

LOCAL ATTRACTIONS

Juneau is a sprawling city, but the downtown area is fairly compact. Right on the cruise ship dock is a small building where you'll find **Juneau's Visitor Information**. A visitor information kiosk is also situated in waterfront **Marine Park** **1**, and the Seadrome Travel Center, which sells local tours, is opposite the floatplane dock. A trolley car departs regularly from the cruise ship dock on 30-minute, round-trip tours of downtown Juneau. Tickets ($14 each) can be purchased from the conductor, and riders can hop off and on along the route. Many choose to stay aboard for the entire narrated tour, then get off and on at various attractions at their leisure. Also on the waterfront is the **Naa Kahidi Theater**, a clanhouse-style theater where performers dramatize traditional native legends. It is located in the **Cultural Arts Park** **2** adjacent to the Alaska Native Artists Market.

   Not to be missed is the **Mount Roberts Tramway** **3** which whisks visitors 2,000 feet above the harbor to an observatory offering panoramic views of Juneau and the surrounding area. Well-marked trails of various lengths lead from the restaurant/theater complex to alpine meadows and the edge of the snowpack. Be sure to stay on the marked trails, both to preserve the vegetation and to ensure your safety. One hiker on the Sheep Creek Trail

The Mount Roberts tramway provides spectacular views and a chance to hike through alpine meadows.

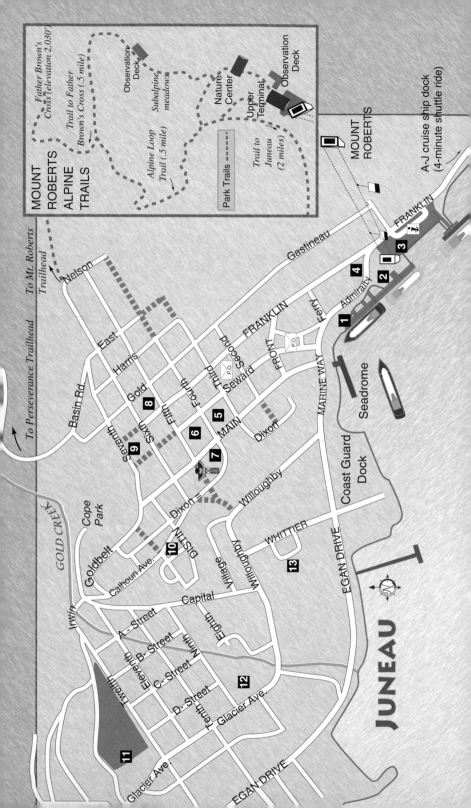

JUNEAU

MOUNT ROBERTS ALPINE TRAILS

Father Brown's Cross (elevation 2,030')

Trail to Father Brown's Cross (.5 mile)

Observation Deck

Subalpine meadows

Alpine Loop Trail (.5 mile)

Nature Center

Upper Terminal

Observation Deck

Trail to Juneau (2 miles)

Park Trails

MOUNT ROBERTS

A-J cruise ship dock (4-minute shuttle ride)

To Mt. Roberts Trailhead

To Perseverance Trailhead

GOLD CREEK

Nelson

East

Harris

Gold

Basin Rd.

Seventh

Sixth

Fifth

Fourth

Third

Second

FRANKLIN

Gastineau

Admiralty

Ferry

FRONT

Seward

MAIN

Dixon

P.O.

P.O.

MARINE WAY

Seadrome

Coast Guard Dock

Cope Park

Goldbelt

Calhoun Ave.

Irwin

Capital

A - Street

B - Street

C - Street

D - Street

Glacier Ave.

Twelfth

Eleventh

Tenth

Ninth

Eighth

Willoughby

WHITTIER

Village

EGAN DRIVE

EGAN DRIVE

Glacier Ave.

DIXON

1 **2** **3** **4** **5** **6** **7** **8** **9** **10** **11** **12** **13**

ventured off the path and headed through thick brush only to lose her footing at the edge of a rock face where she spent a long and windy night clinging to a tree root until rescue workers, at daybreak, found her on the ledge.

From the cruise dock, it's a short walk to the shops on Franklin and Front Streets. These streets are lined with historic buildings such as the restored Alaskan Hotel & Bar which first opened in 1913 and, across the street at 174 S. Franklin, the turreted Alaska Steam Laundry Building, built in 1901. At 202 Front Street you'll find the elegant Valentine Building, built in 1914 by a local jeweller and long-time mayor. In August 2004 a fire erupted in the century-old Endicott Building on the southeast corner of Front and Seward. Fire crews quickly contained the blaze, dousing the roofs of nearby wood buildings built during the Gold Rush era.

The **Red Dog Saloon 4** is one of the first landmark buildings to your left if you're walking up South Franklin Street from the cruise ship dock. This building is not historic but is a popular attraction with its honky-tonk atmosphere and selection of Alaska draft beer.

(Above) Honky tonk piano in the Red Dog Saloon. (Below) St. Nicholas Orthodox Church.

A post office is located on Seward, not far from the main **Juneau Visitor Information Center** which is housed in the **Davis Log Cabin 5**, a replica of Juneau's first public school. One block up, on Fourth, is the **Alaska State Capitol 6**. It was built as the Federal & Territorial Building in 1930 and while it does not have the traditional domed roof of a capitol, it does have an impressive facade of Tokeen marble columns. The ground floor lobby, decorated in blue and gilt, houses an information desk for visitors interested in taking a guided tour. Across from the Capitol, on Main and Fourth, is the **Juneau-Douglas City Museum 7** with displays that capture the city's gold mining era.

On Fifth and Gold, about three blocks from the State Capitol, is the **St. Nicholas Orthodox Church 8**, built in 1894 – nearly 30 years after Russia sold Alaska to the United States.

Governor's Mansion

Although the majority of Russian priests left Alaska at the time of the sale in 1867, they soon regrouped and began returning under the terms of the Treaty of Cession which guaranteed freedom of religion and allowed the Orthodox Church to retain its property and continue its mission in Alaska.

Gold Street leads up to Seventh Avenue where the **Wickersham House** 9 is also open to the public. James Wickersham was a pioneer judge who came to Alaska in 1900. He travelled throughout much of interior Alaska – by sternwheeler in summer and dog sled in winter – and delivered justice to gold mining settlements along the Yukon River.

A respected judge, Wickersham was also a consummate politician who strove tirelessly for Alaska's territorial status, which was granted in 1912. He introduced the first statehood bill four years later and won congressional approval for the establishment of Mount McKinley (now Denali) National Park in 1917. Judge Wickersham spent his final years in Juneau and the house in which he lived is furnished with such items as his 1904 gramophone and his Chickering concert piano, previously owned by the Russian government in Sitka.

Outside the Wickersham House, stairs lead back down to Fifth Avenue, as does Main Street – one block over. A right-hand turn onto Fifth will take you across a pedestrian bypass on your way to the **Governor's Mansion** 10 at the corner of Calhoun and Distin. Built in a colonial style and fronted with white pillars, it's the biggest house in the neighborhood and has a totem pole standing out front. The mansion is the official residence of Alaska's governor and is open for viewing only by advance special request. The one exception is at Christmastime when Juneau residents line up to receive a handshake and cookies from the governor and his wife.

If you follow Calhoun Street up the hillside and across Gold Creek, you'll come to the **Evergreen Cemetery** 11, where the prospectors Joe Juneau and Richard Harris are buried near the east end of the grave-yard. At the other end, off Glacier Avenue, is a monument to their Tlingit guide Kowee. Also buried here are some of those who died in the 1918 sinking of the *Princess Sophia* in Lynn Canal.

A few blocks south along Glacier Avenue, at the corner of Ninth, is the **Federal Building** 🔢. Outside is a bronze sculpture depicting pelicans. It was, according to local tour guides, intended for the Federal Building in Florida but a mix-up in shipping orders sent the eagle sculpture to Florida and the pelicans to Alaska. Florida decided to keep the eagle sculpture, the rationale being that eagles have been sighted there. But, as Juneau residents are fond of saying, these are the only pelicans you're going to see in Alaska.

As for eagle exhibits, you'll find a wonderful one in the **Alaska State Museum** 🔢. To reach this major attraction, carry on down Glacier Avenue, across Gold Creek and proceed along Willoughby to Whittier. Located to the right off Whittier, the State Museum features travelling collections from around the world in addition to its permanent exhibits on wildlife (the highlight of which is an eagle-nesting tree), native culture (the famous Lincoln totem pole is here) and Alaska's Russian heritage.

OUT-OF-TOWN ATTRACTIONS

Mendenhall Glacier is one of Juneau's premier attractions and can be visited by ship-organized tour or on your own by taking the shuttle bus from town ($5 each way). A visit to Mendenhall Glacier is, for many people, their first lesson in how glaciers are formed and behave. The Visitor Center is equipped with books, pamphlets, videotapes and a model display to help explain glacial dynamics. A theater features a videotape on the Mendenhall Glacier and Juneau Icefield, and staff are there to answer any questions.

Outside, nature trails lead to various viewing points. Because Mendenhall Glacier has been retreating about 25 to 30 feet per year since 1750, a half mile of lake water now lies between the Visitor Center and the front of the glacier. The water of Mendenhall Lake reaches 200 feet in depth while the height of the glacier's terminus (snout) is 100 feet above lake level. One-and-a-half miles wide at its

Mendenhall Glacier

snout, Mendenhall Glacier is 12 miles in length and its measured rate of flow is two feet per day. Based on these calculations, the ice at its terminus is about 150 years old.

Another way to view the Mendenhall Glacier is by helicopter. Not only do you get a close look at its icescape of pinnacles and crevasses, you get to walk on its brittle surface. The helicopter will find a safe spot to land and a guide will take you right to the edge of a deep crevasse. Other helicopter tours cover not only the Mendenhall Glacier but some of the other hanging and valley glaciers of the vast Juneau Icefield. Floatplane tours also whisk passengers over the icefield. Below the plane's wings you'll see craggy peaks all but buried in ice and snow, and valleys filled with blue seracs.

One popular flightseeing excursion takes you over the Juneau Icefield to Taku Inlet where you land in front of the historic **Taku Lodge**. Built of logs in 1923, this rustic lodge is well known for its delicious salmon bakes and spectacular vistas, all enjoyed in a peaceful, forested setting.

Dog-sledding excursions are also popular (often selling out) and these entail a helicopter ride to a sled camp on Juneau Icefield where participants are briefed on the basics of the sport before an experienced musher takes you for a spin. Everyone gets to try their hand at mushing and afterwards you can spend a few minutes with the dogs, many of whom have raced in the Iditarod Trail Sled Dog Race. This tour also includes a close look at Juneau Icefield's Taku Glacier and other landmarks during the flight.

Juneau is also the place to go **whalewatching**, with humpbacks feeding throughout the summer in nearby Stephens Passage and Lynn Canal. Wildlife Quest, operated by Allen Marine Tours, offers excursions out of Auke Bay on board specially built vessels equipped with waterjets for speed and maneuverability. The wildlife can be viewed from inside a comfortable cabin with large windows or from the upper deck, while an on-board naturalist provides commentary.

A crevasse on Mendenhall Glacier.

HIKING OPPORTUNITIES

It is possible to hike up Mount Roberts from the trailhead at the end of 6th Avenue, but this two-mile 'Lower Trail,' which ascends 1,600 feet, is uneven and often muddy. The better approach is probably by tram car to the nature center and from there to explore the mountain trails above the tree line.

Other hiking options in Juneau include the Perseverance Trail which starts on Basin Road and winds behind Juneau to a waterfall. Cross over the bridge and follow the trail back towards the waterfront. Walking at a moderate to brisk pace, it takes 30 to 45 minutes to reach the bridge over the falls. You can follow the trail to the eastern part of Juneau and walk back to town, which takes another one to two hours.

The trails at Mendenhall Glacier are also recommended. The Visitor's Center provides a map of the hiking trails. The Loop Trail takes you close to the glacier's snout for outstanding photographs.

(Opposite page) Humpback whale in Lynn Canal; dog-sled camp on the Juneau Icefield. (Below) Hiking trails on Mount Roberts.

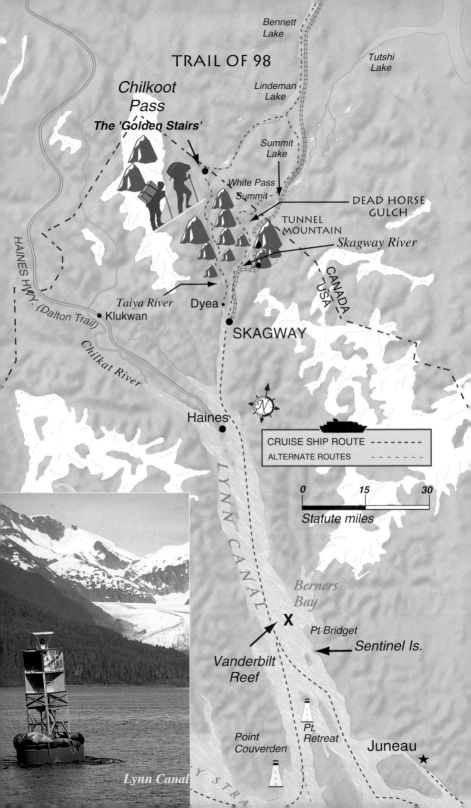

TRAIL OF 98

Bennett Lake

Tutshi Lake

Lindeman Lake

Chilkoot Pass
The 'Golden Stairs'

Summit Lake

White Pass Summit

DEAD HORSE GULCH

TUNNEL MOUNTAIN

Skagway River

CANADA USA

HAINES HWY. (Dalton Trail)

Taiya River
Klukwan   Dyea

Chilkat River

SKAGWAY

Haines

LYNN CANAL

| CRUISE SHIP ROUTE | - - - - - |
| ALTERNATE ROUTES | – – – |

0   15   30
Statute miles

Berners Bay

X   Pt Bridget

Sentinel Is.

Vanderbilt Reef

Point Couverden

Pt. Retreat

Juneau ★

Lynn Canal

STRAIT

CHAPTER SEVEN

SKAGWAY
& THE YUKON

Alaska's colorful gold rush history is an integral part of this northern state's enduring allure, which is why most cruise lines include the port of Skagway, "Gateway to the Klondike", in their Alaska itineraries. Situated at the head of a stunning fjord flanked by snowcapped mountains, the small town of Skagway springs to life each summer with the arrival of the cruise ships. Compact and easy to explore on foot, Skagway came into existence when gold fever swept across North America in the summer of 1897 with the news that prospectors had struck it rich in the Klondike. Skagway was transformed from a single homestead to a bustling port upon the arrival of its first steamship filled with prospectors heading to Canada's Yukon.

Saloons and brothels were quickly constructed and a boom town was born. Soapy Smith and his gang of con men soon controlled the town's activities and Superintendent Sam Steele of the Northwest Mounted Police called it "the roughest place in the world . . little better than hell on earth." Today the streets of Skagway are strolled by law-abiding cruise passengers reliving the town's gold rush days. Many of the original buildings still stand and several of these have been painstakingly restored by the National Park Service. Not only is Skagway a port of great historic interest, its natural setting at the head of Lynn Canal makes it one of the most scenic.

Skagway's Broadway Street is lined with gold rush buildings.

The future site of Skagway before the Klondike Gold Rush.

THE KLONDIKE GOLD RUSH

Captain Vancouver must have been particularly homesick while surveying **Lynn Canal**. Not only did he name Point Couverden at its western entrance for his ancestral home in the Netherlands, he also named Berners Bay and Point Bridget for his mother – Bridget Berners. The inlet itself is named for Vancouver's birthplace of King's Lynn in Norfolk, England. This nostalgic naming of landmarks took place in the summer of 1794, during Vancouver's third and last season on this coast. His health was failing and he no longer joined his officers in the open boats as they ventured up the last few winding channels and twisting fjords still unexplored in their search for an inland waterway.

Homesick as Vancouver and his men no doubt were by this point in their lengthy voyage, the Tlingits who lived here were quite at home. Their main village of **Klukwan** was located at the mouth of the **Chilkat River** near the head of Lynn Canal. Not only was the Chilkat River a fine salmon stream, its valley was a trade route to the interior, where the vast Athabascan region extended across much of the continent to Hudson Bay in northern Canada.

When explorers of Britain's Hudson's Bay Company (HBC) began building forts on the western edges of Athabascan territory, they came face to face with Tlingit tribes. Travelling upriver from their coastal villages, the Tlingits were not pleased to encounter white men taking possession of their fur trade territory. Robert Campbell, a rugged Scotsman hired by the HBC to explore the rivers flowing westward, had several close encounters with the Tlingits, including an 1852 attack by the Chilkats of Lynn Canal on a fort he and his men had built at the junction of the Pelly and Yukon Rivers. Campbell barely survived the attack, but the fort was not so lucky. Abandoned by Campbell and his handful of men, it was quickly demolished by the Chilkats for its nails and ironwork.

Skagway as it looks today, a full century after its boomtown days.

As the fur trade began running out of steam, gold prospectors started trickling into the Yukon area. **Forty Mile** became the largest settlement in the Yukon when gold was discovered in nearby tributaries in 1886. Miners from Alaska and the Yukon converged on Forty Mile, which was the main supply base for the area. The trickle of prospectors was now a steady flow, but the flood was yet to come.

The miners' law of those times is reflected in a notice that was posted downriver at **Circle City**, Alaska : *TO WHOM IT MAY CONCERN: At a general meeting of miners held in Circle City it was the unanimous verdict that all thieving and stealing shall be punished by whipping at the post and banishment from the country, the severity of the whipping and the guilt of the accused to be determined by the jury.*

Frontier justice worked well and peace generally prevailed. Cabins were left unlocked and stocked with firewood. Failure to replace this fuel was a major offense, for the next visitor might arrive so cold and exhausted that only an instant fire could save his life. Miners' meetings were usually held in saloons and if a jail was needed at the conclusion of a hearing, one was quickly constructed. At Circle City, a notice on the jail's door stated that "All prisoners must report by 9 o'clock p.m., or they will be locked out for the night." When Judge James Wickersham arrived in the American part of the Yukon River valley and introduced himself to one old sourdough as "the district judge of the Territory of Alaska" the response was "Oh, the hell you are!"

While the boom towns of Forty Mile and Circle City attracted men and women in search of gold, a different sort of white man was roaming the Yukon River area. His name was **George Washington Carmack.** Born in California, he had witnessed gold fever as a teenager when his father joined California's stampede of 1849. When Carmack arrived in Alaska as a dishwasher on a Juneau-bound steamer, he did not pursue the riches of gold but instead adopted the native way of life.

GOLDRUSH COUNTRY

Dyea to Chilkoot Pass – 16 miles
Dyea to Yukon R. Headwaters – 33 miles
Skagway to Whitehorse – 112 miles

Circle City

Fairbanks

Arctic Circle

Alaska / Yukon

DEMPSTER HWY.

Eagle

Tombstone
Territorial
Park

Blackstone R.

Dawson
City

N. Klondike

Klondike R.

Tok

x

Discovery Claim

Bonanza Creek

Eldorado Creek

KLONDIKE
HWY.

ALASKA

Yukon River

Fort Selkirk

YUKON

Carmacks

ALASKA HWY.

Burwash
Landing

ST. ELIAS MOUNTAINS

Kluane Lake

TERRITORY

MT. LOGAN
∧

Kluane
National
Park

Haines
Junction

1

Whitehorse ★

Trail of '98

Carcross

Bennett Lake

Chilkoot
Pass

White Pass

Watson
Lake

Dyea

Skagway ★

BRITISH COLUMBIA

N

0   100   200

Statute miles

Juneau ★

The Yukon prospectors called him Siwash George. He married a native woman and lived off the land with her people. His closest companions were his brother-in-law, **Skookum Jim**, and another native called **Tagish Charlie**. Jim was a large and powerful man, skilled at hunting and trapping, while Charlie was of smaller stature but gracefully at ease in the wilderness.

In July of 1896, Carmack headed upstream from Forty Mile to the **Klondike River** to do some salmon fishing. There he was joined by Jim, Charlie and his wife Kate. The salmon run was poor, so the men decided to cut timber and sell it to the sawmill at Forty Mile. Jim headed up the Klondike to check out its timber, then turned off at a brook named **Rabbit Creek** which he followed until he found a good stand of spruce. He noticed flecks of gold in the stream and reported this to the others back at camp, but the matter was quickly forgotten.

A few weeks later, on their return trip, they ran out of dried salmon and stopped to hunt. Jim set off with his .44 Winchester and shot a moose which he butchered and cooked beside Rabbit Creek while awaiting the other two men. At one point he knelt beside the creek to take a drink of water and there in the creek bed's gravel was more raw gold than he had ever before seen.

When the other two arrived and Jim told them about his find, their reaction was in keeping with the occasion. Carmack, staring down at the glistening gold, first rubbed his eyes then reached down and picked

(Above) A cairn marks the spot on Bonanza Creek where gold was found in 1896, triggering the Klondike Gold Rush. (Below) William Moore built Skagway's first cabin weeks before stampeders began arriving in July 1897.

up a dime-sized nugget which he put between his teeth and bit on. Charlie grabbed a pan and shovel and almost fell into the creek in his excitement. Carmack grabbed the shovel from Charlie and dug into the loose bedrock. He later described the raw gold as "laying thick between the flaky slabs, like cheese sandwiches." With a full pan of gold and gravel, Carmack set it on the ground and the three men danced around it, performing a combination of "Scottish hornpipe, Indian fox trot, syncopated Irish jig and a sort of a Siwash Hula-Hula."

The next morning Carmack blazed with an axe this message on a spruce tree: *TO WHOM IT MAY CONCERN: I do, this day, locate and claim, by right of discovery, five hundred feet, running up stream from this notice. Located this 17th day of August, 1896.*

G. W. Carmack

Under Canadian mining law, a prospector was allowed only one 500-foot claim per creek, except for the man recording the discovery who could stake two claims. All subsequent claims were then numbered in relation to the discovery claim. At Rabbit Creek – promptly renamed **Bonanza Creek** by Carmack – the discovery claim was shared by Carmack and Jim, but registered in the former's name. Carmack also claimed Number One Below (downstream) while Jim claimed Number One Above (upstream) and Charlie claimed Number Two Below.

When Carmack returned to Forty Mile to register his claim at the mining recorder's office, he decided to stop first at Bill McPhee's saloon. He ordered a couple of drinks at the bar – to calm himself down – then turned to face the crowded, smoky room full of miners. "Boys," he said, "I've got some good news to tell you. There's a big strike up

An Alaska Steamship, loaded with passengers bound for the Klondike, heads up Lynn Canal.

the river." This announcement fell on skeptical ears, for Carmack had a reputation for telling tall tales. In the words of some, he was "the all-firedest liar of the Yukon." But when he held up the gold he had just scooped from Bonanza Creek, everyone believed their eyes – if not their ears. Within a month of Carmack's discovery, 200 claims were staked on the Bonanza and its tributaries. But no one knew which claims would produce gold and which ones were "skunks." Luck determined whether a man struck it rich. A **cheechako** (newcomer) was as likely to hit pay dirt as a **sourdough** (seasoned miner). All each man could do was start working his claim and hope for the best.

Throughout the winter of 1896-97, men of varied backgrounds and nationalities dug into the Klondike's creek beds with picks and shovels. Malnourished and dirty, many suffered from scurvy. They slept in ramshackle huts where lice thrived in their unwashed bedding. But all were driven by gold fever as they scraped away the surface muck and burned fires to thaw the frozen ground to remove gravel covering the bedrock. Upon hitting bedrock, the pay gravel was removed by tunnelling into the side of the creek bank (drifting) and hauling the gravel out with a hand-turned windlass. This was done in winter, when permafrost eliminated the need to shore the shafts and drifts with timbers. When warmer weather arrived and the ground softened, cave-ins became a problem.

This dangerous and backbreaking work continued until spring when meltwater was used for sluicing the piles of bedrock gravel. A sluice is a series of inclined boxes with riffles on the bottom. As the water washed the gravel away, the pieces of gold would fall to the bottom of the boxes and remain trapped there by the riffles.

When the prospectors on Bonanza Creek and its tributaries finished

During the winter of 1897-1898, thousands of stampeders ascended the Chilkoot Trail's Golden Stairs on their way to the Klondike.

Visitors to Skagway relive the excitement of the Klondike gold rush when they board the White Pass and Yukon Railroad.

sluicing their claims in the early summer of 1897, many were rich men. With their moosehide pokes and pickle jars filled with gold, they boarded two stern-wheelers in Dawson and headed down the Yukon to the old Russian port of St. Michael. There they transferred onto two steamships – the *Excelsior* bound for San Francisco and the *Portland* bound for Seattle.

The *Excelsior* reached San Francisco two-and-a-half days before the *Portland* docked in Seattle, where the news had spread and a throng of people was waiting to greet the miners as they filed off the ship with their bags and boxes of gold. People wanted to see, hear and touch these stoop-shouldered, weather-beaten men who had struck it rich in the Klondike.

Gold fever swept the continent and the world. Men and women rushed to the Klondike, stopping at San Francisco, Seattle, Victoria or Vancouver to outfit themselves before heading north. Those who could afford the passage took a steamer to St. Michael, then a paddlewheeler up the Yukon. Others ascended the Stikine and Alsek Rivers or hiked from Edmonton, Alberta through boggy, mosquito-infested wilderness. The majority, however, headed up Lynn Canal to **Skagway**.

In the early summer of 1897, only one family lived in Skagway. William Moore, a former riverboat captain and prospector, had anticipated a gold rush to the Yukon and constructed a cabin and wharf here 10 years earlier. But when the first shipload of prospectors arrived at the 'Mooresville' wharf on July 26, 1897, the surveyors who spilled off the steamer ignored Moore's homesteading claim and quickly laid out a new town which they called Skaguay. The spelling of this Tlingit name (its meaning open to interpretation) was changed to Skagway when a post office was established. Moore, who owned a sawmill and warehouse in addition to the wharf, prospered.

FACING UP TO THE CHILKOOT

Three miles away, at the mouth of the Taiya River, was a small trading post and village of about 250 Chilkoot natives. Called **Dyea**, it competed with Skagway for the gold rush trade. Most prospectors landed at Skagway but set off for the goldfields from Dyea via the 33-mile **Chilkoot Trail** – the 'poor man's route' which included a quarter-mile vertical ascent of 1,000 feet up the 'Golden Stairs' cut into the ice. The **White Pass**, which starts at Skagway, was used by those who had could afford pack horses. This route was 10 miles longer than the Chilkoot but not as steep. Nonetheless, the route's boulders, rocks and muskeg earned it the name Dead Horse Trail during the winter of 1897-98. A stampeder who travelled both trails would later say it didn't matter which one you took, "you'd wished you had taken the other."

Overnight stops (tent cities) dotted the Chilkoot Trail, with stampeders moving their goods in five-mile relays between caches. It could take 20 trips back and forth to cover each leg of the journey. In winter, sledges made hauling supplies a bit easier. It's estimated that 30,000 stampeders crossed the Chilkoot by these two routes, now called the **'Trail of '98.'**

The White Pass trail links up with the Chilkoot Trail at the foot of Lake Lindeman which flows via a narrow rocky stream into **Lake Bennett**, headwaters of the Yukon River. At the **Summit**, the stampeders crossed into Canadian territory. Those without a year's supply of food were turned back by the Mounties.

The majority of stampeders reached lakes Lindeman and Bennett in the spring of 1898 where they whipsawed trees into planks to build boats and rafts while waiting for the ice to melt. When the ice on Lake Bennett broke up on May 29, a flotilla of stampeders set sail down the hazardous Yukon River in their makeshift vessels. A number of these unseaworthy craft capsized and stampeders drowned in the cold churn-

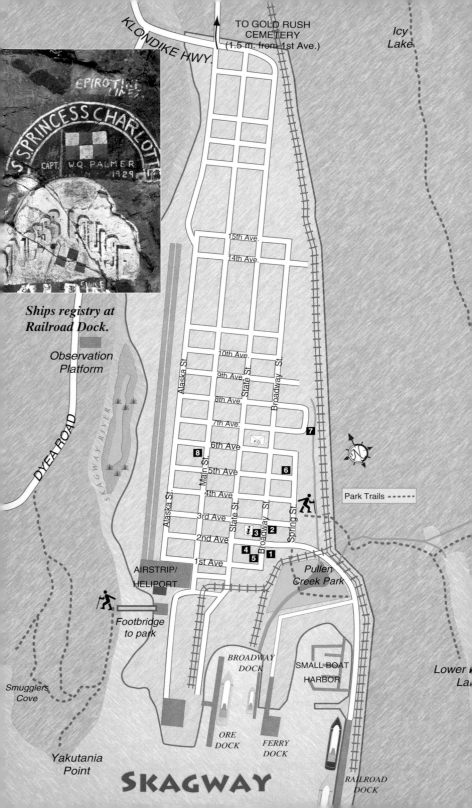

KLONDIKE HWY.

TO GOLD RUSH
CEMETERY
(1.5 m. from 1st Ave.)

*Icy
Lake*

*Ships registry at
Railroad Dock.*

*Observation
Platform*

DYEA ROAD

SKAGWAY RIVER

15th Ave.

14th Ave.

10th Ave.

9th Ave.

8th Ave.

7th Ave.

6th Ave.

5th Ave.

4th Ave.

3rd Ave.

2nd Ave.

1st Ave.

Alaska St.

Main St.

State St.

Broadway St.

Spring St.

State St.

Broadway St.

Alaska St.

P.O.

7

8

6

i

3

2

4

5

1

Park Trails ------

AIRSTRIP/
HELIPORT

*Pullen
Creek Park*

Footbridge
to park

*BROADWAY
DOCK*

SMALL BOAT
HARBOR

*Lower
La*

*Smugglers
Cove*

*ORE
DOCK*

*FERRY
DOCK*

*Yakutania
Point*

SKAGWAY

*RAILROAD
DOCK*

ing waters of **Miles Canyon** and **White Horse Rapids**. The flotilla pressed on, traversing 500 miles of swift-flowing river to arrive, in mid-June, at Dawson City. They had reached the Klondike.

LOCAL ATTRACTIONS

A visitor to Skagway will have no trouble reliving the excitement of the Klondike Gold Rush. Each summer, more than 300,000 people visit this town, which has a year-round population of about 840. Some days, four or five cruise ships are in port at the same time. A short walking tour is a must in Skagway and, with an average annual precipitation of less than 29 inches, a typical summer day here is warm and sunny – perfect for strolling the town's historic streets.

Near the cruise ship docks, at the foot of Broadway, is the **National Historical Park Visitor Center 1** housed inside the old **White Pass and Yukon Route Railroad Depot**, built in 1898 and restored by the National Park Service. Here you'll find exhibits, presentations and written information on the town's historic buildings. Ranger-led walking tours of Skagway Historic District are held throughout the day.

One block up from the Visitor Center is the **Mascot Saloon 2**, built in 1905 and restored for viewing by the National Park Service which has recreated a lifelike bar scene with mannequins dressed as turn-of-the-century locals.

Historic buildings line Broadway, many of them housing private businesses, and across the street from the Mascot Saloon is the Golden North Hotel. Built in 1898, its lobby is decorated with antique fixtures and photographs. Two doors down is the **Arctic Brotherhood Hall 3**, its facade covered

(Below) National Park's Visitor Center and interior of its refurbished Mascot Saloon (right).

with 20,000 driftwood sticks collected and nailed to the front of this 1899 building by an early lodge member. This restored building now houses a **Visitor Information Center**, operated by the Skagway Convention & Visitors Bureau. Ask for a copy of their Walking Tour map. A few doors down from the Visitor Information Center, at the corner of Second and Broadway, is the Red Onion Saloon. One of Skagway's best-known watering holes, it was a dining spot for Robin Williams and fellow cast members when *The Big White* was filmed in Skagway in May 2004.

On the south side of Second Avenue stands Jeff Smith's Parlor **4**, the saloon owned by Skagway's infamous Jefferson Randolph 'Soapy' Smith, who led a gang of criminals that controlled the town. Smith was killed in a shoot-out with surveyor Frank Reid, who died later of his gunshot wounds. On the waterfront, at the foot of State Street, is a marker showing where Reid gunned down Soapy Smith on the evening of July 8, 1898. At the time, Reid and others were guarding the entrance to the Juneau Co. wharf where a mass meeting was being held to organize the townspeople against Soapy Smith and his gang.

Back on Broadway, opposite the Park Headquarters, is the former residence of Martin Itjen **5**. A prominent local businessman, Itjen established the Skagway Street Car company in 1923 when U.S. President Harding came for a visit and was charged 25 cents for a tour in Itjen's car. Soon Itjen was offering tours to "All Points of Interest", and these entertaining excursions in vintage streetcars are still a popular tourist attraction.

Other places of interest include the **Moore Cabin 6**, built by William Moore and his son in 1887; and **Skagway City Hall 7**, built

The Skagway Street Car company has been offering local tours since 1923.

of stone in 1899 by the Methodist Church and now housing the **Trail of '98 Museum**. A number of Skagway's old homes are also featured on the Walking Tour map, as is the **Blanchard Garden** 🔳. Every August the town holds a Gold Rush Garden Club contest.

HIKING OPPORTUNITIES

Skagway's majestic scenery can be enjoyed along several hiking trails within easy walking distance of the port. These range in length and include an easy, one- to two-hour roundtrip hike to Yakutania Point on the waterfront. Another pleasant hike (two to three hours round-trip) is to Lower Dewey Lake. Although the trail starts out steep, the hike around the lake is well worth the brief workout. The mile-and-a-half walk to the Gold Rush Cemetery outside town takes about half an hour and can be a little dusty for the last stretch. However, the walk beyond the cemetery to beautiful Reid Falls is a rewarding sight. There are several other hiking trails in the Skagway area, and a detailed trail map is available at the National Park Service office.

(Above) Golden North Hotel.
(Below) Soapy Smith's gravestone.

Skagway's most famous trail is the Chilkoot, its entire length taking three to five days to hike. Cruise passengers can hike the first two miles on an organized shore excursion that includes a raft ride back to the trailhead in Dyea. Another way to view the Chilkoot Trail and spectacular glacier-covered mountains is by helicopter on a flightseeing excursion.

The array of shore excursions offered in Skagway is extensive, including dog mushing, kayaking, canoeing, cycling and rock climbing.

One of the most popular is the train ride aboard vintage cars of the **White Pass & Yukon Route** (WP&YR) rail line for a scenic trip along the Trail of '98. Construction of this mountain-pass railroad was a massive challenge. Workers, suspended by ropes, chipped and blasted their way through the barriers of rock. Accidents claimed lives and gold

(Above) Rock climbing near Skagway.
(Left) Cycling the Klondike Highway.

fever regularly swept through the work gangs, depleting their numbers.

Against tough odds, the narrow-gauge railroad was completed in the summer of 1900 – after the big rush to the Klondike was over. The rail line transformed Skagway into a shipping port and during World War II thousands of army troops landed here during construction of the Alaska Highway. Shortly after the **Klondike Highway** (from Skagway to Whitehorse) was completed in 1978, the railroad was closed. However it was reopened in 1988 to provide summer passenger service.

The trip is a fascinating blend of dramatic scenery and history. As the train rolls out of Skagway, it passes the **Gold Rush Cemetery** – resting place of Soapy Smith and Frank Reid – then follows the river valley past glacier-fed waterfalls and overhanging rock ledges. The train slowly climbs from sea level to 2,865 feet at the Summit. Along the way, passengers get a close look at the **Glacier Gorge** chasm as the train steams across the abyss and into **Tunnel Mountain**. The ascent continues past **Inspiration Point** (with its mountaintop view of Lynn Canal) and **Dead Horse Gulch** (where 3,000 pack animals died of exhaustion from carrying heavy loads up the steep climb).

Another tunnel – Steel Bridge – is followed by a cliffside glimpse of the famous Trail of '98. Then it's over the **White Pass Summit**, where

The White Pass and Yukon Railroad excursion takes passengers right to Summit Lake in British Columbia.

only those stampeders with a ton of supplies (enough for one winter) were waved on by the Mounties into Canada. This is the turn-around point for passengers taking the three-and-a-half hour rail trip, but the rail line continues to Whitehorse, Yukon Territory. Stops along the way include Fraser Station in British Columbia, where Canadian customs is cleared, and **Carcross** – originally called Caribou Crossing – at the top of Lake Bennett where it flows into the Yukon River. The three natives with George Carmack when they discovered gold on Bonanza Creek – Skookum Jim, Tagish Charlie and George's wife Kate – are buried in the Carcross cemetery. Full-day shore excursions out of Skagway travel as far as Carcross before returning to the ship.

THE YUKON

Whitehorse, the capital of Canada's Yukon Territory, is where Skagway residents do most of their shopping, while Whitehorse residents keep their recreational boats moored at the marina in Skagway. Whitehorse takes its name from the nearby Whitehorse Falls. When stampeders travelled this treacherous section of the Yukon River, they said the frothy white water looked like a horse's mane. To avoid the rapids spilling from Miles Canyon, stampeders hauled their goods on horse-drawn trams past this section of river. The rapids were eliminated in 1958 with construction of a hydroelectric dam, followed a year later with a fish ladder – billed as the world's longest wooden one – which allows migrating salmon to bypass the

dam. Visitors can enjoy the riverside foot trails and suspension bridge now spanning Miles Canyon.

Attractions in Whitehorse include the *S.S. Klondike*, largest stern-wheeler to ply the Yukon River, and the MacBride Museum, a complex of log buildings which includes the first cabin built by Sam McGee – a prospector and friend of Robert Service who was immortalized in Service's famous poem *The Cremation of Sam McGee*. McGee had given permission to Service to use his name, but when he found people were laughing at his namesake, he got even with Service by taking him on a fishing trip near the worst part of Whitehorse Falls before finally putting his terrified passenger ashore.

Whitehorse, home to more than two-thirds of the Yukon's total population of 30,000, is a major stop along the **Alaska Highway**. This famous stretch of highway was built by the U.S. Army Corps of Engineers during World War II, in a race against time and sub-arctic conditions, after Japan bombed Pearl Harbor. With America's west coast shipping lanes vulnerable to Japanese attack, the highway was deemed crucial for securing Alaska and providing a vital supply link. The situation became crucial when Japanese troops invaded the Aleutian Islands in June 1942. American soldiers battled freezing temperatures and rugged terrain to lay a highway across 1,520 miles of mountains and muskeg between Dawson Creek (Mile 0) in northern British Columbia, and Fairbanks, Alaska. Construction began on March 9, 1942, with work crews bulldozing from either end. They met at Soldiers' Summit, near Kluane Lake in the Yukon. A pilot road was opened on November 20 and the following year a permanent road was completed and named the Alcan Military Highway. After the war, the highway was turned over to civilian contractors, regraded, widened and opened to unrestricted travel. Today most of the highway is asphalt-surfaced, but improvements and repairs are ongoing.

A sightseeing boat tours Miles Canyon.

Points of interest long the Alaska Highway, east of Whitehorse, include Liard Hotsprings, where army workers soaked their tired muscles in 1942, and nearby Watson Lake with its famous wall of sign boards. The first signpost was carved by a homesick G.I. in 1942, and hundreds of signs, license plates and other paraphernalia now line the roadside. The Alaska Highway also traces the eastern boundary of **Kluane National Park**.

Kluane is a native name for 'place of many fish,' and this remote wilderness park is also a place of many mountains, containing the most extensive non-polar icefields in the world. The Saint Elias Mountains run through the park where **Mount Logan**, Canada's highest peak at 19,850 feet, stands in ice a mile deep. Winter storms off the Gulf of Alaska bring snowfall so heavy, up to 10 feet can fall in 24 hours. When this happens, "You have to shovel all day long," according to one park warden, "or else you simply get buried."

The Visitor Centre at Haines Junction provides exhibits on the park's spectacular scenery, much of it hidden behind a front range of mountains. The Kluane Range is visible from the Alaska Highway, its peaks including **Mount Kennedy**, named for President John F. Kennedy. In March 1965, his brother Robert, accompanied by seven experienced mountaineers, was the first to ascend this peak. The more distant Icefield Range lies west of the Kluane Range and contains Mount Logan, a massif measuring 100 miles around its base and nearly 10 square miles at its triple-peaked summit, making it one of the largest physical landforms on Earth. It was first climbed by a party of mountaineers in 1925 but remained unchallenged again until 1950. Mount Logan, which takes about 30 days to climb, remains a daunting challenge for serious climbers because of its harsh weather. For most visitors, a flightseeing tour is the best way to view Kluane's magnificent icefields. At the base of these ice-covered slopes, the glaciers are slowly retreating, their melting ice revealing a host of ancient artifacts. The

The Klondike (mid-left) and Yukon Rivers meet at Dawson City.

discovered shaft of a hunting dart dates back 9,000 years, to when herds of caribou, which would gather on the snouts of glaciers to escape swarms of summer mosquitoes, were hunted by humans with bows and arrows. Glacial ice preserves organic material, such as wood, antler, bone, leather and sinew, and the items being surrendered by the retreating glaciers are providing archeologists with direct radio-carbon dating. The ice also preserves caribou dung, massive piles of which have been exposed during the summertime melt.

North of Kluane is the Yukon's Klondike region where **Dawson City** was once the most famous boomtown in North America. The North Klondike Highway, a detour off the Alaska Highway near Whitehorse, traces the Yukon River valley to Dawson City, which sprang to life in the summer of 1897. The Northwest Mounted Police, anticipating an onslaught of stampeders, built a fort here that first summer but in their haste they did a few things wrong. When clearing the land, they scraped away the moss covering the permafrost. This allowed the sun to melt the topsoil and the fort's foundations soon settled into a knee-deep morass. Also, green logs were used in construction and they began to shrink and warp. As buildings fell apart, the Mounties were kept busy reconstructing their fort when they weren't enforcing law and order among Dawson's 30,000 new residents.

Among these new arrivals was a young American prospector named **Jack London**. He lived only briefly in the Yukon but turned his experiences into masterful stories, including his famous novels *The Call of the Wild* (a bestseller in 1903) and *White Fang* (published in 1906). His cabin, built on Henderson Creek in 1899, has been moved to Dawson City and reconstructed to house the Jack London Interpretation Centre. It stands on Author's Avenue, as does the childhood home of **Pierre Berton**, Canada's popular historian who wrote several best-

selling books about the Klondike Gold Rush. The Yukon's most famous poet was the British-born **Robert Service** who immigrated to Canada in 1894. He worked for a bank in Victoria and in other branches in British Columbia before being stationed at Dawson City. Service published his first collection of poems in 1907. Called *Songs of a Sourdough* (republished in 1916 as *The Spell of the Yukon*), this first volume included 'The Shooting of Dan McGrew.' Service, profoundly influenced by Rudyard Kipling, became known as 'The Canadian Kipling' and his restored cabin on Author's Avenue is a major visitor attraction run by

Parks Canada, where his poetry is recited twice daily throughout the summer. Two dozen heritage buildings in Dawson City are maintained by Parks Canada as visitor attractions, including a reconstruction of the 1899 Palace Grand Theatre. Another local attraction is **Diamond Tooth Gerties Gambling Hall,** operated by the Klondike Visitors Association, where the roulette wheels spin and blackjack is played in a gold rush atmosphere of honky-tonk music and can-can dancing.

The **Dempster Highway** stretches north of Dawson City across the Arctic Circle to Inuvik in the Northwest Territories. Completed in 1978, this unpaved two-lane highway sits atop a gravel berm four to eight feet thick, designed to insulate the permafrost and prevent it from melting, which would cause the ground to soften and the road to sink. The Porcupine herd of caribou roam this vast territory and about half of the herd (which numbers 120,000 in total) crosses the Dempster Highway during spring and fall migrations. By August, the green tundra vegetation becomes an explosion of reds and golds, blanketing entire valleys before yielding to winter frosts. At its south end, the highway runs through **Tombstone Territorial Park**, where ridgetop trails provide sweeping views of broad valley floors and black granite peaks.

Established in 1999, Tombstone protects some 1,400 square miles of sub-arctic landscapes in the south Ogilvie Mountains. Tombstone Mountain is the best-known landform in the park, which contains a variety of seldom-seen permafrost landforms such as pingos (small hills) and patterned ground. The Tr'ondek Hwech'in peoples have inhabited this area for at least 8,000 years. Boreal forests in the south provided shelter and firewood, and chert, a rock used to make stone tools, was available at Tombstone Mountain. Fishing was good in the Blackstone River, while the open tundra provided good visibility for hunting the

Beautiful landforms are found in Tombstone Territorial Park.

Eight years before the sinking of Princess Sophia, the Princess May grounded on nearby Sentinel Island but refloated with little damage.

region's large mammals – bear, moose, caribou and Dall sheep. Many species of birds – both boreal and arctic tundra – nest within the park

THE SOPHIA TRAGEDY

When the great gold rush died down in the Klondike, the prospectors gradually sold their claims to mining companies which continued mining the area's pay gravels with machinery. Each fall most of the miners, riverboat crew and others who worked in the Yukon would head south for the winter. On October 23, 1918, a full boatload of people coming out of the Klondike for the winter boarded the ill-fated *Princess Sophia* (a CPR steamship) in Skagway.

Carrying 343 passengers and crew, the *Sophia* was heading down Lynn Canal in a snowstorm when, two hours past midnight, she grounded on **Vanderbilt Reef**. Her distress calls were answered by a variety of smaller vessels which stood by at dawn in choppy seas, waiting for the *Sophia* to transfer her passengers to the waiting vessels. But the seas were too rough to safely launch the small boats and the *Sophia*'s captain decided the passengers would be safer on board the stranded ship. The next night, shrieking winds pushed the *Sophia* off Vanderbilt Reef and she plunged into the icy water. All 343 people on board drowned in the stormy seas, including Walter Harper – the first man to set foot on Mt. McKinley's summit.

HAINES (POP. 1,700)

While the Klondike gold rush was creating the boom towns of Dawson City and Skagway, another entrepreneur named **Jack Dalton** was trying to get a piece of the stampede action in Haines – 15 miles south of Skagway on the west side of Lynn Canal.

Haines had been founded by the Presbyterian missionary Samuel Hall Young in 1880. He was given land for building a mission by the Chilkat natives whom he visited with John Muir in 1879. So impressed were the Chilkat chiefs with Muir's brilliant oratory, they wanted him to run the mission but had to settle for Mr. Young, who named it after Mrs. F. E. Haines – chief fund-raiser for the mission.

When Jack Dalton arrived at Haines, several canneries had been built and a wagon road wound its way from nearby Pyramid Harbor to the Yukon River, following roughly the route of today's Haines highway. He built a few posts along this trail, called it the Dalton Trail, and charged stampeders $2 per head of cattle and $2.50 per horse. Historic stops on the **Dalton Trail** include Glacier Camp – from which 26 glaciers can be seen – and the abandoned native village of Nasketahin, where traditional spirit houses stand in the local graveyard.

The Chilkat tribe of Tlingits display their famous Chilkat blankets and other craftsmanship at the **Center for the Arts** on the Fort Seward grounds. **Fort Seward** was built in 1903 during a border dispute with Canada. This U.S. army post was closed in 1946, then bought by a group of World War II vets who turned the white frame buildings and lawned grounds into private residences and commercial enterprises.

The **Sheldon Museum and Cultural Center**, housed in the original Presbyterian mission, is located at the corner of Main and Front streets.

Northwest of Haines, several thousand bald eagles gather each fall along a five-mile stretch of the Chilkat River to feed on chum salmon. The **Alaska Chilkat Bald Eagle Preserve** protects a 48,000-acre section of this river valley. The eagles can be seen from the Haines Highway, which runs parallel to the river, and the highest concentration of eagles occurs between Mileposts 17 and 22 from Haines.

Passenger ferries run by Chilkat Cruises make regular 35-minute trips between Haines and Skagway.

The town of Haines is dwarfed by the Chilkat Mountains. The large white frame buildings in the background are part of Fort Seward.

Statute miles
0   15   30

BRITISH COLUMBIA
ALASKA

Skagway

N

Grand Pacific
Glacier

Marjerie
Glacier

Muir
Glacier

Takhinsha Mtns

LYNN CANAL

Berners
Bay

Johns Hopkins
Inlet

Mt.
Fairweather

Fairweather Range

GLACIER
BAY

Lituya
Bay

La Perouse
Glacier

Brady
Glacier

Bartlett
Cove

Gustavus

JUNE

Taylor
Bay

Cape
Spencer

CROSS SOUND

Pt. Aldophus

ICY STRAIT

To Hubbard
Glacier

Elfin
Cove

Icy Strait
Point

Hoonah

ADM
ISL

To Sitka

CHICHAGOF
ISLAND

CHATHAM STRAIT

CRUISE SHIP ROUTE - - - - - -
ALTERNATE ROUTES - - - - - -

Peril
Strait

CHAPTER EIGHT

GLACIER BAY

When John Muir discovered Glacier Bay in 1879, it was – and still is – in the process of creation. Glaciers that had filled the entire bay a mere century before Muir's first visit, were now staging a drastic retreat, leaving behind a freshly exposed landscape of newborn islands and inlets.

Neither Muir nor his travelling companions fully believed Sitka Charley when he first described Glacier Bay – at least not the part about the absence of trees. After all, Charley hadn't visited this bay of 'ice mountains' since he was a boy on a seal hunt with his father, and none of them had ever seen a woodless shoreline in this land of rainforests. Nonetheless, they turned up Icy Strait, as directed by young Charley, to see this mysterious bay for themselves. It was the fall of 1879 and John Muir, with the help of Presbyterian missionary Samuel Hall Young, had convinced four native men (Toyatte, Kadachan, John and Sitka Charley) at Fort Wrangell to take him north to see the glaciers. Despite the imminent onset of winter, this brave party piled into a canoe and headed north.

They were just 20 miles from the entrance to Glacier Bay when they pulled into the Tlingit village of **Hoonah** on the southern shores of **Icy Strait**. They were spotted at a distance by the villagers who could tell by the shape and style of their canoe that they were strangers. The Hoonah canoe, designed for sea otter hunting, had a flared hull and

The Fairweather Range comes into view as your ship enters Icy Strait.

moved faster through the water. Like many Tlingit canoes, it was carved out of Sitka spruce because the Western red cedar – a more durable wood – is not found in Tlingit territory west of Chatham Strait.

In the 1990s, Hoonah's local native corporation, Huna Totem, hired logging contractors to clear-cut most of the marketable timber standing on native-owned land. When the logging ended, so did employment opportunities for many of Hoonah's residents, so a new local industry was created with the conversion of a derelict cannery into a museum-mall for the benefit of visiting cruise passengers. Named **Icy Strait Point**, this new port of call received its first cruise ship in May 2004 when Celebrity Cruises' *Mercury* dropped anchor in the harbor and tendered its passengers ashore, where they were greeted by Tlingit dancers and singers. Shore excursions at Icy Strait Point capitalize on the remote wilderness setting and include brown bear sighting, whale watching and salmon fishing

The name Hoonah means 'protected from the north wind' and the village's two original clans had once lived in Glacier Bay until advancing ice forced them to abandon their homes. This likely happened during the Little Ice Age, which began about 4,000 years ago and generally ended in the mid-1700s. Prior to that, numerous advances and retreats of the glaciers took place as the climate fluctuated between cooling and warming. During the height of the Great Ice Age, which began more than 12 million years ago in parts of Alaska, a massive ice sheet extended across half of Alaska's land mass and right across the northernmost Gulf of Alaska. Some of these mountains have never emerged from the Ice Age, supporting almost continuous glaciation for as far back as scientists can determine.

No one knows what the future holds for the glaciers still covering 30,000 square miles of Alaska. Should snowfall increase or the average temperature decrease only slightly, the glaciers could stage another major advance. Our planet is currently experiencing a warming trend that began before the industrial revolution and human interference in the atmosphere. Glaciers worldwide have been receding, including those in Glacier Bay where, in just over 200 years, the ice has melted back more than 65 miles. A few glaciers in the park are, however, advancing due to abundant snowfall in the Fairweather Range.

In his book *Travels in Alaska*, John Muir

A wall of ice blocked Glacier Bay when Captain Vancouver sailed past in 1794.

describes how, upon arriving at the entrance to Glacier Bay, he could see little because of thick weather. Captain Vancouver's chart, "hitherto a faithful guide" was of no use because Glacier Bay had been completely clogged with ice when Vancouver's ships sailed through Icy Strait less than a hundred years before. Only a small bay had indented the ice wall guarding Glacier Bay's entrance.

The wall of ice had now retreated more than 40 miles and this newly landscaped bay awaited discovery by Muir, a man fascinated with glaciers and the way they sculpted the earth. At Glacier Bay he could see the glaciers in action and he no longer had to speculate about their movements as he had done in the Sierra Mountains of California. Here was a living science experiment, proof at last "that this is still the morning of creation." But first he had to convince his travelling companions of the wondrous opportunity before them.

They had come across a camp of Hoonah seal hunters near the entrance to Glacier Bay and Charley, who said the place had changed since he was last there, wanted one of the sealhunters to guide them into the bay. Meanwhile, the Hoonahs were curious about this motley crew "coming to such a place, especially so late in the year." They had heard of Reverend Young but wondered what a missionary was doing in this lonely, desolate bay. "Was he going to preach to the seals and gulls, they asked, or to the ice mountains?"

Muir's native guides explained everything to the Hoonahs and one of them agreed to join Muir's expedition as a guide. Next morning they sailed up the bay in cold, pelting rain and made camp just beyond

John Muir said the world was "still in the morning of creation" after entering the newly exposed waters of Glacier Bay in 1879.

A ship glides close to Marjerie Glacier at the head of Tarr Inlet.

Geikie Inlet. The next day, while the party stayed put due to bad weather, Muir climbed the mountain slopes above their camp for a cloud-fringed view of the bay. It was filled with icebergs and fed by many glaciers, five of which Muir could see.

When Muir returned to camp, Young took him aside and told him their guides were discouraged, fearing this expedition would end in disaster. They questioned Muir's desire to go mountain climbing in a storm and figured he "must be a witch to seek knowledge in such a place as this and in such miserable weather." Rising to his reputation as an eloquent speaker, Muir addressed his demoralized crew. He reassured them that luck always followed him and told them to put away their childish fears. This pep talk worked wonders and, although it was still sleeting rain the next morning, they pushed on towards the head of the bay and the Hoonah sealing grounds.

They spent five days in Glacier Bay, visiting six glaciers and landing on three of them. The others were inaccessible because the fjords had started freezing. Muir was able to study how the rise and fall of the tide sent warmer seawater rushing in and out beneath the snout of the glaciers, gradually melting back the terminus. He climbed the mountainsides for an overall view, and made notes and sketches of the glaciers.

On his second visit to Glacier Bay the following summer, Muir was able to get close to his namesake glacier. After some urging, his native guides paddled within half a mile of its ice-cliff terminus to disembark Muir and Reverend Young on the fjord's eastern shore. A few minutes later, the natives' nervousness was justified as a large chunk of ice crashed into the water. They had to paddle furiously to flee the tossing waves. **Muir Glacier** is fed by the snow-covered slopes of the **Takhinsha Mountains** and, like other glaciers on the east side of

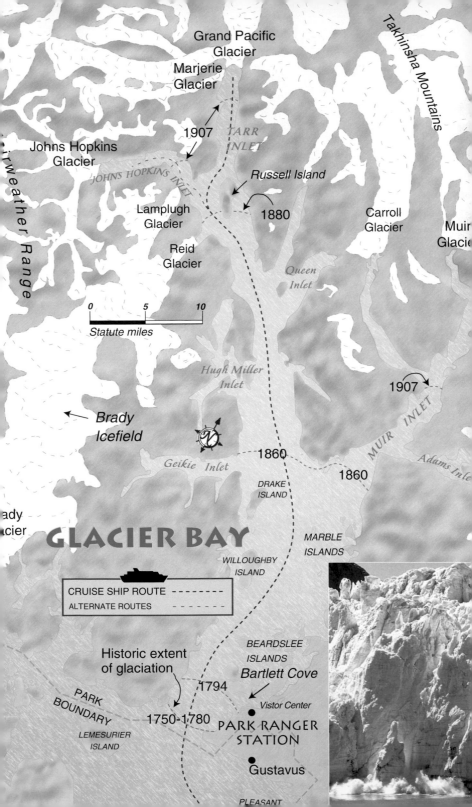

Grand Pacific
Glacier

Marjerie
Glacier

Takinsha Mountains

1907

TARR INLET

Johns Hopkins
Glacier

Russell Island

JOHNS HOPKINS INLET

1880

Carroll
Glacier

Muir
Glacier

Lamplugh
Glacier

rweather Range

Reid
Glacier

*Queen
Inlet*

0   5   10

Statute miles

*Hugh Miller
Inlet*

1907

MUIR INLET

*Brady
Icefield*

Adams Inlet

Geikie Inlet

1860

1860

DRAKE
ISLAND

ady
cier

GLACIER BAY

*MARBLE
ISLANDS*

*WILLOUGHBY
ISLAND*

CRUISE SHIP ROUTE   ----

ALTERNATE ROUTES   - - - -

*BEARDSLEE
ISLANDS*

Historic extent
of glaciation

1794

Bartlett Cove

PARK
BOUNDARY

1750-1780

● Vistor Center

PARK RANGER
STATION

*LEMESURIER
ISLAND*

● Gustavus

PLEASANT

First surveyed by John Muir in 1879, Johns Hopkins Inlet, with its nine glaciers, is one of Glacier Bay's most dramatic inlets.

Glacier Bay, has retreated since Muir's visit. On the west side of Glacier Bay, a few of the glaciers – fed by the **Fairweather Range** – are advancing.

The movement of glaciers is a complex process. No two glaciers are exactly alike and their unique anatomies – determined by the topography of the land they are carving and by localized weather conditions – cause them to often behave quite differently within the same general area. A good example of this is the **Brady Glacier**, which drains into Taylor Bay. This advancing glacier lies outside Glacier Bay but is fed by the same icefield as some of the retreating glaciers within the bay. The Brady Icefield covers much of the spectacular Fairweather Range, which separates Glacier Bay from the Gulf of Alaska.

John Muir (right) and John Burroughs were members of the Harriman Expedition which visited Glacier Bay in 1899.

INSIDE GLACIER BAY

Glacier Bay National Monument was established in 1924 and renamed **Glacier Bay National Park & Preserve** in 1980. The entire park encompasses 3.2 million acres and Glacier Bay lies in the middle of this huge preserve, its many inlets and fjords containing, in total, 16 active tidewater glaciers. Park headquarters are located at Bartlett Cove, just inside the entrance to Glacier Bay on the eastern shore. A ranger station, lodge and campground are located in Bartlett Cove and cruise ships entering Glacier Bay will pause outside the cove to await the embarkation of two park rangers who explain the sights and wonders to the ship's passengers.

Vessel traffic within Glacier Bay is tightly regulated. There are strict limits placed on the number of cruise ships, sightseeing boats and private pleasurecraft allowed into the bay at any one time, and permits must be obtained beforehand. Commercial fishermen are not allowed to trawl in these waters or catch certain marine life, such as herring, shrimp and pollock. The reason for these restrictions is to protect the **humpback whales** that feed in Glacier Bay.

A sudden decline in the number of humpback whales feeding in the bay was recorded in July of 1978 and 1979. Recent studies indicate this may have been a normal seasonal decline, with the whales using Glacier Bay as their early summer feeding grounds. However, to be on the safe side, measures were taken to protect the whales from excessive disturbance to their feeding grounds.

Today the annual number of humpback whales in Glacier Bay varies from 10 to 32. This population is stable and possibly increasing. During the whale season in Glacier Bay – June 1 to August 31 – no vessel is allowed to come closer than a quarter of a mile to a feeding whale or to follow a whale without maintaining a distance of at least one-half mile. Park hydrophones measure vessel noise and its effect on the whales.

A ship's tender brings park rangers aboard at entrance of Glacier Bay.

S *tanding here, with facts so fresh and telling and*
held up so vividly before us, every seeing observer,
not to say geologist, must readily apprehend the earth-
sculpturing, landscape-making action of flowing ice.

John Muir
Travels in Alaska

Harbor seals are a common sight on the ice floes of Glacier Bay, while overhead you'll see gulls (both glaucous-winged and mew), black-legged kittiwakes and Arctic terns. On shore you may spot a brown bear or mountain goat.

As your ship proceeds up Glacier Bay, you will see a raw landscape of freshly exposed rock and soil. Lichens and mosses are the first forms of vegetation to reclaim deglaciated land. They break down the rock and enrich the soil so that small flowering plants and low bushes can grow. Thickets of alder and willow are the next to take hold. They build up the soil and are eventually replaced by spruce trees.

Forests at the entrance to Glacier Bay gradually give way to more recent stages of growth until, near the snout of each glacier, the immediate landscape is one of silt, sand and gravel. In **Tarr Inlet**, at the very head of Glacier Bay, the exposed rock on the northeast side of the fjord is over 200 million years old, while that on the southwest side is about 90 million years old. They belong to separate terranes (fragments of the earth's crust) which nudged their way up the west coast and are now wedged between the Pacific Plate and the North American Plate.

At the head of Tarr Inlet is the **Grand Pacific Glacier** which retreated another 15 miles after Muir first sketched it in 1879, leaving Russell Island in its wake as it retreated up Tarr Inlet. The glacier crossed the border into Canada between 1913 and 1916, then stopped retreating in 1925. It is now back in Alaska, having readvanced, and is on the verge of rejoining the **Margerie Glacier**, from which it separated in 1912. Kittiwakes nest in rocky cliffs between the two glaciers. Here they wait for the glaciers to drop their ice into the sea; this churns up the water and brings baitfish – on which they feed – to the surface.

A glacier's dimensions are constantly changing but the Grand Pacific Glacier is about 25 miles long and one-and-a-half miles wide, with a terminus measuring 150 feet high (above the waterline). The 14-mile-long Margerie is one mile wide with an ice face (terminus) rising 250 feet above the waterline, its base about 100 feet below sea level.

The adjacent inlet – **Johns Hopkins** – is 10 miles long and contains nine separate glaciers. From 1892 to 1929 the ice in Johns Hopkins retreated 11 miles but has been readvancing ever since. **Toyatte, Kadachan, John** and **Charley Glaciers** are all named for Muir's

guides on his first trip to Glacier Bay in 1879. The **Johns Hopkins Glacier** is about 12 miles long and one mile wide, with a terminus that is 200 feet high.

Reid Inlet's glacier is 160 feet high but shallow, so it calves very few icebergs and has a rounded profile – versus the sheer cliffs of blue ice seen at the snout of an actively calving glacier. The Reid Glacier is retreating entirely through melting and evaporation.

Muir Glacier, one of the retreating glaciers that carved **Muir Inlet**, was a big producer of icebergs when John Muir studied it in 1880 and again in 1890, camping in a hut on the shores of

The Lamplugh Glacier lies at the entrance of Johns Hopkins Inlet.

(Above) A ship's officer eases the vessel past chunks of ice found floating near the snout of a tidewater glacier.
(Right) A tourboat gives its passengers a close look at a tidewater glacier.
(Below) A cruise ship slowly approaches Marjerie Glacier at the head of Tarr Inlet.

the ice-filled fjord near the face of the glacier which bears his name. One day he saw a huge blue berg – 240 feet long and 100 feet high – break off the glacier and sail past his camp. Muir noted 33 species of plants in flower in the glacial moraine, and he observed sandpipers on shore, loons and ducks in the water, gulls and eagles overhead. But his attention always returned to the glacier's "crystal wall...thundering gloriously."

Muir made himself a sled so he could travel across the glacier and study its tributaries. He camped at night on the glacier and awoke on the seventh day of this expedition to discover he was nearly blind from the glare of the ice. Everything he looked at had a double image. He kept a snow poultice bound over his eyes and dryly commented in his notes that this was the first time in Alaska he had gotten too much sunshine. His eyes recovered and a few days later, back at his hut, he stayed up all night watching an aurora borealis light the sky above his glorious world of ice mountains.

THE FAIRWEATHER COAST

Cruise ships proceeding through **Cross Sound** provide passengers with a fleeting view of Brady Glacier and its 175 square miles of ice and snow. Less easy to spot is the tiny community of **Elfin Cove** opposite Brady Glacier on the northern tip of Chichagof Island. Elfin Cove is a boardwalk community of about 50 year-round residents. In summer the population swells to 200 with fishboats coming and going to take on fuel, water and provisions. When the sun shines in Elfin Cove, the local shopkeepers sit outside on wooden benches and soak up the welcome rays. A post office, school, store, cafe and laundromat ring the inner harbor where fishermen ready their boats. Some of them head out into the Gulf of Alaska to fish the famous Fairweather Bank. Gentle ocean swells wash into Cross Sound and brown sea otters, floating on their backs, are often seen in these waters.

Cape Spencer marks the northern end of the Inside Passage and the beginning of the Gulf's mainland coast. A light is housed here in a white, square concrete tower atop a rocky islet, and is a welcome sight for fishermen returning from the Gulf to inside waters. Captain Vancouver named this cape in 1794 for a British earl whose descendants would include Lady Diana Spencer.

Cruise ships proceeding north, toward Yakutat Bay or Prince William Sound, sail past the seaward portion of Glacier Bay National Park & Preserve, where an unobstructed view of the **Fairweather Range** is one of Alaska's most spectacular sights. Some of the highest coastal mountains in the world ring the Gulf of Alaska. Their upper slopes covered with ice and snow, they rise abruptly from the edge of the sea, their steep summits towering within 15 miles of the shoreline. Fishboats are dwarfed as they pass beneath the magnificent peaks of the Fairweather Range. The sprawling **La Perouse Glacier** – at the base of

Lituya Bay, on the outer coast of Glacier Bay Park, is plagued by recurring giant waves which are caused by earthquake-induced avalanches at the head of the bay.

Mount La Perouse – is the only tidewater glacier in Alaska that calves icebergs straight into the open Pacific.

About 20 miles northwest of La Perouse Glacier is famous **Lituya Bay**, site of the largest wave ever recorded in Alaska. It was witnessed one July evening in 1958, when an Alaska fisherman was jarred awake by the sudden pitching and rolling of his boat at anchor in Lituya Bay. He rushed to the wheelhouse and looked out at a scene which drove all thought from his mind. The mountains at the head of the bay were moving. Mesmerized by this impossible sight, he watched the massive mountains twist and shake, then heave an avalanche of snow and rock into the water. Up rose a 1,700-foot wall of water which lashed against one mountainous shore and then another before roaring down the bay toward him at 100 mph. The fisherman and his battered boat somehow survived, but two other fishboats were swept from the bay, one of them vanishing.

This was not the first giant wave to strike Lituya Bay, nor will it be the last. An active fault runs through the

Fishboats in the Gulf of Alaska are dwarfed by the Fairweather Range – among the tallest coastal mountains in the world.

Fairweather Mountains at the head of Lituya Bay and another earth-quake could hit at any time. Called everything from "bewitcher" to "death trap," Lituya Bay is breathtakingly beautiful. Mountains stand like snowy sentinels at the head of the bay, their rugged crowns and shoulders draped with glaciers, their lower portions consisting of exposed rock and stands of spruce timber. A line of demarcation between the light green of young trees and the darker green of old growth shows how high the 1958 wave surged up the sides of the bay, denuding the lower slopes.

The Tlingits who once hunted here believed the bay's recurring giant waves were caused by an underwater sea monster who disliked people and occasionally threw a temper tantrum. They established summer villages near the bay's entrance, at what is now called Anchorage Cove, and hoped for the best. Unfortunately, Tlingit legends recall giant waves wiping out entire villages and canoe-paddling men drowning in churning seas at the entrance. This pincer-like entrance is guarded by a submerged bar – the end moraine of the glacier that carved Lituya Bay. The tide rushes in and out of this deep bay with hardly a pause and the tightly-squeezed currents at its entrance can be very treacherous.

In 1786, when the French explorer La Perouse sailed his two frigates through this narrow entrance, the wind shifted in mid-passage and he noted afterwards in his log that "during thirty years experience at sea, I never saw two ships so near destruction." Ten days later La Perouse sent three boats to survey the entrance. He issued explicit instructions to approach the bar only at slack and if no seas were breaking. However, La Perouse's officers were careless and all three boats were seized by an ebb current. One was swept through roaring breakers out to sea but somehow didn't sink or capsize. The other two were wrecked

La Perouse Glacier is the only tidewater glacier in Alaska that discharges its ice directly into the Pacific Ocean.

at the entrance and all 21 men died, their bodies never found. The only traces of the disaster were pieces of the boats that later washed ashore.

No one lives permanently in Lituya Bay, although for years a man named Jim Huscroft lived in a cabin on Cenotaph Island in the middle of the bay. He raised foxes and mined gold in the area. The only boats to pull in now are fishboats and the occasional pleasure boat. Floatplanes sometimes drop off or pick up mountaineering expeditions. A Canadian team of climbers – the first to ascend Mount Fairweather – was picked up at the head of Lituya Bay just hours before the 1958 earthquake struck.

Mount Fairweather – the tallest peak in the range at 15,300 feet – was named by Captain Cook when he sailed along this coast in 1778. Today it marks the border between Alaska and Canada. Northwest of Lituya Bay, the next bay to indent the remote Gulf Coast is Dry Bay, into which the Alsek River flows. This is the northern boundary of the

Elfin Cove is a friendly fishing port located off Icy Strait.

Fairweather Range and of Glacier Bay National Park. The interior boundary of Glacier Bay National Park traces the Alaska/Canada border to the top of Muir Glacier, then veers southeastward through the Takhinsha and Chilkat mountains to Icy Strait. Excluded from the reserve is the town of **Gustavus**, which sits near the entrance to Glacier Bay on a glacial outwash plain – produced when the bay was completely filled with ice.

The terrain here consists of sandy beaches, meadows and forest. Much of this is land that rebounded (lifted) when the ice retreated. The shoreline has risen about 20 feet since the ice started melting 200 years ago. In 1914 these flatlands were homesteaded as a farming community named Strawberry Point, because of the abundance of wild berries. The town's current residents (population about 400) still grow gardens and provide services to fishermen, sightseers and park visitors. Adjacent to the town is the Dude Creek Critical Habitat Area – a stopover each spring and September for thousands of migrating lesser sandhill cranes.

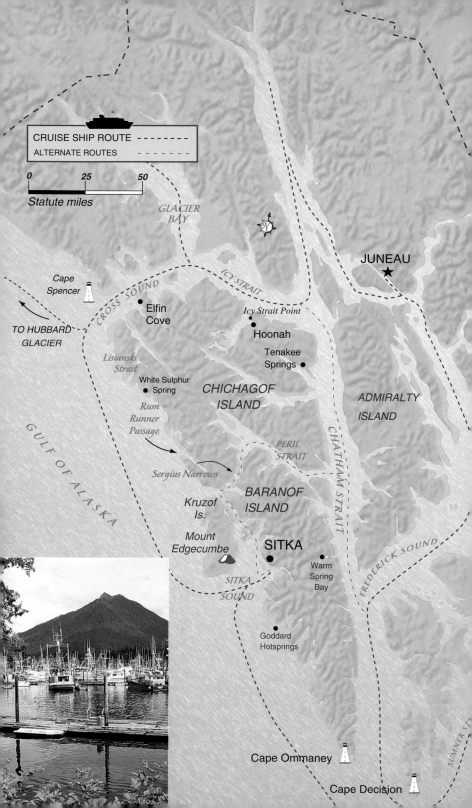

CRUISE SHIP ROUTE -------
ALTERNATE ROUTES -------

0   25   50
Statute miles

GLACIER BAY

ICY STRAIT

JUNEAU ★

Cape Spencer

CROSS SOUND

● Elfin Cove

Icy Strait Point

TO HUBBARD GLACIER

Lisianski Strait

Hoonah

Tenakee Springs ●

● White Sulphur Spring

CHICHAGOF ISLAND

ADMIRALTY ISLAND

Rum Runner Passage

PERIL STRAIT

CHATHAM STRAIT

Sergius Narrows

BARANOF ISLAND

GULF OF ALASKA

Kruzof Is.

Mount Edgecumbe

SITKA ●

● *Warm Spring Bay*

FREDERICK SOUND

SITKA SOUND

● *Goddard Hotsprings*

Cape Ommaney 🗼

SUMNER ST.

Cape Decision 🗼

CHAPTER NINE

SITKA

The Russians gained their first toehold in North America on the outer islands of the Aleutian chain. Following Vitus Bering's expedition of 1741, Russian frontiersmen, called *promyshlenniki*, set off in rickety ships from Siberia's Kamchatka Peninsula (only a few hundred miles distant) to reach this string of volcanic islands. Here lived the Aleuts – skilled hunters of the sea – who were forced by the *promyshlenniki* to hunt sea otters on a scale that quickly depleted their numbers.

Moving east along the stepping stones of the Aleutians, these Russian fur traders – accompanied by their Aleut hunters – eventually arrived at Kodiak Island and, in 1784, established their first sparse settlement at Three Saints Bay. A merchant's clerk named **Grigori Shelikof** led this eastward expansion. He had grand visions of establishing a fur trading company similar to Britain's Hudson's Bay Company. But, whereas the Hudson's Bay Company traded in beaver skins, Shelikof was pursuing the sea otter – whose fur pelts fetched exorbitant prices in Canton.

Shelikof hired a man named **Alexander Baranof** to manage his new settlement at Three Saints Bay. In 1791, at the age of 44, Baranof embarked on his first sea voyage to Russian America. The son of a storekeeper, Baranof couldn't resist the opportunity to escape both an unhappy marriage and his country's rigid class system. He was heading for a new land where social rank was secondary to ambition and hard work.

When Baranof arrived at Three Saints Bay in a *baidara* (a large, open boat), he was sick with pneumonia after enduring seasickness, a diet of raw fish and nights spent sleeping on wet beaches. Yet he was a tough and wiry man who learned the

Sitka celebrates its Russian roots in various forms, including traditional handicrafts.

basics of navigation in the course of the trip and within a few weeks he was back on his feet. His furious energy revived, Baranof set off with 900 natives in 450 *baidarkas* (kayaks) on a tour of the Kodiak coastline to visit the local villages, meet the chiefs and bargain for sea otter pelts.

When a tsunami all but wiped out the Russian settlement at Three Saints Bay, he took this opportunity to move everyone to a new site at the present-day city of Kodiak. From here he continued his preliminary explorations of the region, setting off with a fleet of 90 baidarkas to visit the mainland. While visiting a tribe of Alutiiq in Prince William Sound, Baranof promised to marry the chief's daughter. This was apparently a pleasant task, for she was young and pretty and Baranof gave her the Russian name of Anna.

In the summer of 1795, Baranof sailed to **Sitka Sound**. He had heard much about the beauty of this natural harbor. It was inhabited by a powerful Tlingit clan – the **Kiksadi** – who lived in a village called Shee Atika, atop a hill overlooking Sitka Sound. Backed by mountains and fronted by sea, this Tlingit stronghold was a popular port of call for British and American merchant ships. In exchange for sea otter pelts, these fur traders provided the Tlingit with rum and firearms.

When Baranof journeyed to Sitka Sound four years later with 1,100 men – 100 of them Russian, the rest Aleut or Alutiiq – they were attacked along the way by Tlingits. But this did not deter Baranof who, upon arrival at Sitka, bargained with the local chief for a piece of land six miles north of the village. There, using timbers two feet thick, he built a Russian fortress protected by high watch towers. A stockade encircled its outbuildings and the new settlement was placed under the patronage of **Saint Michael Archangel**.

Baranof returned to Kodiak and an uneasy co-existence pervaded Sitka Sound. For the Kiksadi, it was one thing to trade with white men who came and went by ship, but it was quite another to let these Russians steal the family business by settling on their doorstep with a troop of Aleut hunters. Antagonism erupted into violence in 1802 when the Tlingits attacked the Russian fort and massacred or enslaved about 400 inhabitants. A handful escaped through the woods and were rescued by merchant ships lying at anchor in Sitka Sound.

A British merchant ship took the survivors back to Kodiak where Baranof was informed of the tragedy. Determined to retake Sitka and make it the headquarters for his company, Baranof returned two years later with a fleet of two sloops, two schooners, 300 baidarkas and a Russian frigate, the *Neva*, commanded by Captain-Lieutenant Yuri Lisianski (who had sailed to Sitka Sound from Hawaii).

A bloody battle ensued in which the Tlingits, led by their fearless warrior **Katlian**, withdrew from their village to a fort on the far side of the harbor. Baranof led one of the first charges and took a bullet in the arm for his efforts. Eventually he left Lisianski in charge of military strategy and, under a steady bombardment of cannon fire from the *Neva*'s guns, the Tlingit depleted their ammunition and quietly abandoned their fort in the middle of the night.

Baranof and his men burned the deserted village to the ground and in its place, on the hill overlooking the harbor, a fortified town was built. It was called **New Archangel** and, by 1809, close to 50 ships a year were pulling into port to trade for furs. Baranof hosted the commanders of these merchant ships at his castle on the hill and these banquets became legendary for the amount of food and liquor consumed.

By the end of his tenure as manager of the Russian-American Company, Baranof was known far and wide as the 'Lord of Alaska.' He was not without enemies, however. Many considered him a tyrant. The Orthodox clergy did not approve of Baranof's lifestyle, especially his common-law marriage to Anna and their two illegitimate children. Russian fur traders under his employ at times objected to Baranof's crude management skills and in 1809 a plot to murder him and his family was uncovered.

Baranof sent his wife and children to Kodiak, wrote out his will, then drank his way through the long, dark winter. A man predisposed to black moods, he was now thoroughly demoralized. He resigned his position, but when two of his replacements died en route to New Archangel, he read this as a sign that he was destined to carry on as 'Lord of Alaska.' He turned pious and sent for his wife and children. His son and daughter returned but Anna chose to remain in Kodiak.

Baranof's Castle, standing atop Castle Hill, overlooked Sitka Sound during the days of the fur trade.

(Above) Sitka Pioneers Home. (Left) Aspiring musicians can listen to international artists perform at Sitka's Summer Music Festival. (Bottom) Kayakers enjoy a waterborne view of Sitka Sound.

By 1818, the 70-year-old Baranof was no longer needed by the Russian-American Company. Officials had decided the navy should run the company and two frigates were sent to New Archangel to relieve Baranof of his duties. After running the colony for 27 years, Baranof was ordered to hand over his books. It was rumored that he had embezzled company funds, but an audit revealed the books were in perfect order. Baranof, far from having accumulated great personal wealth, was almost penniless. He had, over the years, paid for improvements to the colony – such as schools – out of his own pocket while making the Russian-American Company the most profitable fur dealer in the world.

It was an emotional farewell for Baranof when the time came to board a ship bound for Russia. His daughter had fallen in love with a Russian naval officer stationed in New Archangel and would remain there for the time being. Longtime friends bid Baranof farewell, including his Aleut hunters, many of whom were devoted to the hard-drinking old Russian. Baranof never made it back to his homeland. He caught a fever during a stopover in Indonesia and died at sea. While a smooth transition to naval rule was taking place back at New Archangel, his body was committed to the Indian Ocean.

Baranof had successfully built the fur trading colony envisioned by Shelikof, but now a different type of management was required to keep it running smoothly. Under naval rule, education and religion were

Castle Hill, a former Russian bastion, was the site of the October 18th, 1867, transfer ceremonies at which the Russian flag was lowered and the Stars and Stripes was raised.

The Bishop's House was built by shipwrights of the Russian navy in 1841 and has been meticulously restored by the Park Service.

advanced and public health became company policy. The wives of naval officers accompanied their husbands to Russian America and brought with them the culture and fashion of St. Petersburg, which earned New Archangel the epithet 'Paris of the Pacific.'

The Tlingits were invited to return to Sitka and they settled at the foot of Castle Hill. The Russian clergy, led by such missionaries as **Bishop Innocent**, built a cultural bridge with the natives by learning their languages and encouraging them to retain their own customs so long as they didn't clash with Orthodox doctrine. Bishop Innocent moved to Sitka from the Aleutians in 1834 and, an accomplished linguist, he quickly learned the Tlingit language. He produced written instructional material in both Russian and Tlingit so the native children could be taught to read and write. The navy built an imposing residence for him. Completed in 1842, it also housed a chapel and seminary for native and creole children.

Bishop Innocent was eventually transferred to Siberia. He left Sitka a few years before the dwindling fur trade prompted Russia's Imperial Government, under Czar Alexander II, to sell its North American colony to the United States in 1867. New Archangel's name was changed back to Sitka, and a period of decline and lawlessness followed as Russian residents returned to their homeland. Gold was discovered near Sitka in 1872 but this was overshadowed by the larger strike in 1880 at Juneau, which eventually became the territory's new capital.

America's purchase of Russian America also brought a change in missionaries arriving in Alaska. The Protestants, led by Sheldon Jackson, had a well-intentioned but different approach to converting the natives, who were no longer encouraged to retain their language and customs, but to adopt those of the country now governing them. However, the presence of the Orthodox church did not vanish with the transfer of political power, and to this day it remains a strong force among the native population – a legacy from Alaska's Russian era.

Neither did the Russian place names disappear. When the United States conducted a survey in 1867 of its newly acquired territory, many of the Russian place names were retained. Islands bear such names as Chichagof, Mitkof, Kupreanof, Wrangell and Zarembo – all naval officers who served in Russian America.

St. Michael's Cathedral, a legacy from Alaska's Russian past, is today a Sitka landmark.

Captain Lisianski, whose survey is responsible for many of the Russian place names, is remembered by an inlet and a strait bearing his name. Grigori Shelikof is honored by a bay named for him on Kruzof Island opposite Sitka. And the island on which Sitka stands is, fittingly, named Baranof.

The islands of Southeast Alaska are called the **Alexander Archipelago,** named this in 1867 by the U.S. Coast Survey to honor Alexander II – the ruling czar at the time. In Sitka itself, much of the architecture and art from its Russian era is preserved. Cruise ships drop anchor in Sitka Sound, where square-rigged schooners once lay at anchor to take on furs for shipment to China. These waters, at one time busy with baidarkas and dugout canoes, now bustle with tenders ferrying cruise passengers ashore.

LOCAL ATTRACTIONS

Centennial Hall, which houses the **Sitka Convention & Visitors Bureau,** was built on the waterfront in 1967 to commemorate Alaska's statehood centennial. It also contains the **Isabel Miller Museum** which

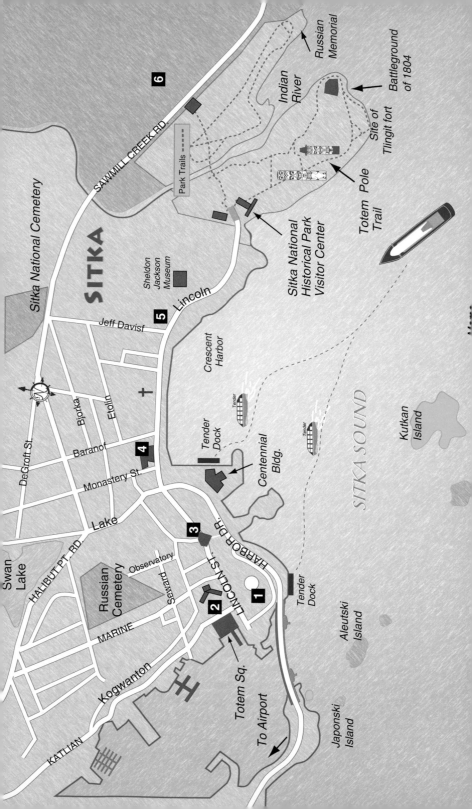

is run by the Sitka Historical Society. Museum exhibits include a scale model of Sitka as it looked in 1867 (the year Alaska was transferred from Russia to the United States), and items from Vitus Bering's historic voyage of 1741, when Russians first set foot on Alaskan soil. Local handicrafts can be purchased in the gift shop.

The stage of the Centennial Building's auditorium is backed by windows overlooking Sitka Sound. This waterfront view of passing fishboats and gliding eagles so impressed the violinist Paul Rosenthal when he performed here in the late '70s with the Arctic Chamber Orchestra, that he founded Sitka's Summer Music Festival. Held each year in the first three weeks of June, these classical concerts attract distinguished artists from around the world. Sitka's **New Archangel Dancers** also perform their Russian folk dances in the Centennial Building. An all-women dance troupe which was formed in 1969, they wear authentic costumes for their crowd-pleasing show.

Between the Centennial Building and the library is displayed a 50-foot **ceremonial canoe** carved by local artist George Benson in 1940. This canoe was carved from a 70-foot cedar log towed to Sitka by a fishboat from Port Renfrew at the southern tip of British Columbia's Vancouver Island.

From here, Harbor Drive winds in a southwesterly direction toward **Castle Hill** **1** which can be reached by a spiral path leading from a parking lot off Harbor Drive. (Stairs off Lincoln Street beside the old post office also provide access.) The sweeping view from this hilltop takes in Mount Edgecumbe – a dormant volcano visible across Sitka Sound on Kruzof Island. This mountain was named in 1778 by Britain's Captain James Cook.

The hilltop was originally occupied by Tlingit natives until they were driven out in 1804 by the Russians, led by Alexander Baranof – manager of the Russian-American Fur Trading Company. Baranof lived here in a wood house filled with fine furnishings, paintings and books until he was asked to retire in 1818. This house was eventually replaced with an enormous two-story log mansion called **Baranof's Castle**. Company officials held gala balls in Baranof's Castle until 1867, when Russia sold its North American colony to the United States. Prince and Princess Maksoutoff were the last occupants of the castle, which later burned to the ground. Its encircling stone walls and mounted Russian cannons are reminders of the past dramas which unfolded on this hilltop.

Stairs lead from Castle Hill down to Lincoln Street where, directly opposite, is the **Sitka Pioneers Home** **2**. It was built in 1934 – the first such facility for elderly Alaskans – and visitors are welcome to stroll the lawned grounds where flower gardens contain native Alaskan plants. A shop in the basement sells handicrafts.

Across the street from the Pioneers Home, on the waterfront, is **Totem Square**. The totem pole displayed here is another carving by

George Benson. One of the pole's crests is the doubled-headed eagle of Imperial Russia. Traditionally, a clan would symbolize an enemy's defeat by borrowing its emblem. Also on display at Totem Square are a Russian cannon and some salvaged anchors from British and American fur trading ships.

Standing prominently in the middle of Lincoln Street like a mid-channel island is **St. Michael's Cathedral 3**. This is a splendid replica of the original church which was built from 1844 to 1848 shortly after Sitka (then called New Archangel) became the diocesan seat of the Russian Orthodox Church in Alaska (then called Russian America).

A fire destroyed the cathedral in 1966, but Sitka residents managed to save most of its valuable icons – religious works of art dating as far back as the 17th century. Many were painted on boards that were gilded with gold and other precious metals, and embellished with jewels. These magnificent icons, and the beautiful domed and spired architecture of the church itself – which took 10 years to rebuild from blueprints – draw thousands of visitors each summer.

Heading east of St. Michael's Cathedral on Lincoln Street, you'll pass the Shee Atika (a Westmark Hotel) and MacDonald's Bayview Trading Company (with a postal substation on the main floor) before reaching the **Russian Bishop's House 4**. Built in 1841-42, this heritage building served as a hospital, school, rectory and place of worship. The first bishop to live here was Father Innocent, who arrived at New Archangel (Sitka) in 1834 as Reverend Veniaminof, after spending 10 years as a missionary in the Aleutians. When his wife died in 1840 he took monastic vows and was consecrated a bishop. He resided

Lincoln Street, in downtown Sitka, is lined with inviting shops and galleries.

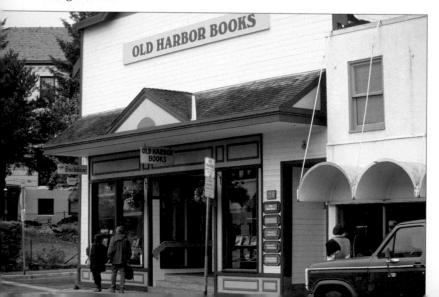

Sheldon Jackson Museum is located on the college campus and contains an impressive collection of native artifacts.

here for the next 18 years before moving to a new diocese in Siberia. In 1868 he became Metropolitan of Moscow – the highest rank in the Russian Orthodox Church – and in 1977 he was canonized a saint.

When the Park Service acquired the Bishop's House, a 15-year restoration project was undertaken to fix its sagging structure and restore the interior furnishings. Hundreds of experts were consulted as the painstaking work was carried out. Blackened icons were sent to an iconologist for cleaning, and teams of specialists at the Park Service's Harper's Ferry Center in West Virginia restored the house's furnishings. The first floor now contains historical and architectural exhibits. In 'The Room Revealed' a cutaway section of the building shows the sturdy scarf joints and other shipbuilding techniques used by Finnish shipwrights during construction. Upstairs is the beautiful chapel where Bishop Innocent and his fellow missionaries spent time in prayer each morning.

From the Bishop's House, the walk heading east on Lincoln Street couldn't be more pleasant. Along the waterfront are lawns, walkways and benches which overlook Crescent Harbor. Across the street, a sidewalk leads past **St. Peter's By-the-Sea** (a pretty stone church with a gift shop out back), followed by the campus of **Sheldon Jackson College 5**, which hosts summer workshops, conferences and events such as the Sitka Summer Music Festival and the Writer's Symposium. In 1983 the college's president, Dr. Michael Kaelke, read that James Michener was interested in writing a book on Alaska but was reluctant

*The trails of Sitka
National Historical Park
provide visitors the
opportunity to view skillfully carved totem poles
in a lovely forest setting.*

to spend time in a cold climate at his age. Dr. Kaelke promptly wrote
the famous author, explaining that winter in southeastern Alaska is
quite mild with temperatures generally above freezing. Michener
accepted the college's invitation to use it as a base from which to
research and write his book *Alaska.*

The **Sheldon Jackson Museum** is an octagonal-shaped concrete
building located on the college campus. It contains a fine collection of
Eskimo, Aleut and Indian artifacts collected by Dr. Sheldon Jackson, a
presbyterian missionary and General Agent for Education, who travelled Alaska by boat, dogsled and on foot in the late 1800s. Sleds,
umiaks and other watercraft hang from the museum's ceiling. Haida
argillite carvings, a Chilkat blanket and the Raven's Head Helmet worn
by Sitka Chief Katlian during the 1804 battle with the Russians, are just
a few of the fascinating items on display.

At the end of Lincoln Street is the **Sitka National Historical Park**.
A visitor center, located at the park's entrance, displays Tlingit exhibits
and presents a recorded slide presentation on Sitka's history. Available
at the visitor center is a booklet called *Carved History*, which explains
each of the totem poles standing along a quarter-mile section of the
park's two miles of trails. Many are replicas of poles collected from
various villages throughout southeastern Alaska for the 1904 Louisiana

Purchase Exposition. They were brought to Sitka the following year and the deteriorating originals are now being preserved in storage.

Just beyond the totem poles is the site of the 1804 battle between the local Tlingits and the conquering Russians. Nearby is the site of the Tlingits' fort to which they retreated under steady Russian bombardment and from which they fled in the middle of the night when their ammunition ran out. From there the trail follows the shores of the salmon-spawning Indian River to a footbridge. Across it are more trails which lead to a Russian memorial for the men who died in the 1804 battle.

Yet another trail connects with the Sawmill Creek Road. A short distance north, at 1101 Sawmill Creek Road, is the **Alaska Raptor Center** . Sick or injured birds of prey are brought here for treatment and rehabilitation before they are returned to the wild. Open houses, demonstration tours and eagle exercise sessions in a nearby muskeg field are held regularly.

An eagle receives rehabilitative care at the Alaska Raptor Center.

Another scenic walk can be taken along the Sheldon Jackson College Forest Trail which follows the Indian River through the college grounds.

OUT-OF-TOWN EXCURSIONS

With the Pacific Ocean at its doorstep, the waters off Sitka offer some of Southeast Alaska's best wildlife viewing. Sea otters are especially abundant and humpback whales are frequently sighted. Boat cruises out of Sitka offer good opportunities to see marine mammals up close, as well as such seabirds as the colorful puffin.

Nearby Silver Bay is a favorite fjord for sightseeing cruises. Here you can view not only the area's wildlife but also an old gold mine, a modern pulp mill and a salmon hatchery.

Sportfishing is fruitful in the bountiful waters off Sitka. Salisbury Sound, 20 miles north of Sitka, is especially good for catching halibut – a prize bottom fish with delicate white meat.

Mount Edgecumbe, a dormant volcano on Kruzof Island, can be seen from Sitka.

OUTLYING PORTS

Sitka is steeped in Russian history but visitors to outlying ports will find themselves soaking in something quite different – the region's natural hotsprings. Long used by natives, then by hunters and trappers, these hotsprings were also retreats for fishermen and gold prospectors.

The **Goddard Hotsprings,** 16 miles south of Sitka on the outer coast of Baranof Island, was one of the first to be developed in the mid-1800s when a few cottages were built to house invalids from Sitka. In the 1920s a hotel was built, which was then turned into an overflow facility for Sitka's Pioneers Home in 1939. Today two cedar bathhouses stand on the hillside and capture the hot mineral waters for visitors arriving by boat.

Beautiful **Warm Spring Bay**, on the other side of Baranof Island, features outdoor rock pools on a tiered hillside overlooking the falls that spill into the head of the bay, near the pier and old buildings of Baranof village. And farther up Chatham Strait, on the east side of Chichagof Island, a community has formed around the local springs. Called **Tenakee Springs**, this hamlet is the former site of crab and salmon canneries, but is now inhabited by retirees and young families. Juneau and Sitka residents arrive by ferry for weekend retreats.

Tenakee's existence centers around the hotspring-fed bathhouse where bathing hours for men and women are posted on the outside door. Visitors soon know them by heart, however, because the bathing hours are promptly told to any strangers arriving in town (it's presumed) for a soak in the springs. The local bathhouse is a more popular

The former cannery town of Tenakee Springs is now a mecca for people seeking relaxation in a hot mineral bath.

topic of conversation than even the weather. It's not unusual to over-hear one resident asking another if he or she has bathed yet that day. Anywhere else this might seem a somewhat personal question, but not in Tenakee Springs.

There are no cars here, but a two-mile road called Tenakee Avenue runs the length of this waterfront village. Only four feet wide in places, the road is travelled by foot, bicycle or three-wheeled motorbike. Near one end of town is a hotel and post office; at the other end is a school. The bathhouse and an old-fashioned general store are in the center of town, just up the road from the ferry dock.

The Alaska State Ferry pulls into Tenakee Springs on its way from Juneau to Sitka. The ferry route includes **Peril Strait** – a twisting chan-nel that separates Chichagof and Baranof islands. This strait was origi-nally named Pernicious by Russia's Captain Lisianski, in remembrance of 200 Aleut hunters who died from eating toxic mussels at its entrance in 1799. They were part of Baranof's expedition who, after establishing a garrison at Sitka, were returning to Kodiak. The site of the initial Russian settlement – a few miles north of the present downtown – is now referred to as Old Sitka and the Alaska State Ferry docks nearby.

Another hotsprings, called **White Sulphur**, exists on the ocean side of Chichagof Island. Some gold prospecting took place on Chichagof, followed by whiskey smuggling when Prohibition took effect in 1918. Piehle Passage (also known as Rum Runner Passage) was named for an adroit smuggler who apparently used this tortuous, rock-strewn passage to evade a revenue cutter.

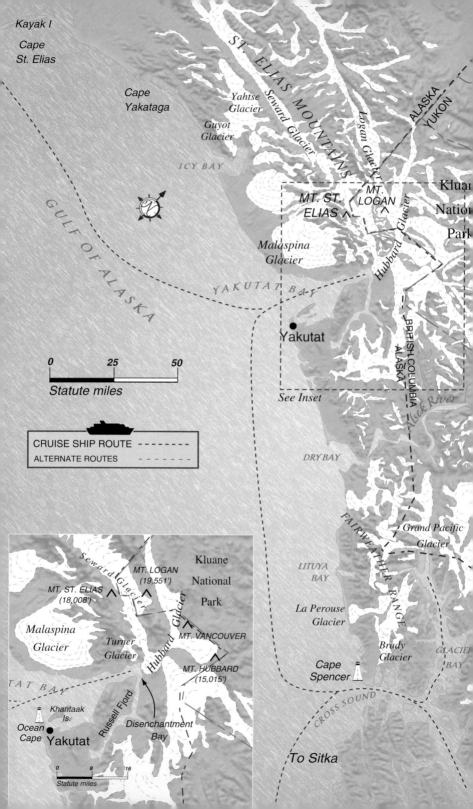

Kayak I

Cape
St. Elias

Cape
Yakataga

Yahtse
Glacier

Guyot
Glacier

ST. ELIAS MOUNTAINS

Seward Glacier

Logan Glacier

ALASKA
YUKON

ICY BAY

Klua

MT. ST.
ELIAS ∧

MT.
LOGAN ∧

Nation
Park

GULF OF ALASKA

N

Malaspina
Glacier

Hubbard Glacier

YAKUTAT BAY

Yakutat

BRITISH COLUMBIA
ALASKA

Alsek River

0   25   50

Statute miles

See Inset

DRY BAY

CRUISE SHIP ROUTE   - - - - - - -
ALTERNATE ROUTES   - - - - - - -

FAIRWEATHER RANGE

Grand Pacific
Glacier

LITUYA
BAY

La Perouse
Glacier

GLACIER
BAY

Brady
Glacier

Cape
Spencer

CROSS SOUND

To Sitka

Seward Glacier

MT. LOGAN
(19,551')

Kluane
National
Park

MT. ST. ELIAS
(18,008') ∧

∧

Hubbard Glacier

∧ MT. VANCOUVER

Malaspina
Glacier

Turner
Glacier

∧ MT. HUBBARD
(15,015')

TAT BAY

Russell Fiord

Disenchantment
Bay

Ocean
Cape

Khantaak
Is.

Yakutat

0   8   16

Statute miles

CHAPTER TEN

HUBBARD GLACIER
& Yakutat Bay

S ome of the most spectacular scenery in the world is found along
Alaska's Gulf Coast on the way to Yakutat Bay. Rising from the
edge of the sea are some of the world's tallest coastal mountains,
their slopes blanketed by North America's largest glaciers.

Few people live along this coast, where the overall landscape is one
of looming mountains and sprawling glaciers. There are but three or
four sheltered anchorages for mariners to pull into and Yakutat Bay
offers the only harbor for large ships. The bay's entrance, over 16 miles
wide, is visible from great distances because it is marked by Mount
Saint Elias, which is 18,008 feet tall and growing. Yes, growing. A
piece of the earth's crust – called a terrane – is sandwiched here
between two tectonic plates. This terrane (called the Yakutat Block)
broke away from the edge of the Continental Plate about 25 million
years ago and, riding on the Pacific Plate, was pushed 330 miles northwest along a fault until it reached the top of the Gulf of Alaska.

About 100,000 years ago, the Pacific Plate began shoving the
Yakutat Block (360 miles long and 120 miles wide) against the
Continental Plate at a rate of about two-and-a-half inches per year.
Something must budge as the dense oceanic plate pushes underneath

the more buoyant continental plate
and, in this case, part of a mountain
range is being forced upward. At a
growth rate of two-and-a-half inches
per year, it would take Mount Saint
Elias quite a while to surpass 20,320-
foot Mount McKinley as the tallest
mountain in North America. Saint
Elias also faces competition from
19,850-foot Mount Logan, only 25
miles away and also rising. All this
bumping and grinding of terranes and
plates is invisible to the human eye
until an earthquake gives the area a
good jolt, which happened at Yakutat

*A fishboat trolls for salmon off the
entrance to Yakutat Bay.*

in September 1899. Living in this remote village on the shores of Yakutat Bay were the original native Tlingits, a few missionaries and some mining prospectors.

The tremors and shocks began on September 3 and lasted four weeks. No lives were lost, even though at least one of the quakes was of the same magnitude as the 1906 San Francisco quake. The small community of Yakutat was at first alarmed and then terrified when, on September 10, the strongest of these quakes sent people rushing from their creaking and groaning homes, while the trees outside swayed like stalks of grass. An eyewitness report by a civil engineer camped at the time in Yakutat was published in the *San Francisco Examiner*. He described native villagers pleading with the missionary to hold church services that morning (a Sunday) to pacify their god, who was obviously "angry at the earth and shaking it." They were horrified when the mission church "rocked until the church bell rang," perceiving this as an omen. When the earthquake ceased, three great waves (tsunamis) rolled in from the ocean and filled Yakutat Bay with whirlpools. Lowlands were flooded as the water level rose 15 feet. The eyewitness engineer reported that "the earthquake was undoubtedly a magnificent sight, but hardly one a fellow would hunt up for the sake of looking at it."

A cruise ship pulls within a quarter mile of Hubbard Glacier's massive snout at the head of spectacular Yakutat Bay.

The U.S. Geological Survey sent a team to inspect the after-effects of the earthquake six years later, and they found that a former tidal zone of beach and barnacled rocks had been raised as much as 47 feet above the high-tide line. This uplifting was felt most dramatically by a group of prospectors camped beside Russell Fjord at the head of Yakutat Bay, not far from **Hubbard Glacier**. When the September 10 quake hit, the men ran from their tents. The glacial moraine under their feet was undulating and the Hubbard Glacier was surging forward. As if that weren't enough, a lake behind the beach spilled from its bed and swept across their abandoned camp. Tons of rock came pouring down as the men fled along the beach. Four days later they made it to Yakutat where they found the residents camped in tents on Shivering Hill, as it was promptly named following the earthquake.

The **Harriman Expedition** had visited Yakutat just 11 weeks prior to the September earthquakes. The scientific party on board the steamer *George W. Elder*, chartered by their host Edward H. Harriman, would have had much to observe and record had they been exploring the shoreline of Yakutat Bay a few months later. As it was, the narrow inlet of **Disenchantment Bay** (at the head of Yakutat Bay) was thick with ice floes when the *Elder* arrived at its entrance and waited for the ice to disperse before proceeding. Meanwhile, some Tlingits paddled along-side in canoes filled with furs and skins for sale. This welcome was similar to that given another scientific expedition a hundred years earlier, when the Spanish explorer **Alejandro Malaspina** visited Yakutat to investigate a rumor that a northwest passage lay at this latitude

A cruise ship approaches Yakutat Bay where Mount Saint Elias was the first point on North America sighted by Vitus Bering in 1741. For decades this mountain served as a navigational marker for European explorers venturing into the Gulf of Alaska.

In the summer of 1791, Malaspina headed north from Acapulco, setting a course that took his two ships directly to Yakutat Bay. When he saw the bay's wide opening at the latitude substantiated by the Academy of Sciences in Paris as being the location of the Strait of Anian (a mythical northwest passage), Malaspina figured he was onto something. The Tlingits living at Yakutat had already dealt with Russian, French and British ships, and they anticipated a brisk trade with this new batch of white men. The Spaniards, however, seemed preoccupied with setting up a base camp and preparing two launches to explore the Strait of Anian. Others were busy collecting specimens and sketching the scenery.

Eventually the Tlingits engaged the Spaniards in barter. However, by the time those manning the two launches returned with disappointing reports of a huge glacier blocking their way, the mood on the waiting ships had also soured. The Spanish were not getting along with the Tlingits and tensions reached a climax when a pair of trousers went missing. A chief was detained and trading was halted until the trousers were returned. The expedition's artist captured the reconciliation scene on canvas – natives approaching in a canoe, one with his arms outstretched in a gesture of friendship, another holding up the stolen trousers. Disappointed but convinced that the 'Strait of Anian' theory was false, Malaspina left. The name he gave the ice-filled inlet at the head of Yakutat Bay reflects his dashed hopes – Disenchantment Bay.

By the time the Harriman Expedition pulled into Yakutat Bay, the wall of ice that had stopped the Spaniards dead in their tracks was now

retreating up the inlet. The *Elder* was able to pick its way through the ice floes and be the first ship to enter Disenchantment Bay. On board was a Yakutat Tlingit named James who had impressed Harriman with his detailed knowledge of the area and was invited to join the elite party of scientists as a consultant to the ship's pilot.

Harriman's scientific party included **John Muir** (described in the guest list as 'Author and Student of

The sheer cliffs of Hubbard's terminus are typical of an actively calving glacier.

Glaciers'), John Burroughs (Ornithologist and Author) and Dr. William H. Dall (Paleontologist of the U.S. Geological Survey). Dall had made several trips to Alaska and his keen observance and recording of what he saw resulted in several animal species receiving his name, such as the Dall porpoise and Dall sheep. Grove Karl Gilbert was the expedition's glaciologist. He made careful empirical studies of each glacier they visited, drawing dozens of maps and taking plenty of his own photographs in addition to those taken by the expedition's two official photographers, one being Edward S. Curtis. Gilbert studied each glacier's topography and the eroded fjords, valleys and rutted plains left behind by receding glaciers. Gilbert's work was a major contribution to the emerging science of glaciology which today measures the thickness of ice with radar, uses aerial photography to monitor a glacier's movements, and employs satellite technology to determine the exact height of a mountain.

The **Hubbard Glacier** at the head of Disenchantment Bay is the longest tidewater glacier in North America. This massive river of ice originates in the St. Elias Mountains of Kluane National Park in Canada's Yukon, and flows for 76 miles before reaching its terminus – an ice-cliff face that is six miles wide. At one time, perhaps as as recently as 600 years ago, the glacier completely covered Yakutat Bay. When the Harriman expedition examined the glacier in 1899, it had just finished retreating and was starting to readvance.

Hubbard received widespread attention in the summer of 1986 and was dubbed the 'Galloping Glacier' when it advanced hundreds of feet within a few weeks. The glacier's snout over-ran a small island and dammed the entrance to Russell Fjord, trapping seals inside what became a huge lake. Its water level rose 83 feet and threatened to overflow, the runoff potentially pouring into the Situk River where salmon would be washed away in a flood of debris. Then, on October 8, the ice dam ruptured and 3,500,000 cubic feet of water per second was dumped into Disenchantment Bay. Shrimp lying on the bottom of this deep fjord were lifted by the turbulent water and thrown onto shore. Scientists speculate that an equivalent discharge of water last took place near the end of the Great Ice Age, when Lake Missoula emptied into the Columbia River.

Surging glaciers are still not completely understood but it's surmised that faulty plumbing is the culprit. A healthy, slow-moving glacier slides on its base while its top layer flows steadily forward, transferring ice from its source (where snow accumulates) to its snout (where the ice melts). When a glacier isn't flowing smoothly, its upper end becomes clogged with accumulated snow and ice. Then, in a year of high runoff due to heavy rain or spring thaw, the glacier's motion is suddenly eased and the glacier is pushed forward as its top-heavy mass of ice surges down the slope.

Hubbard Glacier, longest tidewater glacier in North America, begins its 76-mile journey to the sea on the slopes of Mount Logan, which is Canada's highest mountain and is part of the largest non-polar icefield in the world.

Hubbard Glacier was a major media attraction in the summer of 1986 and the fishermen of Yakutat found themselves chauffeuring reporters and camera crews to the head of the bay. One resident recalls loading a group into his fishboat for a trip to the Galloping Glacier. The two things he remembers are that the reporters didn't like being charged $200 each and that they all held their microphones pointed toward the glacier to record its rumbling noises.

Yakutat is an important port for Alaska's fishing fleet, the only one with dock facilities between Juneau and Cordova (in Prince William Sound). Most of Yakutat's 700 residents run fishboats or work in fish processing plants, and many will tell you that Yakutat is the most beautiful port in Alaska. The town overlooks **Monti Bay**, on the southeast shores of Yakutat Bay, with Khantaak Island lying opposite and acting as a breakwater to the swells which roll into Yakutat Bay off the Gulf of Alaska. Beautiful beaches ring much of the area's shoreline, and stretching across the northern horizon is a breathtaking vista of mountains and glaciers, including **Malaspina Glacier.** It is the largest piedmont (foot-of-the-mountain) glacier in North America, measuring 45 miles from east to west and 30 miles from north to south. Its fan-like terminus is almost 60 miles in circumference and ends within three miles of the Pacific Ocean.

Malaspina Glacier is fed by more than two dozen tributary glaciers. As these smaller glaciers merge with the main glacier, they bring along rock and gravel eroded from valleys. These dark stripes of moraine run in parallel lines like feeder lanes joining a main highway. From the air the Malaspina Glacier looks like an abstract painting with its parallel moraine stripes twisted into swirls or folded into zigzags by surges within the glacier.

Jet planes land daily at Yakutat on regularly scheduled flights. For travellers approaching Yakutat by ship, the landscape looks so uninhabited that the sight of a jet plane coming in for a landing seems completely out of place. These planes touch down on Alaska's longest runway – built during World War II when 15,000 troops were based at Yakutat.

For most of this century, Yakutat's main industry has been the commercial catching and processing of salmon, cod, halibut and crab. The town's first cannery was built in 1904. Timber harvesting is also underway on Tongass National Forest lands between Yakutat and Dry Bay.

Dry Bay lies at the mouth of the **Alsek River** and is slowly being turned into a huge delta. The Alsek River drains 9,500 square miles of Alaska and Canada while carving its way through the Saint Elias Mountains, past glaciers and through canyons, to reach the Gulf of Alaska. Canada's **Tatshenshini River** flows into the upper Alsek. In 1993 it was declared a wilderness park by the British Columbia government after environmentalists opposed an open-pit mine planned for the summit of Windy Craggy Mountain. The Tatshenshini-Alsek watershed, considered North America's wildest river, is now completely protected. Intrepid kayakers occasionally paddle the white waters of this river but it is normally not well travelled. The natives used the Alsek ('Raven's River') as a trade route until a burst ice dam wiped out a riverside village. Afterwards, they restricted their settlements to the river's headwaters and its mouth at Dry Bay.

In August 1999, three hunters on a limited-entry hunt for Dall sheep stumbled upon a remarkable archeological find at the foot of a retreating glacier in Tatshenshini-Alsek Park. They photographed but did not touch the preserved body of an aboriginal hunter who died there, possibly caught in a fierce snowstorm as he was crossing the glacier about 600 years ago. A team of scientists has since been studying Kwaday Dan Sinchi (Long Ago Person Found) – examining everything from his gopher cloak and cedar-and-spruce root hat to his stomach contents. As the glaciers continue retreating, they are expected to reveal more such artifacts and specimens that have been frozen in time.

During the Gold Rush, some prospectors tried to reach the Klondike via the Alsek River. In the spring of 1898 more than 300 men arrived at Yakutat Bay and hauled their mining outfits 50 miles across Hubbard Glacier to the Alsek River. At this point most turned back, but those

Mount Saint Elias looms above the small fishing port of Yakutat, located near the mouth of Yakutat Bay.

who ascended the river set up their winter camp in a desolate area almost devoid of fuel. Freezing and sickness took its toll, with only a handful surviving the ordeal. That spring the survivors reached Dalton Post on the Tatshenshini River. Had they taken a different route from the coast, they would have reached Dalton Trail after a few days of travel.

Some prospectors tried to cross the massive Malaspina Glacier to reach the Yukon. Those who made it were in bad shape – both mentally and physically. When the *George W. Elder* stopped at Yakutat, members of the Harriman Expedition met groups of bedraggled and penniless miners who were hoping to catch the next steamer home. A few were panning for gold in the creeks around Yakutat.

Specks of gold lie in the black sand beaches of **Cape Yakataga** – about 70 miles west of Yakutat Bay. To this day, the residents of Cape Yakataga work their claims by hauling sand and running it through sluice boxes. These modern-day prospectors are mainly summer residents, with about a dozen people living year-round at this remote cape. They grow small gardens in summer, make preserves from wild berries, can or smoke fish and wild game, and collect firewood for their stoves. Stands of spruce and hemlock grow right to the beach, and alder, willow and cottonwood flourish along the river banks. Leisure time is spent beachcombing to see what the gulf has thrown onto the exposed shores of the cape. On clear nights the northern lights can often be seen. In spring and fall thousands of migrating birds – swans, geese, cranes and ducks – stop here briefly.

Cape Yakataga is backed by mountains and flanked on either side by massive icefields – Malaspina to the east, Bering to the west. Lying at the base of Bering Glacier is Cape Suckling. Offshore, jutting into the gulf like a sore thumb, is **Kayak Island**. In July of 1741 a Russian ship under the command of the Danish captain Vitus Bering anchored in the lee of Kayak Island. The ship remained there for only a few hours, just long enough for naturalist Georg Steller to go ashore to sketch and name a few plants and animals, such as the Steller's jay. He was thus the first European to step on Alaskan soil.

Kayak Island rises from the water like a wedge of rock, and **Cape Saint Elias** – one of the most feared capes on this coast – is located at the south end of Kayak Island, where it is connected by a low, narrow strip of land to Pinnacle Rock. Fishermen give this stark cape a wide berth, for strong winds funnel off its sheer cliffs and turbulent currents create erratic waves. This is one of the most dramatic capes on the entire Alaskan coastline and well worth the effort to spot during your cruise. The seas south of Cape Saint Elias were considered perilous until a manned light station was installed in 1916 and later automated by the U.S. Coast Guard in 1974. Today the only inhabitants of Kayak Island are brown bears and foxes.

In waters north of Cape Saint Elias, in Katalla Bay, the famous steamship ***S.S. Portland*** was shipwrecked in November 1910 but its relic wasn't discovered until 2002 by an Alaskan environmentalist exploring this remote shoreline. Nearly buried in silt at the mouth of the Katalla River, and visible only at a very low tide, all that remains of the ship that triggered the Klondike Gold Rush when it pulled into Seattle in 1897 loaded with gold nuggets, are remnants of its wooden hull.

Cape Saint Elias is a feared cape and a famous landmark, being the first place in Alaska visited by Europeans when the Bering expedition stopped here for a few hours in 1741.

PRINCE WILLIAM SOUND

Copper River

MT. WRANGELL

WRANGELL MOUNTAINS

Copper River

RICHARDSON HWY.

Copper Center

Valdez

CHUGACH

MOUNTAINS

GLENN HWY.

1

PARKS HWY.

Palmer

Anchorage

Girdwood

Whittier

Portage Glacier

KENAI PENINSULA

Seward

Sargent Icefield

Columbia Glacier

Harvard Glacier

Barry Glacier

College Fiord

Port Wells

Bligh Is.

Bligh Reef

Cordova

Hinchinbrook I

Cape Hinchinbrook

HINCHINBROOK ENTRANCE

PRINCE WILLIAM SOUND

Knight Island

Chenega I

Sawmill Bay

Montague I

CRUISE SHIP ROUTE
ALTERNATE ROUTES

Statute miles

0   25   50

N

CHAPTER ELEVEN

PRINCE WILLIAM SOUND
& WHITTIER

Prince William Sound is the crowning glory of coastal Alaska. Situated at the top of the Gulf of Alaska, its mainland shores are surrounded by a lofty barrier of mountains and snow, and are indented with dozens of glacier-carved fjords that wend their watery way inland. These fjords contain Alaska's greatest concentration of tidewater glaciers – 20 of which are active.

Glaciers are not the only feature found here in abundance. The numerous forested islands are habitat for Sitka blacktail deer, black and brown bears, wolves, red fox, river otters, mink and other fur-bearing animals. Marine mammals thrive in waters rich with salmon, halibut, red snapper, crab, clams and shrimp. Each summer, thousands of sea otters, Dall porpoises and harbor seals frequent the Sound, along with killer whales and about 50 humpback whales. Overhead bald eagles fly, numbering 5,000 during the summer months, and about half a million marine birds take up residence at the 88 seabird colonies.

Human habitation of Prince William Sound has always been sparse compared to the animal life the area supports. About 3,000 Pacific Eskimos (Chugachs and Eyaks) were living in this area when the first European seafarers arrived. Britain's Captain Cook named Prince

Human habitation is sparse on the glacier-clad shores of Prince William Sound. Shown here is the head of College Fjord.

(Above) A seabird colony at Porpoise Rocks near Hinchinbrook Entrance. (Below) Bryn Mawr Glacier, College Fjord.

William Sound in 1778. When Spanish explorers surveyed part of Prince William Sound in 1790, they left behind such place names as Valdez and Cordova. In 1791 Russia's Alexander Baranof visited Prince William Sound and departed with a new wife – the daughter of a native chief.

A century later, salmon canneries dotted the Sound and herring processing had become a going concern. To compete with European processors, Scottish and Norwegian experts were brought in to teach the locals how to cure and pack herring. A salmon cannery was in operation at **Cordova** when the Harriman Expedition stopped for a visit in the summer of 1899. American railway magnate Edward H. Harriman had chartered the steamship *George W. Elder* for his family's vacation and he invited an impressive collection of scientists to join him in exploring Alaska's coastline. This elite expedition put their time to good use in Prince William Sound. Not only did they name **College Fjord** and its numerous glaciers for the various colleges and universities with which the scientists were affiliated, they also discovered a newly formed fjord.

The *Elder's* captain was using U.S. Coastal Survey charts which showed the navigable waters of Port Wells ending at **Barry Glacier**, located in an inlet adjacent to College Fjord. But when Harriman's expedition pulled up to Barry Glacier, they discovered a narrow passage leading past the glacier's snout. Its wall of ice had retreated since it was last surveyed. Few white people had ever ventured into the upper reaches of

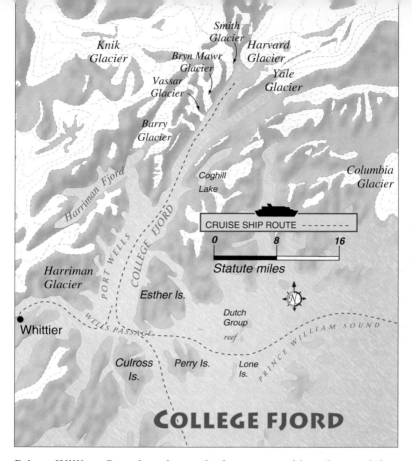

COLLEGE FJORD

Prince William Sound, and none had ever seen this unknown inlet, which was now visible beyond the snout of Barry Glacier. Harriman was a risk taker and he saw this open sliver of water as a window of opportunity. "We shall discover a new Northwest Passage!" he declared. His captain was opposed to taking the ship into uncharted waters where a submerged rock might pierce a hole in the *Elder*'s hull. But Harriman took full responsibility and ordered that they proceed.

Harriman's gamble resulted in their discovery of **Harriman Fjord**. His scientific guests were ecstatic at the sight of more than a dozen glaciers, and expedition members such as John Muir and Grove Karl Gilbert could hardly wait to set up camp on shore and survey these new rivers of ice that flowed into the fjord. Between that summer of discovery and 1914, the Barry Glacier retreated a further four miles. Since then, it has slightly readvanced. The fjord's other glaciers have also retreated, except for Harriman Glacier at its head, which has slowly readvanced. Surprise Glacier was so named because it was the first glacier the Harriman party saw when they entered the fjord.

Today, fishing is the mainstay for most residents of Prince William Sound. In addition to the annual herring and salmon runs are abundant harvests of crab, clams and shrimp. The clam industry suffered a set-

(Top, left) A cruise ship lingers near the snout of a tidewater glacier in College Fjord. (Bottom, left) An on-board naturalist provides glacier commentary.

back when the 1964 Good Friday earthquake raised clam beds 10 feet above the water. The town of **Valdez**, sitting on silt, was shaken so violently that the entire town swayed as if riding ocean waves. Cracks formed in the ground, and began opening and closing, spurting water in the process. Then huge blocks of land slid out to sea, and waterfront buildings and docks collapsed. The final blow came from the tsunamis. Four of these giant, earthquake-generated waves swept ashore, devastating what was left of Valdez.

The town of **Whittier**, on the west side of Prince William Sound, was closer to the quake's epicenter but, unlike Valdez, it was built on bedrock and the ground didn't collapse. The port was, however, hit by a huge harbor wave. A native village on **Chenega Island** was destroyed in the Good Friday earthquake by a tsunami, and was rebuilt at **Sawmill Bay** on Evans Island, on a former saltery site. Valdez was also rebuilt at a new location, about four miles from the original townsite.

In the early '70s, Prince William Sound experienced three bad fishing years in a row, due to poor pink salmon runs. To counteract the cyclical nature of salmon fishing, an aquaculture corporation was formed and over the next few years several large fish hatcheries were built in the western part of the sound. The one at Sawmill Bay, near the native village of Chenega, is one of the largest of its kind in the world in terms of fry released. Salmon runs became so predictable that by the late '80s local fishermen said that catching pink salmon in the sound was more like ocean ranching than fishing.

Meanwhile, a new concern had arisen for fishermen – the presence of oil tankers in their pristine fishing grounds. When oil was discovered beneath the tundra of Alaska's far north, Valdez was chosen as the southern terminus for an 800-mile-long pipeline. Enormous storage tanks were built at Valdez, along with a maze of feeder lines and valves, tanker berths and giant incinerators.

Starting in 1977, crude oil was regularly loaded into tankers and shipped south to refineries. The men and women who fished in local waters were largely opposed to these massive ships traversing the intricate waterways of their fishing grounds. However, measures were taken to ensure their safe movement and for years the transport of oil through the Sound ran smoothly, with no major accidents occurring. Escort tugs and harbor pilots safely saw these tankers (the length of three football fields) through the narrow entrance of the Port of Valdez, past Middle Rock (dubbed the 'can opener') and into open waters. Then, in 1986, things began to change. Budget cutbacks resulted in decreased Coast Guard staff at Valdez, and their radar system was downgraded. Tanker crews, with a proven track record of safety, were no longer required to have a pilot on board past Rocky Point.

Complacency is a mariner's worst enemy and this lesson was learned the hard way in the early hours of March 24, 1989, when the *Exxon Valdez* ran onto **Bligh Reef** and spilled 11 million gallons of crude oil into the pristine waters of Prince William Sound. Currents quickly spread the oil in a southwest direction for 1,200 miles towards the Kenai Fjords, Kodiak Island and the southern tip of the Alaska Peninsula.

Reporters and photographers from around the world converged on Valdez and local residents turned their spare bedrooms into hotel rooms to meet the demand for accommodations. Others arriving at Valdez

Oil tankers in Prince William Sound are now subject to stringent safety measures, including tug escorts and travel restrictions in weather too severe to contain a potential spill.

came to help, and thousands of workers were employed by Exxon to clean the oiled beaches – either by hand or with power hoses. An Alaska state ferry became a floating dormitory for workers.

Fishing fleets were hired to install, clean and repair booms used to corral the spilled oil. As the slick rode the prevailing currents toward the southwestern entrance of Prince William Sound, boats rushed to Sawmill Bay to protect its hatchery with booms. While Alaskans scrambled to keep the spreading oil off their local shores, waterbirds died by the thousands – many so coated in oil they were unidentifiable. Hardest hit of the mammals were the sea otters.

Unlike other marine mammals, sea otters retain their body heat not with blubber but with an insulating fur coat. If this thick fur becomes coated with crude oil, it quickly loses its ability to trap warm air next to the skin and the animal dies of hypothermia. Many of these oil-coated creatures climbed out of the frigid water in an attempt to stay warm. Others inhaled toxic fumes or ingested oil as they groomed their fur.

Exxon spent millions of dollars rescuing the area's wildlife, and extraordinary efforts were made to save the afflicted sea otters. Rushed to emergency headquarters, they were stabilized and sedated before enduring repeated washings with

(Above) Snug Harbor on Knight Island was heavily oiled from the 1989 spill and its streams are still being monitored for lingering after-effects. (Below) A cruise ship plies the scenic waters of Prince William Sound.

a soap solution. Local swimming pools became holding pens for the cleaned otters while they groomed themselves (which restores natural oils) and regained their strength before being returned to the wild. Some were flown to city aquariums for treatment.

The majority of Prince William Sound's shoreline was untouched by the oil spill, and attempts were made to clean the islands and beaches that were in the slick's path. The verdict is still out on the success of this clean-up operation, with a recent government study concluding that lingering oil remains in many streambeds and is dispersed into waterways by tidal action. This residual oil will, according to scientists with the National Marine Fisheries Service, continue to kill or stunt Alaska's pink salmon stocks for generations to come. However, visitors who come to view the pristine beauty and abundant marine life of Prince William Sound will not be disappointed.

One of the Sound's most impressive natural sights also played a major role in the 1989 oil spill. **Columbia Glacier**, largest in Prince William Sound, was named by the Harriman Expedition in 1899. It is over 40 miles long, covers about 440 square miles and terminates at the head of Columbia Bay, a fjord with depths reaching 2,300 feet. The snout of this glacier is six miles across and varies from 160 to 260 feet in height above sea level. The Columbia Glacier has retreated almost a mile in recent years, and scientists predict a drastic retreat of about 20 miles in the next 50 years. This will cause an increase in iceberg production which could potentially block the entrance to the nearby Port of Valdez. Ice discharged from the Columbia has already proven to be a hazard, for the ill-fated *Exxon Valdez* had altered its course to avoid some large ice floes when it hit Bligh Reef. The cruise ships usually keep their distance from Columbia's towering terminus, which is often congested with floating ice, bobbing seals and numerous birds attracted to the fish that feed here on plankton.

Whittier, its port and rail facilities constructed during World War II by the U.S. Army, used to be connected only by a railway tunnel to the rest of Alaska. The tall concrete apartment buildings that comprise the townsite were built to house army personnel and their families, and the 14-story Begich Towers is now home to most of Whittier's year-round population of 300. A highway connection through the 2.5-mile-long tunnel was completed in 2000, providing easy access to Anchorage, which is 65 miles away.

Begich Towers is where most of Whittier's residents live.

Rail cars and motor vehicles head to Whittier after travelling through the mountain tunnel at the head of the Portage Valley.

Traffic in the toll tunnel is one-way and strictly controlled, with vehicles waiting at either end of the tunnel until directed through. Railcars travel through the tunnel on tracks that are straddled by the wheels of cars and buses. Cruise passengers connecting with their ship in Whittier have the option of transferring to or from Anchorage via motorcoach or railcar. Either mode of travel takes you through the scenic Portage Valley, an area covered in Chapter 12.

Valdez (population 4,000) is the most northerly ice-free port in the Western Hemisphere and is connected to the rest of mainland Alaska by the Richardson Highway. A scenic boat ride across Prince William

The Chugach Mountains stretch across the horizon in the Copper River Valley.

Sound transfers passengers from the Whittier cruise port to Valdez if they are heading to the Copper River Princess Lodge. Valdez, nestled at the base of the Chugach Mountains, has been called Alaska's Little Switzerland because of its scenic alpine setting. Attractions include a tour of the Alyeska Pipeline Terminal, the local museum, and a visit to the retreating Valdez Glacier, located about four miles above the pre-1964 townsite. The **Richardson Highway**, running parallel with the pipeline, leads north to Fairbanks. Points of interest along the way include Worthington Glacier, which is accessible on foot, and distant Mount Wrangell, the tallest active volcano in Alaska. Termed a shield volcano because of its broad dome, Mount Wrangell rises more than 14,000 feet and the ice-filled caldera at its summit is nearly 12 square miles. Scientists believe Mount Wrangell's rounded profile is due partly to subglacial eruptions in which the lava flows laterally beneath the ice.

Mount Wrangell's last major eruption was between 2,000 and 10,000 years ago, although it has had several minor eruptions in the last century. The mountain is part of **Wrangell-St. Elias National Park and Preserve**, a vast wilderness of glacier-clad peaks, bordered to the east by the Saint Elias Mountains of Kluane National Park Reserve in Canada's Yukon Territory. The historic copper mining towns of McCarthy and Kennicott are located in Wrangell-St. Elias.

The Richardson Highway eventually converges with the Copper River, which traces the park's western boundary. Park headquarters are at Copper Center (pop. 400), which is also the location of the Copper River Princess Wilderness Lodge where guests enjoy breathtaking views of Mount Drum, a peak standing to the west of Mount Wrangell.

The Copper River Princess Wilderness Lodge is located at Mile 102 of the Richardson Highway.

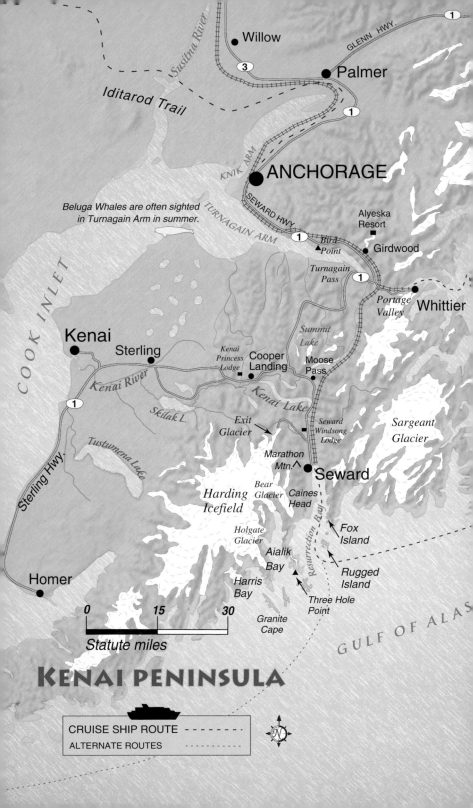

Willow

Palmer

GLENN HWY.

1

3

Susitna River

Iditarod Trail

1

KNIK ARM

ANCHORAGE

Beluga Whales are often sighted in Turnagain Arm in summer.

TURNAGAIN ARM

SEWARD HWY

Alyeska Resort

Girdwood

1

Bird Point

Turnagain Pass

1

Portage Valley

Whittier

COOK INLET

Kenai

Sterling

Kenai River

Kenai Princess Lodge

Cooper Landing

Summit Lake

Moose Pass

Skilak L.

Kenai Lake

Sargeant Glacier

Exit Glacier

Seward Windsong Lodge

Tustumena Lake

1

Marathon Mtn.

Seward

Sterling Hwy.

Harding Icefield

Bear Glacier

Caines Head

Holgate Glacier

Aialik Bay

Resurrection Bay

Fox Island

Homer

Harris Bay

Three Hole Point

Rugged Island

Granite Cape

GULF OF ALAS

0   15   30

Statute miles

KENAI PENINSULA

CRUISE SHIP ROUTE -------

ALTERNATE ROUTES ········

N

CHAPTER TWELVE

ANCHORAGE

Seward, Kenai and the Portage Valley

Anchorage, 'Air Crossroads of the World,' is also the crossroads of Alaska. Not only does its busy international airport handle over 200 flights per day, the city's Lake Hood Air Harbor is the world's busiest floatplane base – handling more than 800 take-offs and landings on a peak summer day. Anchorage is also connected by road and rail to Seward and other communities on the Kenai Peninsula, to Prince William Sound (via Whittier), to Alaska's interior, and to the rest of North America.

As the transportation hub of Alaska, Anchorage is the state's distribution center. Fish and other Alaskan products pass through Anchorage before being shipped elsewhere, and more than 80 per cent of Alaskans depend on Anchorage for incoming freight. In addition to being a major cargo port, Anchorage is the commercial center of Alaska. The city's highrises house the offices of large oil corporations, as well as federal, state and local government agencies. Yet, even with a population of a quarter-million, Anchorage remains refreshingly Alaskan.

Like most Alaskan ports, Anchorage is dominated by the surrounding scenery. The city is situated on the eastern shores of Cook Inlet and backed by the Chugach Mountains, which wrap around Prince William Sound and eventually join another coastal range – the Saint Elias Mountains. South of Anchorage are the glacier-carved and ocean-lapped fjords of the Kenai Peninsula, and to the north is the Alaska Range, home of Mount McKinley and Denali National Park.

A view of downtown Anchorage as seen from across the waters of Knik Arm at Earthquake Park.

The wilderness surrounding Anchorage also makes its way into the city. In winter, moose often show up in the suburbs looking for food, and each spring Anchorage hosts a large population of nesting loons. The city celebrates its close ties to the wilderness with such events as the annual Moose Dropping and Bear Paw Festivals. Best known is the Iditarod Trail Dog Sled Race, an 1,100-mile race from Anchorage to Nome which is held each March. Since the first race in 1977, trained dog teams have mushed their way across two mountain ranges and the pack ice of Norton Sound to reach the finish line at Nome. The race commemorates a heroic rescue mission carried out in 1925 when an outbreak of diphtheria threatened the residents of Nome. A life-saving serum was relayed from Seward, across the Kenai Peninsula and on to Nome, by sled dog mushers who followed an old dog-team mail route that had been blazed in 1910.

Alongside the outdoor activities and festivals of Anchorage, there exists the refinement of big-city hotels, restaurants, and a center for the performing arts. In addition to supporting a symphony orchestra, the city has hosted an impressive list of international artists, including cellist Yo-Yo Ma, soprano Dawn Upshaw, and The Chieftains.

About the only thing lacking in Anchorage is a fishing fleet. The reason is its location at the head of Cook Inlet, where the tidal range is the second largest in the world – second only to Atlantic Canada's Bay of Fundy. Tidal fluxes in Turnagain Arm can surpass 33 feet, and surface waters are in constant motion – travelling at speeds of 10 to 15 mph – with incoming tides often creating a tidal bore (a standing wave) in Turnagain Arm. From November to April, the upper inlet is often frozen or packed with floe ice, and the water's high content of glacial silt is damaging to the saltwater pumps and shaft bearings of fishboat

engines. The water's high silt content was likely a factor in Captain Cook's assuming the inlet was a river when he sailed into this uncharted and boulder-strewn body of water in 1778. His survey was also hindered by recurring thick fog. When Captain Vancouver retraced Cook's route in 1794, he determined that "Cook's River" was actually an inlet and renamed it Cook Inlet.

At one time, the ice in Cook Inlet was 3,000 feet thick. When the ice retreated up Knik and Turnagain Arms at the head of the inlet, shallow estuaries formed as glacial silt was deposited by the retreat-

The Captain Cook Monument over-looks the water at Resolution Park.

ing glaciers. Upon these shores human presence appeared in about 6000 BC when Southern Eskimos first arrived. They inhabited upper Cook Inlet until about 1650 AD, then moved to Prince William Sound when Tanaina natives migrated into the area. Russian fur traders were the next to frequent the region, followed by Russian priests who established a mission near Knik, close to present-day Anchorage, in 1835.

When gold was discovered in 1882 at Crow Creek, about 40 miles south of where downtown Anchorage would eventually stand, prospectors began moving into the area. Then, in 1914, President Woodrow Wilson authorized construction of the Alaska Railroad, with Anchorage the mid-point of a line connecting the coal and gold fields of the interior with the port of Seward. Job seekers flocked to the area and a tent city sprang up on the banks of Ship Creek.

A grid pattern of streets and avenues was laid out by army engineers and a land auction was held, with 655 lots selling for an average price of $225 each. A month later, in August 1915, a poll was held to choose a name for the budding railroad town. The voters chose Alaska City but the federal government decided to keep the existing name of Anchorage. Three years later, the arrival of the first train from Seward marked the completion of the southern line.

World War II brought the next boom to Anchorage. In 1940, Fort Richardson and Elmendorf Air Force Base were built. This military buildup continued with construction of the Alaska Highway in 1942 and, by the end of the war, Anchorage's population had increased five-fold to 43,000 residents.

The Alaska Railroad joined Seward and Anchorage in 1918 and still provides summer passenger service.

In 1951, Anchorage opened its international airport to transpolar air traffic between Europe and Asia, as well as domestic and inter-state air-lines. Seven years later, on June 30, 1958, the Statehood Act was passed and Anchorage celebrated with a 50-ton bonfire. 'North to the Future' was the new state's motto, and the future looked promising for Anchorage. Then, on March 27, 1964, a massive earthquake – the largest ever recorded in North America – hit the city. Situated on glacial silt deposits, downtown Anchorage was devastated. Amid violent shaking, the ground beneath buildings slid into the sea. Sections of 3rd and 4th Avenues collapsed, dropping as much as 10 feet. In the Turnagain area (now Earthquake Park), 75 homes were destroyed, some of them sliding 2,000 feet. Despite such destruction, the city wasted no time rebuilding.

The discovery of North Slope oil in 1968 brought the most recent boom, as oil and construction companies set up headquarters in Anchorage. In 1979, oil revenue began providing the city with such facilities as a new sports arena, a convention center and the Alaska Center for the Performing Arts. The Anchorage Museum of History and Art was expanded and, in 1985, Anchorage was a contender for hosting the 1992 Winter Olympics. The future has arrived for the former tent city of Anchorage.

LOCAL ATTRACTIONS

A tour of downtown Anchorage usually begins at the **Visitor Information Center 1**. Housed in a rustic log cabin with a sod roof, the center is a much photographed sight, with a milepost out front showing directions and flying distances to various cities around the world. Outside the entrance stands a 5,144-pound jade boulder. (Jade, the state gem, is mined around the Arctic Circle.) Adjacent to the Visitor Center is the **Old City Hall**, containing dioramas of Anchorage's old city streets.

The Alaska Statehood Monument commemorates Alaska's 75th anniversary.

Anchorage's Visitor Information Center.

The city's grid pattern (streets running north and south, avenues running east and west) makes downtown Anchorage an easy place to navigate on foot. Hour-long city trolley tours depart every hour on the hour from in front of the 4th Avenue Theater.

Many of Anchorage's original buildings are found on 4th Avenue, and the **4th Avenue Theater** ❷ is a city landmark. Built in the art deco style, it first opened in 1947. Completely refurbished in 1992, the theater contains floor-to-ceiling bronze murals and a ceiling decorated with twinkling lights in the shape of the Big Dipper. This heritage building also houses a restaurant and gift shop. Across the street, at the corner of 4th Avenue and F Street, is the **Alaska Public Lands Information Center** ❸. It was completed in 1939 and is included in the National Register of Historic Places. Formerly the location of a post office and Federal District Court, the building is now a source of park information for visitors planning trips to various regions of Alaska.

Stewart's Photo Shop ❹ (one block east) is housed in the second-oldest downtown building, and its pressed tin ceiling dates from its earlier days as Oscar Anderson's Meat Market. Continuing east along 4th to D Street, you will come across the North Pacific Arc Mural, a huge painting depicting the route of the Anchorage-to-Nome Iditarod Trail Sled Dog Race. On the opposite corner is the **Wendler Building** ❺ (Club 25). Built in 1925 by an early resident, this turreted building was moved here (from the corner of 4th and I Street) in 1984 and is on the National Register of Historic Places. The annual Iditarod Trail Dog Sled Race starts in front of this building and is commemorated with a large, bronze sculpture of a sled dog. Next door, at 446 W. 4th Avenue, is the **National Bank of Alaska** where tapestries depicting Alaska's history are displayed in the lobby. Another lobby worth visiting is that of the **Hilton Hotel**, at 3rd Avenue and E Street, where a stuffed brown bear and polar bear are on display. Across the street is the entrance to

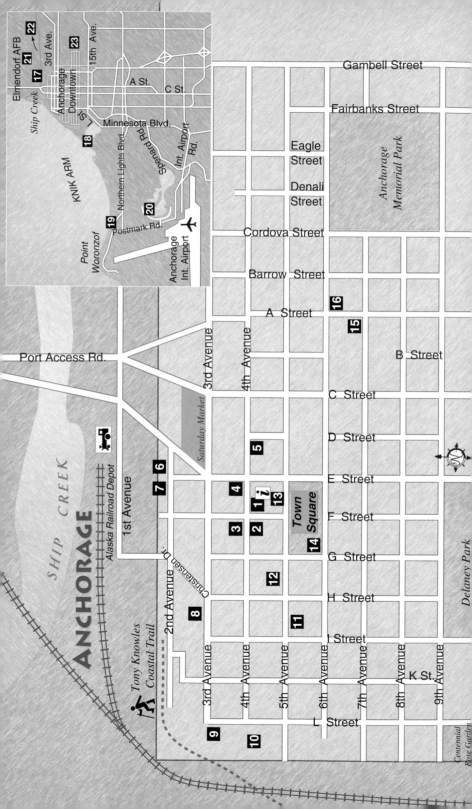

the Saturday Market, an open-air venue of booths selling local handicrafts and other items.

If you continue north on E Street to 2nd Avenue, you will arrive at the **Alaska Statehood Monument** 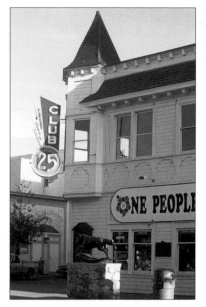, erected in 1990 to commemorate Anchorage's 75th birthday and the 100th anniversary of President Eisenhower's birth. To the west of the monument is the **Ship Creek Overlook** , providing views of the Alaska Railroad Depot to the north and of Ship Creek itself – site of a former fish camp of the Tanaina natives, then a tent city of railroad workers. Today the creek is a popular salmon fishing stream for Anchorage residents. West of the Ship Creek Outlook, on 2nd Avenue, is a small neighborhood of historic homes built around 1917 when the railroad was being developed.

A bronze sled dog marks the Iditarod start line outside the Wendler Building.

Near the western end of 2nd Avenue is the start of the **Tony Knowles Coastal Trail** – eight miles of paved trail which winds along the coast. One block south of the trail's starting point, at the top of Christensen Drive, is the **Port of Anchorage Viewpoint** . This overlooks Knik Arm and the mouth of Ship Creek, where gold rush steamships once anchored while unloading passengers and supplies.

Returning to 3rd Avenue and proceeding west one block to L Street, you arrive at **Resolution Park** and the Captain Cook Monument, commemorating the 200th anniversary of Captain Cook's third and final voyage on board his ship, the *Resolution*. Across the inlet stands Mount Susitna (the Sleeping Lady), its rounded shape carved by glacial ice that once flowed across its summit and lay 3,000 feet deep in Cook Inlet. Three of Alaska's four tallest active volcanoes are also found on the western shores of Cook Inlet – Mount Spurr (11,070 feet), Mount Redoubt (10,197 feet) and Mount Iliamna (10,016 feet). On an island within the inlet stands Mount St. Augustine (4,025 feet) which erupted in 1986, sending ash eight miles high and disrupting air traffic in south-central Alaska. Mount Redoubt erupted in December 1989, dusting Anchorage with ash and disrupting holiday air travel. A more recent eruption came from Mount Spurr in August 1992, with prevailing winds carrying the ash west to Prince William Sound and Yakutat Bay.

Directly south of Resolution Park is **Elderberry Park** 🔟, which contains the Oscar Anderson House – Anchorage's first wood frame house, built in 1915 and now a museum, open daily in the summer. Other points of interest along 5th Avenue are the **Holy Family Cathedral** 🔢, transported from the town of Knik by horse and sleigh in the early 1920s; the **Imaginarium** 🔢, a science discovery center; and the **Egan Convention Center** 🔢, named for William A. Egan, Alaska's first governor elected after statehood. This Center is a hub for cruise passengers connecting with transfers to Whittier or Seward. Across the street is **Town Square**, a municipal park and popular gathering place for locals with its flower-bordered pathways, benches, outdoor amphitheater and the **Alaska Center for the Performing Arts** 🔢 The Kimball Building, Anchorage's first dry goods store, stands at the northeast corner of the park.

At 121 W. 7th Avenue is the **Anchorage Museum of History and Art** 🔢, an impressive museum housing Alaskan and northern art – from prehistoric to contemporary times. A gift shop and cafe are also on the premises. In the next block, at A Street and 6th Avenue, is the **Russian Orthodox Museum** 🔢. **Ship Creek Salmon Viewing & Waterfowl Nesting Area** 🔢 along Ship Creek, is where salmon can be viewed swimming upstream from June through September. At nearby **Westchester Lagoon Waterfowl Sanctuary** 🔢, wild geese and ducks live year round.

Earthquake Park 🔢, located between Northern Lights Boulevard and the shores of Knik Arm, is the site of Anchorage's worst destruction during the 1964 earthquake. Here buildings were leveled by landslides. Rather than rebuild in this area, Anchorage residents decided to

The Egan Center is across the street from flower-filled Town Square.

turn it into a park with an interpretive display. The Tony Knowles Coastal Trail runs along the park's shoreline.

Lake Hood Air Harbor 20, located between Earthquake Park and the International Airport, is the world's largest and busiest floatplane base. A shoreside park offers visitors a view of the lake and its aerial activity. **Alaska Aviation Heritage Museum** on the south shore of Lake Hood (4721 Aircraft Drive) contains an observation deck and fascinating displays featuring historic aircraft and pioneer aviators.

Northwest of downtown Anchorage is the **Elmendorf Air Force Base Wildlife Museum 21** which features mounted animals, and the **Alaska Native Heritage Center 22**, where indigenous art and architecture can be viewed in a parklike setting. This attraction can be reached by free shuttle service from downtown.

One mile east of downtown is **Merrill Field** 23, named in honor of a pioneer pilot who was the first to fly a commercial flight west of Juneau and the first to attempt a night landing in Anchorage. He also discovered, in 1927, a key pass in the Alaska Range which bears his name. With half of Alaska's licensed pilots living in Anchorage, Merrill Field is a busy small plane base.

Regular flights are available from Anchorage to Alaska's far-flung northern communities, such as **Nome**, a town rich in Eskimo culture and gold-rush history. Located on Norton Sound, an arm of the Bering Sea, Nome (pop. 3,500) is the location of the finish line of the Iditarod Trail Dog Sled Race. In winter, Nome residents can ski on the frozen Bering Sea and watch the Northern Lights dance across a winter sky. In summer, the sun never sets, or at least it appears not to because it dips just below the horizon. At summer solstice the sun is up for more than

Lake Spenard, where floatplane rides are available, is part of the Lake Hood Air Harbor.

Nome's tent city appeared after gold was found on the beach in 1898.
The gold rush lasted four years and attracted 20,000 prospectors.

22 hours and during the short night the sky doesn't darken, giving the appearance of 24 hours of daylight from June through early August.

TURNAGAIN ARM

The scenic **Seward Highway** runs between Anchorage and Seward, and was designated an All-American Road in 2000, an honor given to the nation's most outstanding highways. The Alaska Railroad follows basically the same route as the Seward Highway, which starts just south of Anchorage and traces the northern shore of Turnagain Arm. There are several turnouts and scenic overlooks along this stretch of road, with views across Turnagain Arm to the Kenai Mountains.

Beluga whales are often sighted in Turnagain Arm, where tides can range up to 38 feet, exposing vast expanses of mud flats at low tide. People are warned not to venture onto these exposed mud flats which can become quicksand. More than one person has lost their life after getting stuck in the mud and drowning as the water level rose before rescue crews could save them. Beluga Point and Bird Point are good spots to view Turnagain Arm's bore tides, which arrive at Beluga Point about an hour after low water at Anchorage.

Tidal bores occur regularly in Turnagain Arm due to the large tidal range in Cook Inlet. When the rapidly rising tidal waters in Cook Inlet flow into the narrow, shallow, gently sloping basin of Turnagain Arm, this creates an incoming wall of water ranging from six inches to 6 feet in height, depending on the size of the tide and other factors such as wind strength and direction. Also along this stretch of the Seward Highway are several gunmounts, used to hold 105mm recoilless rifles for shooting down accumulated snow and reducing the occurrence of random avalanches, which close the highway for short periods.

At the highway's junction with the **Alyeska Highway** is the town of **Girdwood**, a former mining camp and now a recreational center attracting skiers in winter and hikers in summer. At the far end of town, nestled at the base of **Mount Alyeska**, is the Alyeska Prince Hotel, a luxury resort featured in the cruise lines' land tours. Adjacent to the resort is the Alyeska Tramway which operates daily in summer and provides panoramic views from a mountaintop complex. Also in Girdwood is the Chugach National Forest's District Office where a wealth of information is available on the area's natural attractions.

PORTAGE VALLEY

A connecting road worth exploring while travelling the Seward Highway is the **Portage Glacier Road**, which leads to Portage Lake. Near this junction is the former townsite of Portage – a railroad town that was once part of a natural trade route across the Portage Valley between Cook Inlet and Prince William Sound, used by natives, Russian fur traders and gold prospectors. The land underneath Portage sank during the 1964 earthquake and, flooded by Turnagain Arm, the town was abandoned. The marshy land is now ideal habitat for waterfowl. The area's **Alaska Wildlife Conservation Center** is a good place to see indigenous birds as well as large mammals, including moose, caribou and brown bear. The animals living at this center are orphaned or injured when brought here for rehabilitation.

(Below) Alyeska Resort. (Right) A roadside view from the Seward Highway.

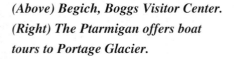

(Above) Begich, Boggs Visitor Center.
(Right) The Ptarmigan offers boat
tours to Portage Glacier.

The turnoff to **Portage Lake** is about three miles south of the former townsite, and the paved highway weaves across the valley floor, past campgrounds, trout ponds and salmon streams to **Begich, Boggs Visitor Center** overlooking Portage Lake. Named for two Congressmen whose plane disappeared in the area in 1972, the Center provides information on the Chugach National Forest and the glaciers lining Portage Valley. The retreating **Portage Glacier** flows into Portage Lake and can be viewed on hour-long boat tours operated by Holland America under a special-use permit with the Forest Service. **Byron Glacier** can be accessed on foot, following an easy-to-moderate mile-long trail that traces the glacier's meltwater stream to its snout.

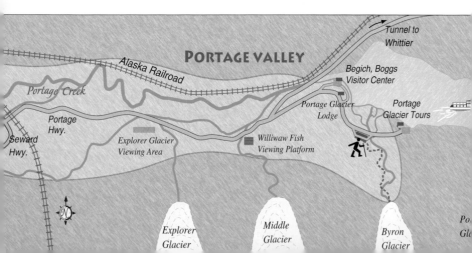

It's possible to walk right onto the glacier's snout but be aware of the avalanche danger – a distant rumbling sound would be your cue to leave. The **Williwaw Fish Viewing Platform** is a good place to see spawning salmon from late July through early September.

Not far from the Begich, Boggs Visitor Center is the Portage Glacier Lodge, a day lodge with a cafe and gift shop. The Portage Highway continues eastward, along the shores of Portage Lake to a mountain tunnel that leads to **Whittier**. Until 2000, when modification of the tunnel was completed, there was no road connection to Whittier and vehicles would ride on flat cars through the tunnel.

KENAI PENINSULA

A popular recreational area for Anchorage residents, the Kenai Peninsula has been called "Alaska in miniature" for the diversity of its scenery, habitat and wildlife. The Seward Highway wraps around the head of Turnagain Arm before turning inland and ascending 1,000 feet to Turnagain Pass, then

A young hiker pauses on the trail to Byron Glacier.

meandering southwestward past mountain lakes and creeks. The rail line diverges with the highway at the head of Turnagain Arm, paralleling the Placer River, which drains the many streams of Placer Valley. Points of interest along the Seward Highway include a scenic viewpoint overlooking Lower Summit Lake, and a stop at the Summit Lake Lodge, a landmark log structure with views overlooking Upper Summit Lake. There are also several hiking trailheads along the highway.

Near Quartz Creek bridge the stands of red-rust spruce trees along this stretch of highway have been ravaged by spruce bark beetles. More than a million acres of spruce forests on the Kenai Peninsula have been killed by these beetles. Their larvae, the size of rice grains, destroy the tree's ability to transport nutrients, causing it to die.

(Above) Park visitor walks past the snout of Exit Glacier. (Below) Angler tests his luck in the Kenai River.

The **Sterling Highway** turn-off leads westward along the shores of the Kenai River where anglers will find some of the best freshwater fishing Alaska has to offer. Nestled on the banks of this beautiful river is the Kenai Princess Wilderness Lodge, where the setting is sublime and excursions include lake kayaking and river rafting, as well as nature hikes and horseback trail rides, all offering a close-up look at the area's green valleys, snowcapped mountains and turquoise lakes. Much of this area lies within the Kenai National Wildlife Refuge, first established as the Kenai National Moose Range in 1941 to protect the area's moose population. More than 200 species of wildlife live in this 1.92 million-acre refuge, its headquarters located in Soldotna (pop. 4,000), one of several rural communities situated in the western reaches of the Kenai Peninsula. Nearby Kenai (pop. 7,000), on the shores of Cook Inlet, is an historic homestead town containing a century-old Russian church and art galleries. Homer (pop. 4,700) is another enclave for local artists. This scenic fishing port is at the far end of the Sterling Highway and its famous spit extends halfway across the mouth of Kachemak Bay. Above this rise the glaciated peaks of the Kenai Mountains.

Seward, headquarters for Kenai Fjords National Park, is the southern terminus of the Seward Highway, 127 miles from Anchorage. Located at the head of Resurrection Bay at the foot of the Kenai Mountains, Seward was established in 1903 as an ocean terminal for the planned Alaska Railroad. Named after Secretary of State William Seward (who arranged the purchase of Alaska in 1867), the town of 2,800 is today a commercial fishing and cargo port.

The waters in and around Resurrection Bay are prime fishing grounds, with huge salmon runs and halibut weighing over 300 pounds. The Seward Silver Salmon Derby, held each August, is Alaska's most prestigious fishing event, drawing thousands of anglers. Halibut, a seafood delicacy, is served fresh from the sea in Seward's modern, waterfront restaurants overlooking the bustling boat harbor.

At the south end of town is the new **Alaska SeaLife Center**, a research and educational complex operated by the University of Alaska-Fairbanks. Sick, injured or stranded sea mammals and birds are brought to the Center to be cared for by a team of veterinarians. Those animals unable to return to the wild will find a permanent home at the Center where rookeries are designed to mimic the region's natural habitat, featuring pools of clear sea water and secluded areas where animals can mate and rear their young.

The **Park Visitor Center** provides information on **Kenai Fjords National Park**, which was established in 1980 and is best seen from the water. Seward's sightseeing boats take visitors to see the park's rugged capes, sea arches and tidewater glaciers. The massive **Harding Icefield** covers an area of 30 by 50 miles and is a remnant of an icecap that completely covered the Kenai Mountains at the end of the last ice age. As recently as 1909, the Kenai Fjords were still ice-filled bays. Fifty years later these glaciers had staged a major retreat, leaving in their wake fjords which contain new islands and cliffs freshly scoured by ice.

In addition to this dramatic glacial action, tectonic plates are colliding in

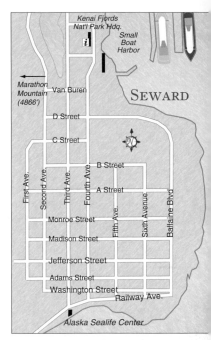

(Below) The Alaska SeaLife Center provides a close look at Steller sea lions and other species indigenous to the region.

the area. The Kenai Mountains rest on the subsiding edge of one plate and, as they are pulled under, glacial-carved cirques become halfmoon bays and former peaks are reduced to craggy islands. The Kenai coast is slowly slipping into the sea. All this happens very slowly of course, except when an earthquake hits.

When the 1964 Good Friday earthquake struck, the ground underneath Seward – perched on the edge of a submarine slope – lost its shear strength and became part of a massive underwater slide. The Seward shoreline dropped six feet within 30 seconds, taking with it the town's harbor and fuel docks. This was followed by a series of tsunamis that wiped out the remaining waterfront industries, including the railroad docks. Seward's death toll was 13 and a plaque in remembrance of these victims rests in the center of town near the rebuilt harbor.

The natural forces at work along the Kenai coast are manifested in dramatic landmarks that compete for sightseers' attention. First there is **Aialak Cape**, a granite intrusive formed 60 million years ago, which looks like a huge boulder shoved skyward from the earth's crust. Then there is **Three Hole Point** – a towering sea arch formed by wave erosion. And of course there are the glaciers, many of which are still unnamed. Sea mammals thrive in these waters and more than 200,000 seabirds – including horned and tufted puffins – nest on the rocky islands and capes of the Kenai Peninsula. The **Chiswell Islands** are also used by sea lions, and **Barwell Island**, off Cape Resurrection, is a murre colony. In Resurrection Bay, sea otters are a common sight.

Resurrection Bay was once used by Russian fur traders for ship building. Before that it was inhabited by a small population of Southern Eskimos called Unegkurmit. In 1918, the artist and adventurer

Three Hole Point is one of several dramatic landmarks viewed on a boat tour of Kenai Fjords National Park.

Rockwell Kent lived with his son and a fox farmer on **Fox Island**. His book *Wilderness: A Quiet Adventure in Alaska* describes his winter experiences here. Alaska Heritage Tours offers boat tours to Fox Island and overnight stays at its lodge.

On the western shores of Resurrection Bay, six miles south of Seward, is **Caines Head State Recreation Area**. This steep headland, with its strategic view of the bay, was chosen by the United States Army for building a Harbor Defense System during World War II. Seward was an important wartime port, for it was Alaska's only year-round transportation center before completion of the Whittier Tunnel and Alcan Highway. A half-dozen other locations were also chosen for guarding Resurrection Bay, including an iron bunker installed opposite Fox Island near the bay's eastern entrance.

Kenai Fjords National Park encompasses Exit Glacier, located northwest of Seward where the Exit Glacier Road intersects with the Seward Highway. Near this junction is the Seward Windsong Lodge, providing excellent accommodations and dining. At the far end of Exit Glacier Road is the entrance to the Exit Glacier fee area which includes a ranger station with exhibits and interpretive programs. A network of hiking trails leads to the terminus of the glacier, which is retreating and actively calving large chunks of ice. Visitors are warned to stay off the ice but it is possible to get very close to the edge of the glacier while remaining on park pathways.

(Below) Seward Windsong Lodge, located along Exit Glacier Road, offers excellent meals and accommodation. (Right) A sign outside a Kenai-area hair salon.

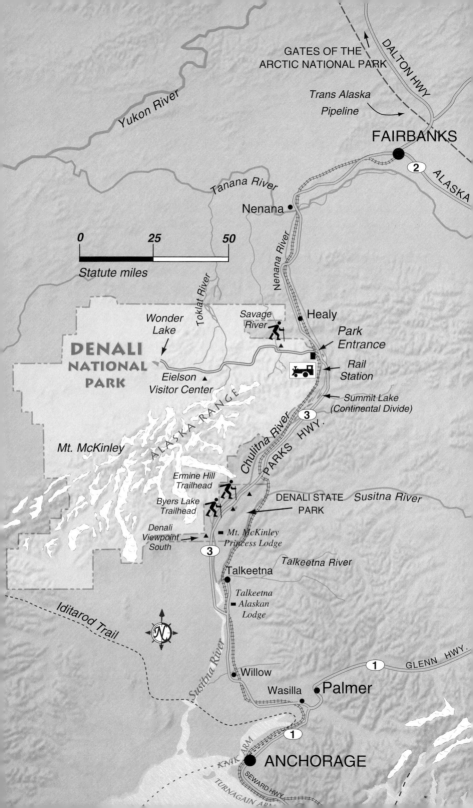

CHAPTER THIRTEEN

DENALI NATIONAL PARK
& Fairbanks

Denali National Park and Preserve is symbolic of the wilderness that once dominated North America. As vast tracts of the New World's land were explored and colonized, a movement arose to preserve pockets of wilderness where the imprint of humans was barely noticeable. In Alaska, these pockets are mighty big. Of America's 95 million acres of designated wilderness areas, 57.6 million are in Alaska. By comparison, Ohio has 77 acres and some eastern states have none.

The need to preserve wilderness is deeply rooted in American thought. Thomas Jefferson, Ralph Waldo Emerson and Henry David Thoreau were the philosophical fathers of environmentalism, a movement that gained momentum in the late 19th century, with John Muir and President Theodore Roosevelt among its early proponents.

In 1916, the National Park Service was established, and the following year Mount McKinley National Park was created, largely through the efforts of naturalist and conservationist Charles Sheldon who first visited the Denali region in the summer of 1906. As chairman of the Boone and Crockett Club of New York, Sheldon led a 10-year campaign to preserve the Denali wilderness and finally, in 1917, Congress

Mount McKinley, highest peak in North America, is the centerpiece of Denali National Park and Preserve.

approved a bill to establish a national park. Although Sheldon wanted the name of Denali for the new park, it was called the Mount McKinley National Park from 1917 until 1980. In that year the boundary of the park was tripled in size from 1.9 million acres to six million acres and became the Denali National Park and Preserve.

Denali is a native word meaning 'high one' and it refers to **Mount McKinley**, named after President McKinley, which rises 15,000 feet above the surrounding countryside. Its twin peaks stand in isolation, often shrouded in clouds that collect around the tallest mountain in North America. The north summit is 19,470 feet high and the south peak rises to 20,320 feet. The Denali National Park and Preserve is huge and, at six million acres, is larger than Massachusetts.

Mount McKinley is part of the six-hundred-mile long **Alaska Range** and its massive size is likely due to its location in a bend of the Denali fault system, where one crustal block has shoved against another. McKinley is an impressive sight and a challenging climb for mountaineers, who first reached the North Peak in 1910 and the South Peak in 1913. Summer weather on Mount McKinley is cool, wet and windy.

The park contains habitat for 37 species of mammals – caribou, grizzly bear, moose, wolf and Dall sheep among others – and 155 species of birds, including golden and bald eagles. These animals live in the taiga (white and black spruce intermingled with aspen, birch and

Alaska Range

poplar) and tundra (willow, dwarf birch, sedges and grasses), alongside the lakes, rivers and alpine glaciers of the park. A 90-mile road traverses the park, providing visitors with breathtaking sights of **Wonder Lake**, **Savage River Canyon** and **Muldrow Glacier**, which descends 16,000 feet from the upper slopes of Mount McKinley.

GETTING TO DENALI

The entrance to Denali National Park is located 240 miles north of Anchorage (120 miles south of Fairbanks) and can be reached by road, rail and air. From Anchorage, the rail line and Glenn Highway (#1) trace the shores of Knik Arm, where the **Matanuska Valley** lies at its head. This lush valley, about 40 miles northeast of Anchorage, was settled in the 1930s by midwest farmers. The growing season here is only four months but the long daylight hours produce giant vegetables – turnips over seven pounds and 70-pound cabbages. **Palmer** is the valley's trading center and hometown of Olympic champion skier Tommy Moe. The turn-off to Palmer is at the junction of the Glenn Highway (#1) and George Parks Highway (#3), the latter running between Anchorage and Fairbanks. About seven miles past this junction along Highway #3 is the town of **Wasilla**, an Anchorage bedroom community with about 6,000 residents. It is also the headquarters of the Iditarod Trail Sled Dog Race. About 25 miles past Wasilla is the town of

(Above) George Parks Highway. (Below) Talkeetna is an interesting stop on the road to Denali.

Willow, chosen by voters in 1976 as a new site for the state's capital, which is currently located in Juneau. However, the projected cost of such a move prevented it from happening.

Talkeetna, located about 20 miles south of Denali State Park, is a major stop along the Alaska Railroad. Here passengers often disembark to visit one of several lodges in the area where the views of Mount McKinley are superb. Two excellent choices are the Princess Mt. McKinley Wilderness Lodge and the Talkeetna Alaskan Lodge. Shuttles are available from these lodges to Talkeetna (pop. 800) where the town's pioneer past is well preserved in its original log cabins and one-room schoolhouse now housing the local museum. Talkeetna is a base for mountaineering expeditions to Mount McKinley, and flightseeing excursions depart regularly from its small airstrip. River rafting and dog sledding demonstrations are also offered.

The Talkeetna Forest Ranger Station, located two blocks west of the town's museum, is the place to obtain information on **Denali State Park**'s trails and natural attractions. Denali State Park was established in 1970 and expanded to its present size in 1976. The park shares it western boundary with the much larger Denali National Park and Preserve. The Parks Highway runs though Denali State Park and offers superb vantage points for viewing the Alaska Range. The roadside viewing area at Milepost 134.8, with an interpretive board, is probably the best place to pause in your journey and gaze at snow-crowned McKinley and other peaks of the Alaska Range.

Denali National Park is the highlight of land tours available to cruise passengers embarking or disembarking in Seward or Whittier. The main staging area for visitors is just north of the park entrance where a number of lodges and services are situated. Regular bus shuttles take lodge visitors into the park where a visitor center is located near the entrance. Free shuttle buses serve the entrance area, which encompasses the Railroad Depot, Park Headquarters and several miles of trails.

If you arrive at Denali with an organized cruisetour, you will have the option of numerous excursions into the park that are arranged by the lodge. A bus will pick you up at the lodge and take you into the park, stopping at several spots where you can wander awhile and observe this beautiful landscape. The buses move along the park road at a leisurely pace, pausing at the various viewpoints along the way.

There are many species of wildlife you will be able to see from roadside vantage points. Caribou and moose often feed within a few miles of the road and occasionally a brown (grizzly) bear might be spotted along a ridgetop or valley floor. The park is also home to wolves, but during summer months they generally hunt individually and at night, so a sighting is rare.

The park also supports a variety of birds, some of which have migrated great distances, including the arctic tern (from

South Denali Viewpoint at Mile 134.8 provides superb views of Mount McKinley and the Alaska Range.

Bus excursions into the tundra of Denali National Park offer travellers a chance to spot moose, bear and, as shown above, caribou. (Below) Savage River Trail.

Antarctica) and jaegers which have arrived from southern oceans. More common are the ptarmigan (a small goose-like bird), grouse and jays. Some birds of prey, such as golden eagles, can also be seen riding the updrafts along ridgetops in search of food.

The Eielson Visitor Center is the most common turnaround point and is an eight-hour round trip that provides spectacular views of Mount McKinley and the surrounding tundra. Longer day excursions extend to Wonder Lake, about 170 miles or 11 hours round trip. Although there are restrooms and drinking water available at the park centers, there is no food service. So, in addition to warm clothing, you should be sure to pack a lunch if it is not being provided on the excursion.

If you arrive at Denali by car, you can drive as far as the Savage River parking lot at Mile 15. Private vehicles are restricted beyond this point and one of the park's shuttle buses must be taken to travel further into the park. These buses depart regularly from the visitor center and seats

SAFE HIKING

When hiking in Denali, keep in mind that weather conditions can change quickly and that crossing glacial rivers can be dangerous. Sturdy footgear is a must. Never approach or feed a wild animal. Make noise when hiking so you don't surprise an animal, especially a bear. If you encounter a bear, do not run; however, if a moose charges at you, run. Check with the visitor center for information on trails and bear safety. Ranger-led walks and hikes are offered throughout the summer.

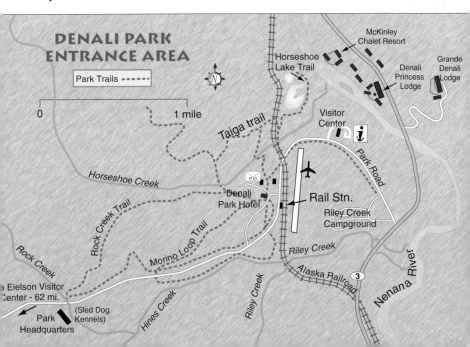

are in heavy demand, so an advance reservation by phone or through the lodge where you are staying is recommended. If you are considering overnight camping in the backcountry of the park, permits must be obtained in person at the visitor center.

Several good trails lie within the park's unrestricted entrance area and are easily accessible by private vehicle or by shuttle bus from the visitor center. Horseshoe Lake Trail is a 1.5-mile roundtrip hike through taiga forest and entails a 200-foot descent to an oxbow lake. This lake, an abandoned meander of the Nenana River, was part of the river's main channel until the accumulation of silt and the building of dams by beavers caused the river to carve a new course.

At mile 15 on the Park Road is the Savage River Trail, which follows the floor of a V-shaped canyon once filled with glacial meltwater. The trail runs along both sides of the narrow river which is spanned by a footbridge at the loop end of the trail, which is three miles roundtrip and an easy one-hour hike along flat terrain.

DENALI'S SLED DOGS

Denali's most popular interpretive program – one that began in 1939 – is the sled-dog demonstration held three times a day throughout the summer at the park's kennels (reached by shuttle bus from the Visitor Center). These working dogs have played an important role ever since rangers began patrolling the park in 1921 to discourage the poaching of wildlife. When the size of Denali National Park was tripled in 1980, the original two-million-acre park was designated a wilderness area, which restricted the use of motorized equipment and mechanized transport within its boundaries.

Alaskan huskies make superb sled dogs.

Thus, rangers would carry out their winter patrols by dog sled team – a traditional mode of transport that has proven to be more reliable than snow machines. Trained sled dogs can sense a snow-obscured trail beneath their paws and find a patrol cabin during a wind-driven whiteout. They don't run out of gas or have mechanical parts that freeze up. Food, water and booties to protect their feet are all that's needed. Their thick fur keeps them warm when camping along the trail, and a sled dog is born to run. Those at Denali are bred not for looks but for performance, with long legs and tough feet for breaking a trail through deep snow. A friendly temperament is also required for greeting the thousands of park visitors who come to meet them each summer.

Sternwheel tour boats take Fairbanks visitors on attraction-filled rides along the Chena River.

FAIRBANKS

Situated on a flat river plain, Fairbanks is a sprawling city – the second largest in Alaska with a borough population of 75,000. Named for the Indiana Republican Senator Charles W. Fairbanks (who became Vice President to Theodore Roosevelt), the town was founded during the gold rush. Enjoying a strategic position on the banks of the Chena River, Fairbanks became a major trading center for miners.

During World War II, the military built airfields and roads around Fairbanks, and this construction boom produced jobs for the local civilians. Fairbanks also benefited from the Cold War era when renewed defense spending expanded the area's existing bases, and radar systems and missile sites were installed. Today its airforce base serves as the site of a joint American-Canadian-Russian training program for coordinating search and rescue operations in the Arctic.

In 1967, the Chena River overflowed and flooded Fairbanks. With the help of federal aid, local businesses were rebuilt and homes were restored. A year later oil was discovered near Prudhoe Bay, and Fairbanks was once again in a strategic position for the proposed pipeline. When construction began in 1974, the population surged. The heyday ended in 1978 and Fairbanks plummeted into a recession with widespread unemployment.

The hot and cold nature of Fairbanks' economic past is also reflected in its climate. Just 90 miles south of the Arctic Circle, winter days are short and bitterly cold. In contrast to the dark chill of winter are the long, hot, sunny days of summer with daylight in June and July lasting about 21 hours. The aurora borealis is regularly seen in the skies over Fairbanks.

LOCAL ATTRACTIONS

With its local sites fairly spread out, Fairbanks is best seen by car or coach tour, although guided walking tours are offered by the Fairbanks Convention & Visitors Bureau. Popular attractions include **Alaskaland Pioneer Park,** established in 1967 to commemorate the centennial of Alaska's purchase. Admission is free to this 44-acre park encircled by its own small-scale railroad to provide transportation for visitors. Sites include: Gold Rush Town, where shops and cafes are housed in relocated pioneer cabins; Palace Theater & Saloon, which holds summer musical reviews; the sternwheeler *Nenana*, which is drydocked in the middle of the park; the Pioneer Museum; and Northern Inva, where native athletes demonstrate their heritage sports.

The **University of Alaska Museum**, one of the state's top 10 visitor attractions, houses displays of Alaska animals, plants, natural history, native culture and gold rush history. Also located on campus, is the Geophysical Institute – a center for earthquake research – and the **Large Animal Research Station** where you can view musk-ox, reindeer and caribou from raised platforms The University of Alaska Fairbanks began as an agricultural college in 1922 and grew into a major institution for higher learning in Alaska.

Local **sternwheeler cruises** include a four-hour-long, narrated cruise of the Chena and Tanana Rivers aboard an authentic sternwheel riverboat, from the decks of which you will see log cabins, fish wheels and the 'Wedding of the Rivers' where the Tanana – carrying 100,000 tons of glacier sediment – meets the mouth of the Chena. Stops along the way include a dog-sledding demonstration at the kennels of Susan Butcher, four-time Iditarod champion.

A few miles west of Fairbanks is the **Cripple Creek Resort** (also known as the Ester Gold Camp). Listed on the National Register of

Visitors can pan for gold at Gold Dredge Number 8, which operated in the Goldstream Valley near Fairbanks from 1928 to 1959.

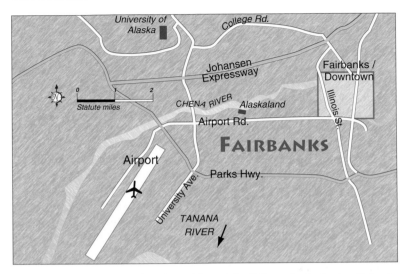

Historic Places, its authentic gold rush buildings include the Cripple Creek Hotel and the famous Malemute Saloon. Continuing southwest along the Park's Highway, travellers arrive at **Nenana** where the local railroad depot houses the official State of Alaska Railroad Museum. Built in 1923, it too is listed on the National Register of Historic Sites.

An hour's drive east of Fairbanks along the Chena Hot Springs Road takes you to the **Chena Hot Springs**. Rustic cabins provide accommodation and soaking facilities include two jacuzzis, a hot tub and a swimming pool. The springs here circulate through fractures in the granite to depths of two miles where the rock is hotter than the surface boiling point of water.

Circle Hot Springs, discovered by a prospector in 1893, are reached by the Steese Highway which leads in a northeast direction from Fairbanks. **Manley Hot Springs** are located a 45-minute flight northwest of Fairbanks or via a detour off the **Dalton Highway**, which leads north to Prudhoe Bay. A trip along the Dalton takes you across the Yukon River, the Arctic Circle, the rugged Brooks Range, rolling foothills and a vast, tundra-covered plain. Called the "Haul Road," it was a supply route for trucks serving work camps during construction of the **Trans-Alaska Pipeline**.

Construction of the pipeline was Alaska's most important economic boom since the gold rush. Built by a conglomerate of oil companies, called Alyeska Pipeline Service Company, it was a major engineering feat and was designed to prevent thawing of the permafrost which covers much of Alaska's interior. Other factors in construction were the region's drastic temperature range (from 90° F to -60° F) and high earthquake activity. Last but not least were concerns that the pipeline would damage the region's fragile ecosystem and disrupt migration of caribou and other animals.

The discovery of oil in 1968 set a series of events into motion. In 1971, the Native Claims Settlement Act resolved the grievances of Alaska's natives who felt that neither the Alaska Purchase nor the Statehood Act had established their land rights. The 1971 Act established 13 native-owned corporations, and granted the native peoples $1 billion in revenue and 40 million acres of land.

In November 1973, Congress passed the Pipeline Authorization Act and construction of the 800-mile pipeline began. About half of its length was raised on stilts joined in a zig-zag pattern for flexibility when the pipeline expands and contracts with drastic temperature changes. The accordion-like pattern also allows the pipeline to absorb earthquake waves with minimal damage.

The oil started to flow in 1977, with friction from the pumping pressure keeping the oil at about 140° F. To absorb this heat rather than transfer it into the ground (and melt the permafrost), the stilts supporting the pipeline contain a special liquid that absorbs the oil's high temperature and releases it into the air through radiator fins. The pipe itself is protected by a layer of galvanized steel and nearly four inches of insulation. Over the years the pipeline has been shot at more than 50 times, leaving indentations but never a puncture hole until, in October 2001, someone fired at it with a .338-calibre rifle. Oil spraying from the small bullet hole was spotted by a surveillance helicopter crew about 75 miles north Fairbanks, and four hours later a 37-year-old man was arrested and charged. He apparently had no motive for the shooting and

The Alaska Pipeline and Dalton Highway wind past Galbraith Lake on the north slope of the Brooks Range.

appeared to be intoxicated. The pipeline is buried underground at regu-larly spaced intervals to allow for crossings by caribou, which reported-ly will not pass beneath a raised structure. The caribou herds that migrate across the North Slope appear to be unaffected by the pipeline's presence and are flourishing. However, environmentalists remain opposed to any oil drilling within the **Arctic National Wildlife Refuge** for fear this would jeopardize the coastal calving ground of the Porcupine caribou herd. Nonetheless, polls indicate that the majority of Alaskans are in favor of drilling.

The oil discovered at **Prudhoe Bay** was a long time in the making. Its source is a rich shale deposited during early Jurassic time, which was eventually covered with 6,000 feet of sandstone and other rock during the geological formation of Alaska. A chemical process (not yet fully understood) transforms organic material into oil which, being lighter than water, will float through available pores and fractures in the rock above and collect in reservoirs.

Barrow (pop. 4,500) lies about 200 miles west of Prudhoe Bay and is the northernmost U.S. settlement, situated 350 miles above the Arctic Circle and unconnected to any other community by road. The Inupiat Eskimos who founded this Arctic community have traditionally hunted whales, walruses and polar bears, and are noted for their carvings in ivory and bone, as well as their production of mukluks (boots made of sealskin). Barrow's Eskimo culture, along with the opportunity to see polar bears, northern lights and the midnight sun, draws air travellers to this remote port on the edge of the Arctic Ocean. A monument opposite the airport is dedicated to humorist Will Rogers and aviator Wiley Post, whose plane fatally crashed near Point Barrow in 1935.

Mount McKinley

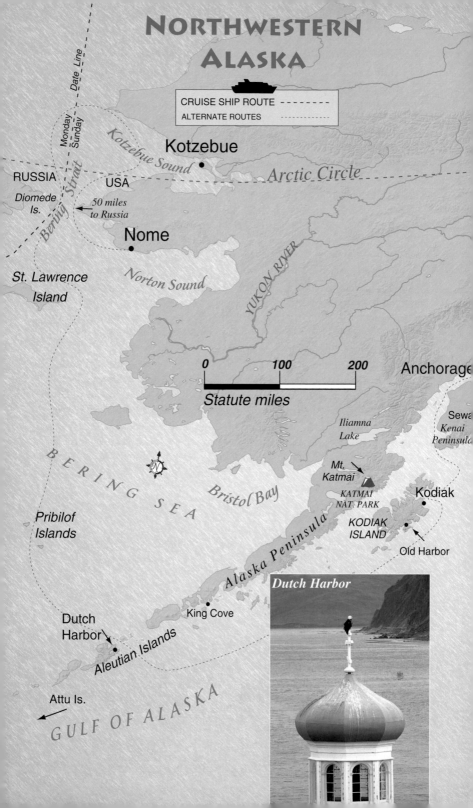

NORTHWESTERN ALASKA

CRUISE SHIP ROUTE - - - - -
ALTERNATE ROUTES · · · · · · ·

Date Line

Monday Sunday

Kotzebue Sound

Kotzebue

Arctic Circle

RUSSIA

USA

Diomede Is.

Bering Strait

50 miles to Russia

Nome

St. Lawrence Island

Norton Sound

YUKON RIVER

0   100   200

Statute miles

Anchorage

Iliamna Lake

Sew
Kenai Peninsula

Mt. Katmai

KATMAI NAT. PARK

Kodiak

KODIAK ISLAND

Old Harbor

B E R I N G   S E A

Pribilof Islands

Bristol Bay

Alaska Peninsula

Dutch Harbor

King Cove

Aleutian Islands

Dutch Harbor

Attu Is.

GULF OF ALASKA

CHAPTER FOURTEEN

EXPEDITION CRUISING
Kodiak, Katmai, Aleutians and Bering Sea

lthough most ships conclude a Gulf of Alaska cruise at Seward
or Whittier, there are still thousands of miles of spectacular
coastline to explore west of Cook Inlet. Beyond is the Alaska
Peninsula and such famous places as the McNeil River – where brown
bears congregate each fall to feed on salmon runs – and Katmai
National Park & Preserve containing 2.5 million acres of volcanic
mountains, caldera lakes, caribou herds and the largest unhunted population of brown bears in the world. Few places are more remote than
Katmai Park, except perhaps the outer islands of the Aleutian chain
which stretches for 1,000 miles along the edge of a deep-sea trench
separating the Gulf of Alaska from the Bering Sea.

A few cruise companies offer adventure expeditions to Kodiak
Island, the Aleutians and the Bering Sea, where isolated islands contain
Eskimo and Aleut villages, as well as huge populations of seabirds and
sea mammals. Here is a sampling of what awaits visitors to the more
remote waters of coastal Alaska.

KODIAK ISLAND

As a cruising destination, Kodiak Island remains undiscovered. Called
"Alaska's Emerald Isle", this mountainous island is covered by a dense
growth of grass, berry bushes, alder thickets and wildflowers. At the
island's southernmost end, heath and tundra cling to the thin topsoil.
Some adjacent, smaller islands contain spruce forests, but most of

Port of Kodiak

Kodiak Island itself is devoid of trees, the land scoured by glaciers in the last ice age. From the water, Kodiak's verdant slopes look like manicured golf links. However, upon stepping ashore, visitors quickly discover that the grass is chest high.

The lush vegetation of Kodiak Island (second largest island in the U.S. after Hawaii) is also prime habitat for the largest carnivorous land mammal in the world – the Kodiak brown bear, which grows as large as 10 feet (when standing upright) and weighs up to 1,500 pounds. Roads here are found only in the port towns, leaving the mountainous interior the sole domain of bears and other wildlife.

The waters around Kodiak are also rich with animal life. Humpback whales, Dall porpoises and sea otters are frequent sights as are colorful puffins. In the Port of Kodiak, where the state ferry docks, Steller sea lions are regular visitors. These large mammals swim near the fishboat docks, scavenging for fish scraps. Several summers ago, a local fisherman was squatting on the dock when a sea lion grabbed him by the backside and pulled him into the water, dragging him six feet under before letting him go. Such tales don't endear sea lions to fishermen, but Steller sea lions are a protected species in Alaska, having suffered a drastic population decline in recent years.

Kodiak is a colorful fishing port – one of the largest in America – and it attracts college kids each summer in search of lucrative deckhand jobs. Many of the greenhorns, however, end up working in the canneries. At Larsen Bay, site of Kodiak Island's oldest operating cannery, summer workers are housed in wooden dormitories set on pilings and joined by boardwalks to the cannery buildings. When the fish tenders pull in loaded with salmon, the assembly lines roll – regardless of the hour.

Alaska's Russian history is closely tied to Kodiak, which was the colonial capital of Russian America before Alexander Baranof moved

Larsen Bay Cannery is a summer home for college students from the Lower 48 who work here during the salmon season.

it to Sitka. Kodiak's Baranof Museum is the oldest Russian structure remaining in Alaska, built by the Russian-American Company in 1808 for storing fur pelts. Of solid log construction, it overlooks a stone wharf once used by sailing ships of the fur trade.

Behind the museum a sweep of lawn leads to the local Russian Orthodox Church – a vital presence in Kodiak since 1784 and a moderating influence on Russian fur traders who were often brutal in their treatment of natives. The Orthodox missionaries helped the natives preserve their traditions and the church has retained a faithful following among the indigenous population. Native fishermen display icons on their vessels and often ask the local priest to bless their boats before heading out.

The town of Kodiak has a history of adversity. When Mount Katmai erupted in 1912, falling ash blackened the skies for two days and residents could barely breathe. The ground shook and homes collapsed under the weight of ash that piled 18 inches thick on level surfaces and many feet deep in slides. During the 1964 earthquake, part of the town dropped two feet and seismic sea waves washed boats in the harbor onto shore. Outlying ports were also hit by tsunamis. At the native village of Old Harbor, residents climbed up the mountainside and watched a series of huge waves wash away their homes. The village church stood its ground against waves surging past its windows and the people of Old Harbor say it was a miracle that the church survived. It served as a refuge until outside help arrived, and to this day the church plays a major role in the community.

In 1784 the first Russian settlement in Alaska was established just a few miles from Old Harbor at Three Saints Bay. An important battle took place at which the invading Russians defeated the native Alutiiqs, who had inhabited Kodiak Island for some 7,000 years and whose traditions included the partaking of a *banya* (sauna). This tradition is still

Glacial erosion shaped Kodiak and its neighboring islands, which are a geological extension of the Kenai Peninsula.

practised in Old Harbor, where visitors are often invited to someone's home for a steam in the family's *banya*. Prominent visitors to Old Harbor include James Michener (while researching his book Alaska), singer John Denver (who arrived here in the wake of the 1989 oil spill), and David Rockefeller (who pulled into port in the summer of 1991 as the leader of a sailing expedition).

KATMAI NATIONAL PARK

Lying 25 miles across Shelikof Strait from Kodiak Island is the Alaska Peninsula. The Aleutian Range of snow-capped mountains forms the backbone of this peninsula and runs its entire length, from Cook Inlet to the Aleutian Islands. Best known of these peaks is Mount Katmai, around which a national park has been established.

Mount Katmai erupted on June 6, 1912, and drastically altered the surrounding valleys, lakes and rivers with material spewed from its volcanic core. For a week before Katmai's massive eruption, the surrounding area was rocked by earthquakes that were felt 130 miles away. When Katmai erupted through a vent in its base, the sound explosion was so deafening that, had it taken place in New York City, residents of Chicago would have heard it plainly. Glowing hot lava, ash and gas burst skyward from Mount Katmai, its summit collapsing as the mountain's magma chamber emptied. Residents of Kodiak Island, 100 miles distant, were rained with ash so thick that for two days a person couldn't see a lantern held at arm's length.

Fishboats often anchor in the numerous bays of Geographic Harbor – part of Katmai National Park – where large brown bears wander the isolated beaches.

It was one of the greatest volcanic eruptions in recorded history, but because of Katmai's remote location, no human lives were lost. However, plant and animal life was destroyed as molten material flowed over the surrounding terrain. For several days the skies over much of the Northern Hemisphere were darkened by a haze of ash and gas that continued spewing from Novarupta – the new cone that had formed over the vent at the base of Mount Katmai. In the end, hot ash covered an area of 40 square miles to depths of 700 feet.

Four years later, the National Geographic Society sent a scientific expedition, led by Robert Griggs, to study the aftermath of this cataclysmic event. They were awestruck at the sight of a valley completely filled with ash and thousands of smoking fumaroles, their steam still soaring 500 feet into the air. It was named the Valley of Ten Thousand Smokes and on September 24, 1918, President Wilson established Katmai National Monument to preserve this unique area of historical and scientific interest. In 1931 the monument was enlarged to protect its significant population of brown (grizzly) bears and other animals, such as moose and caribou. Presidents Roosevelt and Johnson each enlarged the preserve further and, in 1980, President Carter granted the area National Park status.

A mainly roadless region, Katmai Park is not the most accessible national park in America, but it does attract visitors from around the world who specifically research and seek out this unique corner of the globe. Brooks Camp – located inland on Naknek Lake, about 300 air miles southwest of Anchorage – is the hub of the park with a Visitor Center and a road leading to the Valley of Ten Thousand Smokes. Adventure cruise expeditions pull into Geographic Harbor for a close look at the volcanic ash which lies on the park's rugged slopes and beaches. The local beachcombers here are brown bears, which are frequently seen ambling along the foreshore in search of food.

THE ALEUTIANS

Extending westward from the Alaska Peninsula, the Aleutian chain is a lonely stretch of submerged mountains, their peaks marking the edge of a deepsea subduction zone called the Aleutian Trench. The weather here is an ongoing battle between the Bering Sea's cold Arctic air and the Gulf of Alaska's warmer Pacific air. Vicious winter storms are replaced with the dense fog of summer.

Japanese troops invaded the Aleutians in June 1942, the first foreign occupation of American soil since the war of 1812. The United States had anticipated such a move and installed two secret airfields (disguised as canneries) on either side of Dutch Harbor. The Japanese, thinking the nearest American airfield was at Kodiak, were repelled in their attack on Dutch Harbor but did land on the islands of Attu and Kiska. When American pilots attempted to retake the occupied islands, violent gales and poor visibility were more of a hazard than enemy fire.

Colonized by Russian fur traders, Dutch Harbor on Unalaska Island is one of the few good Aleutian harbors.

Throughout the winter of 1942-43, Japanese troops defended their positions against American air attacks. Dashiell Hammett, author of *The Maltese Falcon* and *The Thin Man*, was stationed at the Aleutians during the war and wrote about this northern battlefield in *The Capture of Attu, Tales of World War II in Alaska*. "Modern armies had never fought before on any field that was like the Aleutians," he wrote. "Bad weather fought against us – air reconnaissance was almost impossible."

Finally, on May 11th, 1943, 11,000 American troops landed on Attu and, after 18 days of fighting, 2,600 Japanese troops were reduced to 800. In the end, only 28 were taken as prisoners – the rest died in combat or committed suicide to save their honor. About 550 American soldiers were killed retaking Attu, and several thousand were wounded. On Kiska, east of Attu, the Japanese had secretly abandoned the island under cover of dense fog. When American troops landed on Kiska's shores after weeks of heavy shelling, they found the place deserted.

An earlier invasion of the Aleutians took place in the 1700s, when Russian fur traders subjugated the Aleuts as hunters of sea mammals. The islands' Russian history is evident in the onion-domed, wooden churches that still grace the native villages dotting the green slopes of these misty islands. One of the Aleuts' oldest settlements was at Dutch Harbor, where the Russian fur traders based their operations. Today Dutch Harbor is a major fishing port – consistently ranking at the top of U.S. ports for value of commercial fish landed.

During the king crab boom of the 1980s, hundreds of fishboats passed through Dutch Harbor on their way to the Bering Sea. In 1987, they bought a total of 80 million gallons of fuel. Strategically located between the Bering Sea and the North Pacific Ocean, and with a geographic proximity to the Orient and the U.S. Northwest, this busy harbor is a major service center for the harvesting and processing of groundfish and crabmeat.

THE BERING SEA

The largest Aleut population exists not on the Aleutian Islands but on the Pribilofs, in the Bering Sea. The ancestors of these people were brought here by Russian fur traders to harvest seals. The islands' huge fur seal colonies still bring visitors to the Pribilofs, but now they come to discreetly watch these animals from special blinds. On St. Paul Island, hundreds of thousands of fur seals spend the summer at 14 different rookeries and haul-out locations. Large males – "beachmasters" – arrive in late May and establish their territories. The females arrive in June to bear their young. Reindeer and Arctic blue fox also inhabit the tundra-covered Pribilofs, along with more than two million seabirds which arrive each summer, some migrating from as far away as Argentina. Species commonly sighted include horned and tufted puffins, rock sandpipers, red-legged kittiwakes and crested aukluts.

During World War II, after Japanese troops invaded the western Aleutians, the U.S. Navy evacuated the Pribilof Aleuts to Funter Bay on Admiralty Island in Southeast Alaska where they were interned for two years, living in the bunkhouses of an old cannery. After the war, reforms led to self-government for the Pribilovians.

Adventure cruises don't end at the Pribilofs, but carry on across the Bering Sea to the Diomede Islands, where both the Alaskan and Siberian mainlands are visible in clear weather, and to St. Lawrence Island, where the natives are Yu'pik-speaking Eskimos whose dialect is similar to the natives of Provideniya on the nearby Siberian coast. At least one cruise expedition visits the Russian Far East and transits the Bering Strait, proceeding far enough north to cross the Arctic Circle.

(Below) Arriving at Boxer Bay on St. Lawrence Island. (Right) Local islanders.

Empress of the North –
1,295 tons, 235 passengers

Carnival Spirit, 2000 – 88,000
tons, 2,124 passengers

Summit, 2001 – 91,000 tons
1,950 passengers

AMERICAN WEST STEAM-BOAT CO. The stern-wheeler ship *Empress of the North*, carrying 231 passengers in all-outside staterooms, debuted in Alaska in 2003. It offers seven-night roundtrip cruises from Juneau, and 11-night cruises between Seattle and Juneau, stopping at major and minor ports. www.alaskacruisetour.com

CARNIVAL CRUISE LINES: Owned by the largest cruise corporation in the world, Carnival positions its 88,000-ton *Carnival Spirit* (launched in 2001) on 7-day line cruises between Vancouver and Whittier, with glacier viewing in Prince William Sound and stops at Ketchikan, Juneau, Skagway and the less-visited port of Sitka. *Carnival Spirit* also sails round-trip from Vancouver on a seven-day Inside Passage itinerary which includes a day in Glacier Bay. Carnival ships, which attract a high number of first-time cruisers, are popular with young people and families who enjoy the line's excellent children's facilities. Officers are Italian and service staff are international. www.carnivalcruises.com

CELEBRITY CRUISES: Founded in 1990 by the Greek line Chandris Inc., Celebrity Cruises is now owned by Royal Caribbean International. An upscale cruise line offering gourmet cuisine and sophisticated service, Celebrity's Alaska fleet consists of *Mercury* (77,713 tons; 1,870 passengers) and two Millennium-class ships, *Infinity* and *Summit*. At 91,000 tons, these spacious ships carry 1,950 passengers and offer an array of onboard amenities including indoor and outdoor swimming pools, whirlpools, health spa and youth center. *Mercury* and *Infinity* cruise on 7-day round-trips from Seattle and Vancouver respectively, with the glacier visit being Hubbard Glacier. *Infinity* stops at Ketchikan, Juneau and the former Russian port of Sitka, while *Mercury* stops at Juneau, Skagway, Ketchikan and Prince Rupert. *Summit* offers 7-day Gulf of Alaska cruises between Vancouver and Seward with stops at Hubbard Glacier, Icy Strait Point, Skagway, Juneau and Ketchikan or Sitka. Officers are Greek and service staff are international. www. celebritycruises.com

CRUISE WEST: The late Chuck West, founder of this family-owned company, was known as Mr. Alaska for his long and colorful career which began as a bush pilot in 1946. A pioneer of leisure travel to Alaska, West founded the state's first tour company which eventually became Westours and was sold to Holland America in 1973. West then founded Cruise

Spirit of Alaska – 97 tons
70 passengers

West, this line of small ships providing close proximity to the shoreline, taking passengers off the beaten path along narrow channels and pristine fjords, and pulling into small ports and fishing villages. This Seattle-based company offers a variety of itineraries along the Inside Passage and beyond to Prince William Sound, Kenai Fjords, Kodiak Island, the Aleutians and remote islands in the Bering Sea. The ships, all with outside cabins, carry 78 to 114 passengers. The onboard atmosphere is casual and evening presentations are designed to enhance the daytime sights and activities which include wildlife viewing by Zodiac. Officers and service staff are American. www.cruisewest.com.

HOLLAND AMERICA LINE: This company's presence in Alaska began with the acquisition of Westours in 1973. Today, Holland America has a totally integrated operation for its customers with support services including tour coaches, domed rail cars and the Westmark chain of hotels. This premium cruise line currently positions eight ships in Alaska. Its 7-day roundtrip itineraries from Seattle are serviced by

the *Oosterdam, Westerdam* and *Zaandam,* with ports of call being Ketchikan, Juneau, Sitka and Victoria, and a visit to either Glacier Bay or Hubbard Glacier. Servicing the Inside Passage on 7-day return trips from Vancouver are the *Ryndam* and *Zuiderdam,* with stops at Juneau, Skagway, Glacier Bay and Ketchikan. On one-way line cruises between Seward and Vancouver, HAL has three 55,000-

Statendam, 1993 – 55,000 tons
1,264 passengers

ton sisterships (*Statendam, Ryndam* and *Veendam*) on varied itineraries. In business since 1873, HAL operated transatlantic service from Rotterdam to New York for decades before turning to cruises in the late 1960s. Holland America's Dutch officers and service staff of Indonesians and Filipinos have built a solid reputation of well-run, immaculate ships with a high level of elegant service. HAL's spacious ships have classic lines, contain extensive artwork and are finely appointed with conveniences that include a bathtub in most staterooms. www.hollandamerica.com

NORWEGIAN CRUISE LINE: NCL was one of the first lines to invent modern cruising with trips from Miami to the Bahamas in the

mid-1960s. The line currently positions three mainstream ships in Alaska, two of these homeported in Seattle. *Norwegian Sun* and *Norwegian Star* offer round-trip 7-day cruises from Seattle. The *Sun* stops at Ketchikan, Juneau, Skagway, Prince Rupert and Sawyer Glacier in Tracy Arm. The *Star* visits Glacier Bay, Juneau, Skagway, Prince Rupert and Victoria. The *Norwegian Wind* offers a 7-day roundtrip cruise from Vancouver that stops at Ketchikan,

Norwegian Star, 2001 – 91,000 tons, 2,240 passengers

Juneau, Skagway and Sawyer Glacier in Tracy Arm. Officers are Norwegian and service staff are international. www. ncl.com

PRINCESS CRUISES: Princess's experience in Alaska began when *Princess Italia* first steamed north in 1969. At its inception, Princess relied on chartered ships and took its name from one of these – Canadian Pacific's *Princess Patricia.* From the start, Princess estab-

lished a reputation for a high standard of service and the line experienced phenomenal growth in the 1970s when the company permitted the television series *The Love Boat* to use its ships for onboard settings. Princess operates seven ships in Alaska, four of them on line cruises between Vancouver and Whittier (Anchorage). Seven-day loop cruises from Seattle are on the *Sun Princess* and *Dawn Princess*. Their

Sun Princess, 1995 – 77,000 tons, 1,950 passengers

route from Seattle takes them past the west side of Vancouver Island as they head to Alaska's Inside Passage. Also available are 10-day Inside Passage loop cruises from San Francisco on the 70,000-ton *Regal Princess*. All Inside Passage itineraries include glacier viewing in Tracy Arm and a stop at Victoria. One-way Gulf of Alaska cruises between Vancouver and Whittier are available on the 113,000-ton *Diamond Princess* and *Sapphire Princess,* and on the 88,000-ton sisterships *Coral Princess* and *Island Princess.* This seven-day itinerary takes in Glacier Bay along with the many glaciers of College Fjord in Prince William Sound. Princess Cruises' extensive and integrated tourist services provide coaches and domed rail cars for its cruisetour passengers who stay at the company's custom-built lodges. Officers and service staff are international. www.princess.com

RADISSON SEVEN SEAS: This luxury line made its Alaska debut in 2000, where it currently positions the 50,000-ton *Seven Seas Mariner.* This luxurious ship accommodates 700 passengers – all in outside suites and each with a balcony and bathtub. It offers seven-night loop cruises from Vancouver, and seven-night Gulf of Alaska cruises between Vancouver and Seward or Whittier. Ports of call include Ketchikan, Juneau, Skagway and Sitka, with glacier viewing in Tracy Arm and Yakutat Bay. Officers are Italian and service staff are international. www.rssc.com

ROYAL CARIBBEAN INTERNATIONAL: In 1995 RCI brought the largest ship of its time to Alaska with the arrival of the 70,000-ton *Legend of the Seas.* Power lines across Seymour Narrows, a major pass of the Inside Passage, had to be raised 20 feet to accommodate this ship. Quite a few larger ships have arrived on the scene since, but RCI still maintains a big presence with three large ships cruising to Alaska, all outfitted with RCI's trademark rock-climbing wall on the funnel.

The 90,000-ton *Serenade of the Seas* offers 7-day roundtrip cruises from Vancouver with stops at Skagway, Juneau and Ketchikan as well as a visit to Hubbard Glacier and Misty Fjords. The 78,000-ton *Vision of the Seas* offers 7-day roundtrip cruises from Seattle and visits Tracy Arm, Juneau, Skagway, Icy Strait Point and Victoria. *Radiance of the Seas* sails on 7-day line cruises between Vancouver and Seward. These handsome modern megaships offer spacious and impressive public areas

Serenade of the Seas, 2003 – 90,000 tons, 2,500 passengers

such as a multi-deck atrium with glass elevators and the company's hallmark Viking Crown Lounge – a glass-wrapped observation lounge located on the highest deck to provide passengers with a panoramic view of the passing scenery. Family suites and a spacious playroom and teen center make these ships ideal for passengers with children. Officers are Scandinavian and service staff are international. www.royalcaribbean.com

SILVERSEA: Consistently rated the #1 Small Ship Cruise Line by Conde Nast Traveler, this luxury line offers a variety of Alaska itineraries, from 7 to 12 days in length, on board the 28,000-ton *Silver Shadow*, which accommodates 382 passengers in all-outside suites, most with private balconies. Base ports are Vancouver and San Francisco, with ports of call including Sitka, Wrangell and Victoria. www.silversea.com

INDEX

PHOTO CREDITS:

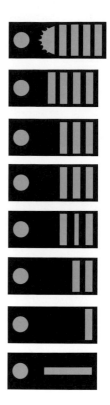

CAPTAIN
1st in Command
STAFF CAPTAIN
2nd in Command
SENIOR FIRST OFFICER
Senior officer of the Watch
FIRST OFFICER
Senior officer, navigator
SENIOR SECOND OFFICER
Senior officer of the Watch
SECOND OFFICER
Junior officer of the Watch
THIRD OFFICER
Junior officer of the Watch
DECK CADET
Trainee officer of the Watch

To distinguish officers on board your ship, the above striping, as displayed on the officer's sleeve or epaulet, will indicate rank.